THE CRIMINOLOGICAL IMAGINATION

For Ira and a life of the imagination

THE CRIMINOLOGICAL IMAGINATION

Jock Young

polity

First published in 2011 by Polity Press

Polity Press
65 Bridge Street
Cambridge CB2 1UR, UK

Polity Press
350 Main Street
Malden, MA 02148, USA

ISBN-13: 978-0-7456-4106-5 (hardback)
ISBN-13: 978-0-7456-4107-2 (paperback)

A catalogue record for this book is available from the British Library.

Typeset in 10 on 12 pt Adobe Sabon
by Servis Filmsetting Ltd, Stockport, Cheshire
Printed and bound in Great Britain by MPG Books Group Limited, Bodmin, Cornwall

For further information on Polity, visit our website: www.politybooks.com

Contents

Preface

This is the last book of a trilogy; the first, *The Exclusive Society* examined the extraordinary mechanisms of exclusion in late modern society, where sections of the population, whether indigenous or immigrant, are culturally absorbed, then summarily rejected as an underclass, detached, despised and unwanted in a process of inclusion and exclusion, the social bulimia of late modernity. The second, *The Vertigo of Late Modernity*, traced how such a process of othering relates to the vertiginous insecurities of our time. The tribulations of the economy and the insecurities of social life in late modernity where the old securities of family, work and community are undermined, generate a need for certainty and a secure ontology. It seeks firm social categories: the 'real' nature of marriage, the appeal to an absolute 'right and wrong', the true differences between the sexes; it is concerned with fixed demarcations and rigid distinctions. In reality, social categories are rarely distinct lines of demarcation between groups of people; social mores and social actions never clear and this is particularly true in the late modern world where norms are increasingly blurred, overlapping, changing and contested. Often, this desire for certainty is expressed in an essentialism of self and of others which is rooted in class, gender, race, ethnicity or nation. Such an othering involves a distancing and a diminishing. Binaries are created of them and us where there is seen to be an economic, social and moral hiatus between the superior and inferior, normal and deviant parts of the population.

It was while writing *Vertigo* that it dawned on me that such a process of othering which demanded clear lines and sharp demarcations was paralleled in the positivist movement in the social 'sciences', the nomothetic impulse to create universal laws and a science of society. For science requires distinct divisions between its subjects of study, whether atoms or species, and a consensus of definition to maintain its objectivity;

science abhors the blurred, the constantly contested and the subjective. So the binaries of society are readily imported into the academy. Furthermore sociology is frequently a subject where the social scientist looks downwards at the poor and supposedly more problematic parts of society. There is distance and there is diminishing. The criminological gaze all the more so; its traditional lens focuses on those who are seen to inhabit special universes economically detached, spatially segregated and morally reduced, consisting of individuals who by disposition, lack of socialization or circumstance are less than us. This process involves a detachment of individuals from the social structure, a denial of history, a loss of meaning; it forgoes transformative politics and concentrates on amelioration and accommodation. It is, as we shall see, precisely the opposite of the methodology which C. Wright Mills championed in *The Sociological Imagination*.

The sociological imagination can be engendered by social marginality, it flourishes at times of rapid change and environments of diversity; it can be obscured by academic isolation far from the maelstrom of late modern life, it can be forcefully suppressed by government intervention, it can be rung out of the budding scholar by a tedious apprenticeship within the discipline – a so-called professionalization – which prioritizes quantitative methods and digital distancing over human contact, *verstehen* and patient ethnography. For Mills a key indice of loss of such imagination was the rise of abstracted empiricism where reality was lost in method and measurement, where the tools of the trade become magically more important than reality itself, where to put it metaphorically, the telescope becomes of greater importance than the sky.

I have traced in this book how abstracted empiricism has expanded on a level which would have surely astonished Mills himself. How in much of the social sciences reality has been lost in a sea of statistical symbols and dubious analysis. I have, in part, focused on developments in criminology because it is here where abstracted empiricism has flourished to the greatest extent, producing a new genre of research and a novel breed of journal which has all but forgotten a great legacy of scholarship, where theory has been banished to the passing nod and the perfunctory and critical work significantly marginalized. But such a process has, as we shall see, spread to mainstream sociology and has clear resonances throughout the social sciences.

I have pointed to several areas which have been ill served by the hubris of abstracted empiricism. The understanding of the AIDS epidemic and methods of containing it were not helped by sampling frames which ignored precisely such groups which were most likely to be key to its spread and surveys which gave palpably false portrayals of human sexual activity, the debate over deleterious drug use is not enhanced by self-report studies whose validity stretches credibility, and the inability to satisfactorily explain the fall of the crime rate in the US and the UK is a story replete with ethnocentrism; it is, as I will seek to demonstrate, a tale of a conceptual toolbox which is exceedingly limited in its instruments and tardy in its theory.

It has to be said that many funding bodies are simply not getting a decent return in terms of their policy concerns. That they would, in fact, get better advice if researchers were considerably more wary about their use of numerical data, much more reflective in their interpretation of the figures which they produce and who utilize statistical analysis in a much more limited and circumspect way. At the very least they must take cognizance of the fact that survey methods are riddled with problems and their results must be interpreted with caution, that regression analysis is limited in its capability and that recipe book statistical testing is controversial both in its scientific basis and its ability to test hypotheses and establish causality. As it is much of the 'precision' and statistical 'sophistication' is an elaborate window dressing which obfuscates rather than illuminates reality. It is, to be blunt, largely a waste of money in policy terms and in many cases actually produces results which are counterproductive and dysfunctional.

The criticisms of social surveys, statistical testing and mathematical modelling abound. Their limitations are debated in economics and among statisticians but precious little of this seems to get across to the journals of mainstream criminology and sociology. Intriguingly there are hints in the textbooks that all is not as settled and secure as might seem to be the case but such hesitations are quickly glossed over in the haste to get on with the job. For, as we shall see, the phenomenon of skating on thin ice, of sensing that one's premises are insubstantial and precarious, is combined with the notion that somehow the hubris of science will speed us safely across the pond. If I can, in this book, create a moment of hesitation and contribute somewhat to the growing scepticism with regards to the widespread desire to quantify every aspect of the human condition I will have succeeded.

Acknowledgements

This book was written first of all in New York, then in London, then back again, it is a product of work at the University of Kent where I was Professor of Sociology and the City University of New York where I am Distinguished Professor of Criminal Justice. I owe a lot to discussions with post-graduate students at both institutions and particularly to my classes at the CUNY Graduate Center, where students have taught me as much as I have taught them and the subsequent debates spiced with gossip which, with some sort of inevitability, ended up in O'Reilly's or Jakes. My colleagues at the Centre for Criminology, Middlesex University, where I cut my teeth on survey research, particularly John Lea and Roger Matthews have been constant intellectual companions long after the institution itself has sadly been diminished and neglected. At John Jay College, Dave Brotherton and Michael Flynn have been an inspired source of support and of ideas as well as great fun to work with. Talking to Jim Lynch was a wonderful opportunity to bounce ideas about statistics; I can think of no more agreeable person to disagree with. Andrew Karmen was kind enough to look at my chapter on the New York miracle and offered very pertinent advice. Catriona Woolner was, as always, a great help and a good friend. Adam Edwards, Stanley Aronowitz, Frank Wilson, Peter Squires, John Hagedorn, Peter Marina, Cyann Zoller, David Downes, Paul Rock, Lynn Chancer, Phil Carney, Simon Hallsworth, Luis Barrios, Michael Jacobson, Michael Rowan, Brenda Vollman, David Fonsesca, Barry Spunt, Chris Stone, Rick Rosenfeld, Erich Goode, Carla Barrett, Nachman Ben-Yehuda, Mark Hamm, Louis Kontos, Chris Hale, Mitch Librett in no particular order, variously agreed or disagreed with me but everyone helped. What can I say about Jeff Ferrell, Keith Hayward and the late Mike Presdee other than their immense enthusiasm for cultural criminology made this book possible. Jayne Mooney is my closest friend and my greatest critic, our children Joseph and Fintan seem to be taking the prospect of spending their teenage years in New York with great equanimity, my eldest son Jesse finished his PhD at the same time I finished this book but much more importantly, he and Stella brought Ira into the world and it is to him that this book is dedicated.

Jock Young, Brooklyn, October 2010

Introduction: The Legacy of C. Wright Mills

Fifty years ago, C. Wright Mills published *The Sociological Imagination* (1959), a book which has both haunted and beguiled sociologists ever since. It is a volume resonant with forebodings as to what was happening to sociology, and predictions as to what might happen in the future. It has had a tremendous impact: most students of sociology have heard of it, although perhaps today few have read it. Warnings of the perils of Grand Theory and Abstracted Empiricism are deep in the consciousness of most academic sociologists – emerging every now and then as question marks set against their actual practice.

Mills was a sociologist's sociologist, a man of energy and commitment, a 'radical nomad', in Tom Hayden's words (2006). He was the constant advocate of 'sociology as a vocation', a man of political commitment and personal vulnerability, a passionate proponent of intellectual craftsmanship. He idealized such craftsmanship: the joy of writing, the excitement of weaving together theory and research, conceptually insightful and empirically grounded. Yet he was simultaneously a role model and a bitter critic of the way that craftsmanship and scholarship were being undermined; that the sociological imagination, so much needed, was being lost.

What was this imagination, and what was the necessity for it? Let us say from the start that, although many people are only too willing to endorse Mills' advocacy of 'imagination' (indeed who wouldn't?), it is rare that the actual nature of such imagination is understood, or the radical implications of his analysis. My aim in this book is to examine the way in which Mills' predictions have panned out today, and to gauge the extent to which his warnings have been heeded. In doing so, I will tend to focus on criminology – as one of the most rapidly expanding parts of the social sciences – but not at all totally, as we shall see shortly. But let us first tease out the elements of Mills' sociological imagination.

For Mills, the key nature of the sociological imagination was to situate human biography in history and in social structure. The role of such imagination was to bridge the gap between the inner life of human actors and the historical and social setting in which they find themselves. It is this fundamental triangle of the individual placed in a social structure at a particular place and time that is at the centre of Mills' work. He dismisses the notion of the individual abstracted from society as either a creature of ahistorical reason or inner unruly forces. Rationality is shaped by society and setting, in our time, adaption to the rationality of the great bureaucracies may produce individuals who are like 'cheerful robots', their very rationality of career and lifestyle reflecting their profound alienation. Nor can we turn to some universal psychology to comprehend our predicament: It is true, as psychoanalysts continually point out, that people do often have 'the increasing sense of being moved by obscure forces within themselves which they are unable to define'. But it is *not* true as Ernest Jones asserted, that 'man's chief enemy and danger is his own unruly nature and the dark forces pent up within him'. On the contrary: 'man's chief danger today lies in the unruly forces of contemporary society itself, with its alienating methods of production, its enveloping techniques of political domination, its international anarchy – in a word, its pervasive transformations of the very "nature" of man and the conditions and aims of his life' (1959, pp. 20–1).

He talks of 'the earthquakes' of social change, and of widespread feelings of people feeling themselves adrift, of being unable to understand what is happening to them, of individualizing their problems, whether it be in employment, or marriage, or community. 'Nowadays men often feel that their private lives are a series of traps', he writes at the beginning of *The Sociological Imagination*. And he continues:

> They sense that within their everyday worlds, they cannot overcome their troubles, and in this feeling, they are often quite correct: What ordinary men are directly aware of and what they try to do are bounded by the private orbits in which they live; their visions and their powers are limited to the close-up scenes of job, family, neighborhood; in other milieux, they move vicariously and remain spectators. And the more aware they become, however vaguely, of ambitions and of threats which transcend their immediate locales, the more trapped they seem to feel. (1959, p. 3)

They feel trapped, often disillusioned – they cannot make sense of their lives. It is absolutely no coincidence that, although Mills – true to his times – uses the masculine pronoun, almost at the same time Betty Friedan, in her pathbreaking book, *The Feminine Mystique* (1960), asked herself, almost guiltily, as she ferried the kids on the school run, to the play dates, to soccer and to the Guides: *'Is this all there is?'* The sociological imagination proposed that sociology, if it is to be of any significance, must link the inner lives of people to the structures of power and ideology and the historical period in which they live – a project which Feminism so powerfully addressed in the process of making 'the personal the political' over the subsequent years. Indeed, any social analysis worth its salt must do this. 'For that imagination', as Mills put it:

> is the capacity to shift from one perspective to another – from the political to the psychological; from examination of a single family to comparative assessment of the national budgets of the world; from the theological school to the military establishment; from considerations of an oil industry to studies of contemporary poetry. It is the capacity to range from the most impersonal and remote transformations to the most intimate features of the human self – and to see the relations between the two. Back of its use there is always the urge to know the social and historical meaning of the individual in the society and in the period in which he has his quality and his being. (1959, p. 7).

Such a consciousness is not merely the province of some elite of public intellectuals, it is an insight which is glimpsed in the flux of rapid social change which makes up the modern world. For, if the downside of such a momentum is feelings of entrapment and alienation, the upside is an increased reflexivity, a dereification of the social world, and an awareness of the ever-present possibility of change.

> In large part, contemporary man's self-conscious view of himself as at least an outsider, if not a permanent stranger, rests upon an absorbed realization of social relativity and of the transformative power of history. The sociological imagination is the most fruitful form of self-consciousness. By its use men whose mentalities have swept only a series of limited orbits often come to feel as if suddenly awakened in a house with which they had only supposed themselves to be familiar. Correctly or incorrectly, they often come to feel that they can now provide themselves with adequate summations, cohesive assessments, comprehensive orientations. Older decisions that once appeared sound now seem to them products of a mind unaccountably dense. Their capacity for astonishment is made lively again. They acquire a new way of thinking, they experience a transvaluation of values: in a word, by their reflection and their sensibility, they realize the cultural meaning of the social sciences. (1959, pp. 7–8)

Finally, out of this analysis emerges one of the most forceful distinctions of the sociological imagination: that between 'the personal troubles of a milieu' and 'the public issues of social structure'. Without such an imagination, the focus on the local milieu and the obfuscation of the wider structure, personal troubles remain as they are – personal, individual, isolated pains often tinged with self-blame and doubt, with imaginative help, the personal troubles of the many become collective issues: the personal becomes the political. But here too Mills moves backwards and forwards from the micro to the macro, from the local to the system as a whole, and back again:

> Do not allow public issues as they are officially formulated, or troubles as they are privately felt, to determine the problems that you take up for study. Above all, do not give up your moral and political autonomy by accepting in somebody's else's terms the illiberal practicality of the bureaucratic ethos or the liberal practicality of the moral scatter. Know that many personal troubles cannot be solved merely as troubles, but must be understood in terms of public issues – and in terms of the problems of history-making. Know that the human meaning of public issues must be revealed by relating them to personal troubles – and to the problems of the individual life. Know that the problems of social science, when adequately formulated, must include both troubles and issues, both biography and history, and the range of their intricate relations. Within that range the life of the individual and the making of societies occur; and within that range the sociological imagination has its chance to make a difference in the quality of human life in our time. (1959, p. 226)

Let us pause for a moment and think of the relevance of this analysis for today, at the beginning of the twenty-first century. The speed of change has considerably heightened; there is, in Todd Gitlin's phrase, 'a new velocity of experience . . . a new vertigo' (1980, p. 233). I have charted such feelings of dizziness, of instability, in *The Vertigo of Late Modernity* (2007): a world characterized by instability in all the three spheres of work, family and community, of economic uncertainty where reward appears arbitrary, random, and where all measures of distributive justice seem askew. A new world where self-development, self-invention and identity become a prime goal, yet where all the props of identity in the three spheres become more insubstantial and phantasmagoric, and the shock of pluralism is hastened by the forces of globalization. In short, a late modern social order where there is a chaos of reward and of identity. Here, too, people face an existential quandary: their uncertainty can easily be interpreted in terms of self-blame and individual failure, yet the widespread nature of economic and cultural instability and its daily dissemination in the global media, facilitate feelings of connectedness and of recognizing the parallel nature of the human condition, despite a plurality of social worlds and values. So that, if one response to uncertainty is the construction of hardened identities based on religion, nation, race or gender – the creation of barriers of difference by othering all that is outside of our chosen camp – the other is to deconstruct such cultures, to welcome human creativity and celebrate difference. Surely, in a late modern world of heightened insecurities and competing fundamentalisms, the necessity for a sociological imagination becomes that much greater? Witness the need to link the local to the global, to situate, for example, terrorism – religious fundamentalism, poverty, AIDS, crime, heroin addiction – in personal biography, historical context and social structure. To connect together personal troubles in various parts of the world with collective issues across the globe, to make the personal political.

But let us return to Mills' discussion of the response of sociology to such a challenge, when he was writing in the middle of the twentieth century. His assessment of the situation is famously sceptical and acerbic. He identifies two diametrically opposed tendencies in the academic sociology of the time, both of which lose contact with social reality. Whereas the sociological imagination involves the movement from the local milieu to the total system and back again, one tendency – Abstracted Empiricism – concentrates solely on the local yet as we shall see in a strange and distant way, and the other – Grand Theory – focuses on the system, while both manage to abstract themselves from their objects of study.

Let us take Grand Theory first. Mills famously begins his demolition with a translation of sections of Talcott Parsons' *The Social System* (1951). He takes a slab of verbiage from the text and translates it in a few words into plain English. What is of interest here is the banality of much of what is being said once the dense prose is radically pruned, and how glaring omissions – such as the nature of power and its legitimation – are more easily overlooked. But what makes for a narrative so opaque and turned in on itself, written in a style which is almost defensive, having what Mills calls a 'protective advantage'? It certainly is conservative in its implications, but it is not so in a proselytizing fashion. The vitriol poured upon Parsons at the time, by scholars of the left, manifestly overestimated his influence. Indeed *The Social System* seems purposely written for a small scholarly audience of academics and students. It is rather like the language of the mediaeval alchemist, designed to pass on an esoteric knowledge, cautious and intricate, hidden under a carapace of scholarship and learning. It is abstracted from history and social structure, distanced from social reality. Thus Mills writes:

> history can be altogether abandoned: the systematic theory of the nature of man and of society all too readily becomes an elaborate and arid formalism in which the splitting of Concepts and their endless rearrangement becomes the central endeavour. (1959, p. 23)

He distinguishes semantics and syntax: semantics are words about reality, syntax are words in relation to each other. 'Grand Theory', he writes, is 'drunk on syntax, blind to semantics' (1959, p. 34). Thus typologies have a reality of their own, concepts chatter with each other, the academician ponders over subdivisions without questioning what is being divided. All of us working in sociology (or any of the social sciences or humanities for that matter) know of the extraordinary solipsis of the academy. It is seen in debates which are almost entirely self-referential, it is encountered in obfuscation and erudite vacuity, it seems to thrive on splitting hairs and dancing on pins: it is the reason, for example, why commentaries on Durkheim are invariably more complex than reading Durkheim himself, and how the latter-day Foucauldians have taken an outrageous and iconoclastic thinker and turned his writings into some sort of Talmudic parody of contested interpretation. In his appendix on intellectual craftsmanship, Mills caustically warns us against: 'using unintelligibility as a means of evading the making of judgments upon society – and as a means of escaping your readers' judgments on your own work' (1959, p. 224). And earlier in *The Sociological Imagination* he points in the most scathing terms to those intellectuals who stubbornly refuse to acknowledge the world outside of the academy. American democracy, he notes, may not (at this moment in the 1950s) have a plethora of movements and progressive parties, but at least there is the form of democracy, the legal possibility of free speech and public criticism. The contrast was with the Soviet Union at that time. Thus, he writes:

> We ought not to minimize the enormous value and the considerable opportunity these circumstances make available. We should learn their value from the fact of their absence in the Soviet world, and from the kind of struggle the intellectuals of that world are up against. [And, he adds scornfully:] We should also learn that whereas there many intellectuals are physically crushed, here many morally crush themselves. (1959, p. 191)

In this book I will be on the lookout for evidence of the persistence of Grand Theory, the dissociation of concepts from reality. It reappears, we shall see, sometimes with totally different political valences, and it crosses over into new shapes and forms. But let us, now, look at Mills' second violation of the sociological imagination: Abstracted Empiricism. Here the structure fades out of sight, history is banished from thought, and the myopic eye of the researcher focuses on the immediate. For, if in Grand Theory the concepts dissociate from reality, become 'The Concept' and the concepts proceed to talk together, in Abstracted Empiricism the methods detach from reality, method becomes methodology, and 'the method' becomes absorbed in itself.

Let us sum up Mills' argument with regard to imagination. He insists on the need to see the individual in the context of the social structure and place this in historical period; he demands an analysis which moves from the macro to the micro and back again; he points to the gross inequities of our time in terms of the domination of a political elite in an intensely divided class society; he sees the sociological imagination not just as an attribute of the highly trained sociologists (indeed often the reverse) but as a world view which can arise out of the individual's attempts to make sense of a dizzying world; he sees two particular tendencies in academic sociology as directly obfuscating such an imagination; and last *but not least* he ties this imagination to transformative politics directed at attending to the gross economic and political inequities of the social order. The irony is, as Erich Goode (2008) has trenchantly pointed out, that mainstream sociology has trumpeted Mills' notion of the sociological imagination in every introductory textbook but has dropped the transformative politics which are so central to understanding Mills' mission. Furthermore, his methodological critique, so close to his politics has been likewise ignored. Indeed, abstracted empiricism has become the dominant tendency in sociology.

For Mills the central philosophical tenet of abstracted empiricists is their claim that their investigations are 'science'. Indeed, Mills is perhaps the first to depict such physics envy among sociologists. Thus, he writes:

> Probably no one familiar with its practitioners would care to deny that many of them are dominated by concern with their own scientific status; their most cherished professional self-image is that of the natural scientist. In their arguments about various philosophical issues of social science, one of their invariable points is that they *are* 'natural scientists', or at least that they 'represent the viewpoint of natural science'. In the discourse of the more sophisticated, or in the presence of some smiling and exalted physicist, the self-image is more likely to be shortened to merely 'scientist'. (1959, p. 56)

In his critique of positivism, Mills points to the rise of a new stratum of technical functionaries, and the decline of the scholar as intellectual craftsman engaged directly in research where theory and research constantly interact and develop. This bureaucratization of research involves costly research projects, extensive research teams, large surveys and databases. The aim is to collect, in an unreflexive way, findings – like building blocks – which supposedly automatically gain the larger picture. The research administrator no longer has direct contact with the data, the interviews are carried out on his or her behest by semi-skilled interviewers with little training, or indeed insight. *Precision is seen to be truth:*

Those in the grip of the methodological inhibition often refuse to say anything unless it has been through the fine little mill of The Statistical Ritual.
It is usual to say that what they produce is true even if unimportant. I
do not agree with this; more and more I wonder how true it is. I wonder
how much exactitude, or even pseudo-precision, is here confused with
'truth'; and how much abstracted empiricism is taken as the only 'empirical' manner of work. If you have ever seriously studied, for a year or two,
some thousand hour-long interviews, carefully coded and punched, you
will have begun to see how very malleable the realm of 'fact' may really
be. Moreover, as for 'importance', surely it is important when some of the
most energetic minds among us use themselves up in the study of details
because The Method to which they are dogmatically committed does not
allow them to study anything else. Much of such work, I am now convinced, has become the mere following of a ritual . . . (1959, p. 72)

And as for the new social scientists entering the profession, the
apprenticeship dumbs curiosity and dims the imagination. Here his
condemnation is complete:

I have seldom seen one of these young men, once he is well caught up,
in a condition of genuine intellectual puzzlement. And I have never seen
any passionate curiosity about a great problem, the sort of curiosity that
compels the mind to travel anywhere and by any means, to re-make itself
if necessary, in order to *find out*. These young men are less restless than
methodical; less imaginative than patient; above all, they are dogmatic – in
all the historical and theological meanings of the term. Some of this is of
course merely part of the sorry intellectual condition of so many students
now in American colleges and universities, but I do believe it is more
evident among the research technicians of abstracted empiricism.

They have taken up social research as a career; they have come early
to an extreme specialization, and they have acquired an indifference or a
contempt for 'social philosophy' – which means to them 'writing books out
of other books' or 'merely speculating'. Listening to their conversations,
trying to gauge the quality of their curiosity, one finds a deadly limitation
of mind. The social worlds about which so many scholars feel ignorant do
not puzzle them.

Much of the propaganda force of bureaucratic social science is due to
its philosophical claims to Scientific Method; much of its power to recruit
is due to the relative ease of training individuals and setting them to work
in a career with a future. In both instances explicitly coded methods,
readily available to the technician, are the major keys to success . . . But
once a young man has spent three or four years at this sort of thing, you
cannot really talk to him about the problems of studying modern society.
His position and career, his ambition and his very self-esteem, are based
in large part upon this one perspective, this one vocabulary, this one set of
techniques. In truth, he does not know anything else. (1959, pp. 105–6)

I have quoted extensively from this passage because I want to underscore the direction and acerbity of Mills' critique. Over the last half century, C. Wright Mills has become something of an icon and, like all icons, he has become all things to all people. Nobody quarrels with the need for imagination – like integrity, or objectivity – it's everyone's favourite, no one denies the need to relate the micro to the macro level (although this is most frequently interpreted in the most stolid and least humanistic manner), everyone likes the distinction between personal problems and public issues (yet, as we shall see, the thrust of the analysis is towards the personal and the individual). But what seems to be missing in the legacy of Mills is the critique of what is going on within the social sciences. For people will applaud imagination, yet fail to address that which systematically undermines it. They will make a nod of abeyance to the work of Mills, yet ignore what is happening in front of their eyes. Let us leave this for the moment and end this chapter with Mills' injunction about intellectual craftsmanship, which sums up his position:

> Be a good craftsman: Avoid any rigid set of procedures. Above all, seek to develop and to use the sociological imagination. Avoid the fetishism of method and technique. Urge the rehabilitation of the unpretentious intellectual craftsman, and try to become such a craftsman yourself. Let every man be his own methodologist: let every man be his own theorist; let theory and method again become part of the practice of a craft. Stand for the primacy of the individual scholar; stand opposed to the ascendancy of research teams of technicians. Be one mind that is on its own confronting the problems of man and society. (1959, p. 225)

Now let us fast forward from the 1950s to where we are now: the beginning of the twenty-first century, and judge what has happened . . .

I

Closing Down the Imagination

$$Y_{it} = \alpha + \beta_1 Time_t + \beta_2(Time_t)^2 + \sum_{k=3}^{5} \beta_k(QT_{kt}) + \beta_6 Unemp_t \qquad (1)$$

$$+ \sum_{k=7}^{10} \beta_k Risk_{ki} + \beta_{11}Nuisance_i + \beta_{12}Close_{it} + \beta_{13}Dosage_{it}$$

$$+ \sum_{k=14}^{27} \beta_k Duration_{kit} + \sum_{k=28}^{83} \beta_k(Risk_{ki}*Duration_{kit}) + \sum_{k=84}^{89} \beta_k(Dosage_{it}*Duration_{kit})$$

This equation is taken from an article in the journal Criminology on the effectiveness of police raids on reducing drug dealing around nuisance bars: 'Estimating Intervention Effects in Varying Risk Settings: Do Police Raids Reduce Illegal Drug Dealing at Nuisance Bars?', Criminology 41(2) pp. 257–92, May 2003, by J. Cohen, W. Gorr and P. Singh. The key to the equation is as follows:

'Y_{it}	=	*number of drug-related 911 calls in target area 'i' at time 't';*
$Time_t$	=	*index of months 't' from 1 to 36 (January 1990 = 1);*
$QT2_t$	=	*1 if month is March, April or May and = 0 otherwise;*
$QT3_t$	=	*1 if month is June, July or August and = 0 otherwise;*
$QT4_t$	=	*1 if month is September, October or November and = 0 otherwise;*
$Unempt$	=	*citywide unemployment rate in month 't';*
$Riskki$	=	*risk factor score 'k' in study area 'i' (k = 7 for land-use risk in target area 'i', k = 8 for guardianship risk in target area 'i'; k = 9 for land-use risk in buffer area surrounding target area 'i', k = 10 for guardianship risk in buffer area surrounding target area 'i');*

$Nuisance_i$ = *1 if target area 'i' contains any nuisance bars and = 0 otherwise;*

$Close_{it}$ = *1 if target area 'i' contains any closed nuisance bars at time 't' and = 0 otherwise;*

$Dosage_{it}$ = *number of police raids in target area 'i' at time 't';*

$Durationk_{it}$ = *1 if target area 'i' at time 't' is the kth month in an observation sequence and = 0 otherwise (k = 14 to 17 for Pre months 1 to 4 before an enforcement period, k = 18 to 23 for Enforcement months 1 to 6 during an enforcement period, k = 24 to 27 for After months 1 to 4 following an enforcement period);*

$Interactionk_{it}$ = *product of* $Prek_{it}$, *Enforcementk_i t, and* $Afterk_{it}$ *duration months times: k = 28 to 41 for* land-useki *risk in target area, k = 42 to 55 for* guardianshipki *risk in target area, k = 56 to 69 for* land-useki *risk in buffer area, k = 70 to 83 for* guardianshipki *risk in buffer area, and k = 84 to 89 for* dosageit *level.'* (2003, p. 275)

Note the delightful quasi-scientific usage of 'dosage' for the number of police raids. The findings, incidentally, were 'that police intervention suppresses levels of drug dealing during periods of active enforcement but the effects largely disappear when the intervention is withdrawn' (2003, p. 257). No comment.

I was sitting in the library of John Jay College of Criminal Justice, City University of New York, on 10th Avenue, browsing through the journals. I turn to *Criminology*, perhaps the most prestigious journal of world criminology, when an article catches my eye or, at least, an equation does. (I have reproduced it above.) It is cutting edge stuff, although not at all atypical of its contents, and its authors are well-published and respected.

The article simply fascinates me. The confetti of Greek letters, beta, lambda, epsilon, the masquerade of science, the strange litany of indicators: Time, Unemp, Risk, Nuisance, Closed, Dosage and Duration seems in a different universe from the louche bars, dope smokers, snitches and police harassment of downtown Pittsburgh. It is, of course, a full-blown example of abstracted empiricism. In 1954 Mills wrote: 'Sociology, judging by the books of its practitioners, is a strange field of learning. In the libraries of the professors you will find books containing announcements like this: $p^1(= p^2ij)$' (1963, p. 68 [1954]). I don't know what he would have made of the full-on rhetoric of a modern day behavioural equation. Here the data mysteriously detach themselves from their

subject matter and lose all context in an abstraction of reality, existing in some cyber-universe of computer and database which only very
elliptically touches the rich social tapestry of bars, drug takers and the
squads that pursue them. A few weeks previously I had read a fascinating
PhD dissertation by Mitch Librett entitled 'The Spoils of War: Divergent
Lifeworlds and Identity Formation Among Undercover/Vice Cops in
the 'Burbs' (2005). Librett, himself an undercover cop during his ethnographic research, obviously lives in a totally different world to Cohen,
Gorr and Singh. Yet his contact with the drug scene was daily and
intimate, while their relationship was one of distance; indeed I strongly
suspect that their sense of their own objectivity stemmed very largely
from this fact of hiatus. Thus, paradoxically, the less their contact with
the subject matter the more knowledgeable they feel.

If one looks closer at the article, the more mysterious it becomes, for
there is not just distance here, there is a strange tunnel vision. The theory
behind the article is a poor atrophied thing, a smattering of deterrence
theory, the assumption of rational choice, a smidgeon of routine activities
theory. The explanatory narrative is appallingly thin: a series of observations characterized by their obviousness are straight-facedly referenced as
if to build a case: bars are an attractive setting where buyers and sellers
can meet, displacement may occur to other nearby drug markets, while
routine activities theory 'provides a useful theoretical framework for
considering why bars are expected to be suitable places for drug dealing'
(2003, p. 258). Whole swathes of theory and controversy are simply not
mentioned: that the war against drugs is the most massive and global
manifestation of the failure of deterrence is not touched upon, that drug
busts are frequently racist in their targets is not referred to, that such
strategies may be counterproductive is not glimpsed as a possibility, that
police corruption and connivance is commonplace and can easily undermine the simple equation of quantity of police busts ('treatment' in the
text) set against the amount of illicit activity goes under their radar. This
is a study of deviant behaviour without deviance.

Most of the article is on research design and methodology, graphs
abound, and although the narrative itself is very simple: what effect does
policing (independent variable) have on drug dealing (dependent variable), the text becomes more and more convoluted. Let me give you just
a short taste – not too much or you will probably feel tempted to close
the pages of the book:

> To control for potential bias from unmeasured differences among the bars,
> the estimating equation is expanded to include separate main and interac-
> tion effects for Long Enforcement and Short Enforcement nuisance-bars.
> Tables 7a and 7b report the OLS parameter estimates for this modified

model. Most of the effects estimated for all bars emerge only for the Long Enforcement bars (Table 7a), and very few interaction effects are evident for the Short Enforcement bars (Table 7b). In the only substantial change from the model in Table 5, the main effect of Dosage loses significance in Table 7. Increasingly stronger suppression effects during successive months of enforcement periods persist among the bars that experience at least one enforcement period lasting at least 5 months, but are not evident among the short-enforcement bars.

Likewise the interactions between Enforcement Month and Dosage from Table 5 continue in Long Enforcement, but not in Short Enforcement bars. Also the interactions between Risk and Enforcement Month from Table 5 remain significant for Long-Enforcement bars in Table 7. The net effects (figures not presented) for Long-Enforcement bars are similar to those found in model 1, and no similar decreases in drug calls occur among the Short-Enforcement bars. Persistence of these results after we introduce additional controls for unobserved heterogeneity provides further evidence in support of increasing suppression effects on drug dealing activities with increasing duration of enforcement. (2003, pp. 286–9)

You have to dig deeper into the article to discover what is happening: it is a dense text and a desperately thin narrative. Yet when you do, the base seems terribly fragile and unsubstantial. The dependent variable, for example, is measured by the number of public-initiated 911 drug-related calls to the police – a fairly shaky indicator if you were to ask me. The very fact that in high drug-use areas you may get less likelihood of 'phoning the police and vice versa is scarcely touched upon. One gets the feeling that the authors are at least subliminally aware that they are skating on thin ice, but that the more quasi-scientific the rhetoric, the more sophisticated the statistics, *the more that they are distanced from what they are studying*, the more secure they feel.

My fascination is not with the actual article, whose explanatory power is perhaps unsurprisingly very limited, but how one explains the occurrence of the article itself. What concerns me is not the article's explanation, but the explanation of the article. How, indeed, does such a strange formulation of human behaviour occur in such secure and auspicious parts of the academy – particularly in this age of late modernity where human behaviour, far from pursuing some deterministic logic and mathematical trajectory, has an ever-increasing accent on creativity and self-invention?

Where does this fit Mills' predictions? One suspects that in this new statistically sophisticated Abstracted Empiricism, 'method' has become, as Mills put it, 'methodology', and methodology begins to take on all the verbiage of Grand Theory. Indeed, as theory itself atrophies, methodology and the complexities of statistical manipulation become a substitute for theory. And what of Mills' three guidelines of the imagination? The individual with his or her narrative, in a social structure situated at some time and place in history. Here, alas, there is no history: the scenario depicted is an empty stage upon which the actors – police and drug dealers – appear from out of nowhere. They have no past, and their future is a mundane world structured by the pushes of deterrence or the lack of it. The war against drugs, the most poignant overreaching history, is not even mentioned – the history of the area, the vicissitudes of employment, of neighbourhood, of poverty, ethnic identity, migration and adaption not even hinted at. As far as the police are concerned, we have no knowledge of overall police policy, the history of police–public relations and, going down the structure, anything about the particular police department or, more specifically, no inkling of the goings on in the drug squad – the temptations and discontent, the pride and privations of the officers concerned. Indeed the officers are caricatured as 'doses' in the formula or at best act out orders like robots in an equation. As for the drug dealers themselves they are creatures of calculation and opportunity, they exist in a wafer-thin narrative. They may well be drug users themselves, but we do not know that; why, we don't even know what drug they are using. They may know members of the drug squad, sometimes over-well, they may probably have suffered the privations of prison; the raids may anger them and reinforce their subculture, be part of a long drawn out battle, evoke anger, resistance, treachery. They may even know of the raids in advance; we just don't know. But there are, of course, reasons for this. For what the researchers are looking for are universal generalizations independent of people, structure, history and place: the very opposite of Mills' admonitions. What they are seeking is the nomothetic, the scientific, a social world circumscribed by law-like generalizations, just like the natural world. It is the dream of the new orthodoxy within much of the social sciences, a positivism which looks to natural science and to econometrics. Let us contrast this for one moment with Philippe Bourgois' wonderful study of crack dealers in East Harlem, *In Search of Respect* (1995), which arose out of the emerging tradition of critical anthropology. Here we have a rich narrative and biography, a history of immigration set in the context of the decline of manufacturing industry in Manhattan from the 1980s onwards. All of this has as a backcloth the American Dream and the loss of respect among second generation Puerto Rican immigrants living in the sullen and violent streets of East Harlem. The actors are profane, lusty, angry; they have love lives, quarrels, take and enjoy drugs, cannot quite make out why Philippe, a white middle-class man from the Upper Eastside, who speaks as though he were on television, is studying them. They reflect on him, he reflects on them. They are real people not numbers on a computer; they search for respect, for the American Dream, in a world where there are precious few means of success available to them; they improvise through drug dealing, they create a structure, a subcultural world which both frees them and imprisons them. There is plenty of reflexivity there; Philippe frowns at their sexism and violence, Primo and Caesar smile at his naivity and prudishness. One has, indeed, entered a totally different world to that of lambda, epsilon, doses of police and bad bars to be treated.

Let Me Introduce You to the Datasaur

The datasaur, Empiricus Abstractus, is a creature with a very small head, a long neck, a huge belly and a little tail. His head has only a smattering of theory, he knows that he must move constantly but is not sure where he is going, he rarely looks at any detail of the actual terrain on which he travels, his neck peers upwards as he moves from grant to grant, from database to database, his belly is huge and distended with the intricate intestine of regression analysis, he eats ravenously but rarely thinks about the actual process of statistical digestion, his tail is small, slight and inconclusive.

Recently there has been a series of articles which question the capability of statistical modelling in the explanation and prediction of crime rates. Foremost of these is the work of David Weisburd and Alex Piquero (2008), of particular pertinence because their doubts and criticisms are from two scholars prominent among the ranks of quantitative researchers. They analyse the level of explanatory power measured as the level of variance by the multivariate models used in the journal *Criminology* between 1968 and 2005. Their findings are astonishing: the average predictive capacity of the models is under 40 per cent with 60 per cent of crime unexplained; indeed one-quarter of the studies explain less than 20 per cent and one-tenth at less than 10 per cent. They add that it is worth noting that each model included control variables such as age and gender as well as the variables associated with the theory being tested, so that there is a built-in over-estimation of their level of prediction. Further, that there has been a *decline* in the variance explained over time which, as they put it, raises 'serious questions for criminologists. In short, criminology does not appear to be following a strictly science-based model over time, one centred on improvement' (2007, p. 31). They sum up their analysis by the query: 'Are low levels explained by variance due to inadequate theory, poor data and measurement, or is there some more general principle operating that limits our ability to explain crime?'(2007, p. 9). My answer to this, as I have sought to demonstrate in this book, is that they are absolutely right on all three levels of deficiency.

Eminently forthright are the acerbic commentaries of Ted Goertzel (2002, 2004; Goertzel and Goertzel, 2008) a writer who excels in pointing to the Emperor's new clothes. His main point is that the acid test of statistical modelling is prediction, yet what actually happens is that researchers take past events and constantly readjust their model until it fits the data. He focuses on multiple regression research into the deterrent effect of the death penalty on homicide, where scholars make various mysterious yet definitive forecasts of the effect of one execution on the number of future murders. Some say eight murders are deterred per execution, some say three, some say five, and some say none at all. He notes how the data are severely limited and hopelessly inadequate, the data chosen are selected to fit the favoured model and the model is finessed and meticulously adjusted to fit the data. One person's model is used to falsify another person's model. Goertzel additionally examines a series of celebrated findings in the areas of the effects of guns, legalized abortion and imprisonment on crime rates. All have the same failings; all are welcomed as truth if they confirm the preconceived beliefs of the assessor. He concludes by citing the distinguished quantitative sociologist David Freeman, who wrote: 'I do not think regression can carry much of the burden in a causal argument. Nor do regression equations by themselves give much help in controlling for confounding variables' (1999, p. 292). And he adds the apposite remark of Richard Berk that Freeman's contention: 'will be very difficult for most quantitative sociologists to accept. It goes to the heart of their empirical enterprise and in so doing puts entire professional careers in jeopardy' (1999, p. 315).

The Elevation of the Journal and the Rise of the New Genre

Over the last decade there has grown up a peculiar formula for writing journal articles. The introduction usually presents two theories in competition, but they are strange one-dimensional creatures almost unrecognizable compared to the real thing, by virtue of being rendered simple and decontextualized for the purposes of operationalization. This acephalous introduction, this headless chicken of an argument, is then followed by an extensive discussion of measures, the practicalities of measurement become more important than what is being measured, while the data themselves are usually outsourced from some past study, or bought in from a survey firm, an obligatory recession analysis follows, an erudite statistical equation is a definite plus, and then the usually inconclusive results are paraded before us. The criminologists themselves are far distant from crime out there, hidden behind a wall of verbiage and computer printout, the barrier graphited with the Greek letters of statistical manipulation. What can we do to get out of this sanitized redoubt? What is needed is a theoretical position which can enter into the real world of existential joy, fear, false certainty and doubt, which can seek to understand the subcultural projects of people in a world riven with inequalities of wealth and uncertainties of identity. What we need is a method which can deal with reflexivity, contradiction, tentativeness, change of opinion, posturing and concealment. A method which is sensitive to the way people write and rewrite their personal narratives. Our problems will not be solved by a fake scientificity, but by a critical sociology, honed to the potentialities of human creativity and meaning.

Perhaps I should not say this – and certainly not so early on – but the title of this book, *The Criminological Imagination*, is something of a misnomer. Not 'imagination' because I have a lot to say about imagination, and the lack of it, but 'criminological'. For I will certainly not concern myself solely with crime and criminological matters. Indeed my argument pivots around strange findings in the sociology of sex and, on the way, we will encounter examples from anthropology, cultural studies and general sociology. Of course Mills himself had his doubts about titles: 'I hope my colleagues', he writes, 'will accept the term "sociological imagination". Political scientists who have read my manuscript suggest "the political imagination", anthropologists "the anthropological imagination" – and so on.' But, he adds: 'The term matters less than the idea. . . .' (1959, p. 19, n. 2). So be it.

I will be concerned both with quantitative and qualitative studies taking a critical eye both to survey work and ethnography. Thus we will examine the famous and acrimonious debate over what Margaret Mead actually encountered in Samoa, as well as looking at the work of the Birmingham School, and more recent ethnography. I think I shall make it clear that the problems of social scientific investigation are not confined to criminology nor that the magic wand of ethnography will transport us easily away from the deep-seated problems of quantitative research. Nor should it be thought that criminology is alone in the social sciences with the affliction; sociology also suffers from this blight, one has only to look, say, at *The American Sociological Review*, or *The American Journal of Sociology* to see similar manifestations of the positivistic method. Let me give an example from a while back, from an article in *The American Journal of Sociology* by Eugene Kanin, a pioneer in the study of date rape. I quote it not merely because it is unintentionally amusing, but because it succinctly places reality in a subaltern position to method:

The levels of erotic intimacy were telescoped into three categories – (1) necking and petting above the waist, (2) petting below the waist, and (3) attempted intercourse and attempted intercourse with violence – in order to satisfy requirements for chi-square. (1957, p. 198 n. 2)

Things have changed quite drastically since the early days of classic American sociology. Just compare *The American Sociological Review* in the past and *The American Sociological Review* today. Consider 'Social Structure and Anomie', perhaps the most cited article in sociology, published by Merton in 1938. It is a brilliant article, I still read it with delight – it is surely intellectual craftsmanship that fits C. Wright Mills' canon to perfection. It was written during the period when Merton shared many of Mills' opinions on methods, on sociology and politics as well (Young, 2010). It talks of problems of the system and problems of the individual, it manifestly connects private troubles to public issues, it places the American Dream in the context of American history, it is comparative in that it hinges around the comparison with crime rates in Southeastern Europe; above all it is imaginatively conceptual, the famous forms of adaptation from conformist to ritualist, from retreatist to innovator. But would it be published today? One can imagine the letter from the editor, the reports from the peer reviewers: 'Dr Merton talks interestingly about differential crime rates in the United States and Southeastern Europe, but where are the Gini Coefficients, where are the statistical tests, where are the formulae which systematically sum up his argument? Where is his evidence that the American Dream is "a sop for those who might rebel against the entire structure were this consoling hope removed"(1938, p. 679 n. 15) and, perhaps, isn't this rather too political for a scientific article?' But we need go no further because some of this work has already been done for us. For in fact, we can have a reasonably good idea what would be expected of Merton today when we read present day 'clarifications' of his work. Thus Eric P. Baumer in an article entitled 'Untangling Research Puzzles in Merton's Multilevel Anomie Theory' 'untangles' Merton thus:

$$Y_\infty = \beta_0 + \beta_1(Y_3) + \beta_2(Y_4) + \beta_3(Y_3Y_4) + \beta_4(Y_3Y_4Y_5) + \beta_5(Y_3Y_4Y_2) + \beta_6(Y_3Y_4Y_6)$$
$$+ \beta_7(Y_3Y_4Y_7) + r$$

$$\beta_0 = \gamma_{00} + u_0$$

$$\beta_3 = \gamma_{10} + \gamma_{11}(X_2) + \gamma_{12}(X_3) + \gamma_{11}(Y_1) + u_1 \quad (2007, p82)$$

It is beyond me how such a fanciful elaboration aids the understanding of Merton's lucid and parsimonious piece. There has to be a point where disentangling becomes mangling, where one suspects some other motive, scientistic and nomothetic, has taken over.

But still I come back to criminology, only in part because that is the area in which I have spent most of my academic life and feel most at home. More importantly it is because the tendencies of obsessive concern with natural scientific and statistical method, of numerical othering, of distancing from the subject matter, of bracketing off issues of power and inequality, of abstracted empiricism are more pronounced in criminology than elsewhere. And then there is the paradox: the criminological gaze is more exposed to problems of power, stigmatization, pluralism and the contest of values than perhaps any other area of the social sciences. Indeed, there is a certain privileged vantage point of criminology and the sociology of deviance of which it is part, for it is here that norms are formed and norms are broken, where norms are disputed and selectively enforced, where deviance is enacted and deviance concealed. Here nothing seems like it purports to be (a fact of tremendous importance in evaluating the interview, the questionnaire or the superficial first glance of ethnography) – and deviance seems to bubble below every crack and crevice of the taken-for-granted social structure. It is here, late at night, where the rule of law breaks down in the crack of the night stick, it is the traffic stop where its arrogant prejudice is caught for fleeting moments on video camera; it is the prison yard, in the arms of the law, where drugs, rape and violence are more prevalent than outside its walls. It is the hidden economy of factory and the street, the everyday corruption of politicians and the powerful. It is the place where nothing really looks like it should and where the world is not what it seems to be.

All of this would seem a marvellous starting point for a critical perspective to emerge. And indeed, during the 1960s and early 1970s, the new criminology and the sociology of deviance were very much to the centre of debate within sociology as a whole. This was the time of a cultural turn which resonated throughout the social sciences from anthropology through to labour history. Explicit in this endeavour was a stress on the interpretative rather than the mechanistic and the positivistic. Thus both a reduction of human action to a reflex of the material situation or a positivistic enactment of a pre-given culture was ruled out of court. Rather, an interpretative analysis focusing on the way in which human actors generate meaning becomes paramount. It was an exceptional period in the sociology of deviance consisting of two radical strands: subcultural and labelling; on the one hand the theories of Albert Cohen and Richard Cloward arising out of the inspirational work of Merton, at that time still influenced by Marx and a radical interpretation of Durkheim (see Young, 2010) and on the other the phenomenological tradition of Becker, Kitsuse and Lemert, supplemented by the social constructionist work of writers such as Peter Berger and Thomas Luckmann. I will expand on this later but suffice it to say that this scholarship was extraordinarily influential involving, as it did, the existential sense of freedom curtailed and constructed by the labels and essentialization of the powerful. Deviancy was a human creation, granted meaning; social control involved a denial of meaning and the imposition of a deterministic essence. By the mid 1980s such a humanistic sociology, buttressed by strong critiques of positivistic methods was a major force within criminology. Let me list briefly some of the theoretical insights and advances which were the common currency of the time:

- that statistics are social constructions
- that deviance is not a quality inherent in an act but a quality bestowed upon it
- that meaning is dependent on social context
- that the human subject is a creative actor albeit in circumstances beyond his or her control
- that explanation has to place the actor in a wider social structure and cannot remain on the level of the individual
- that we live in a pluralistic society of contested definitions of deviance and normality
- that agencies of social control attempt to maintain and enforce the definitions of the powerful.

Furthermore, the actual world around us has reinforced such insights. Mass immigration has brought pluralism to our streets, the mass media has brought it to our eyes and our ears while the late modern stress on creativity and lifestyle has mobilized a dazzling array of subcultures to intrigue or dismay us. The world changes fast, social definitions have no fixity, people's lives are disembedded, they change jobs, communities, families more frequently, they constantly rewrite the narratives of their lives. We do not live in a world of solidity and essences however much we may hanker for them. None of this is conducive to the perspectives which would allow positivist views to survive easily, let alone thrive. Since then, however, there was been a considerable shift back to positivism. It is not that critical criminology has disappeared. Far from it: as we shall see, it flourishes, but positivism, once seemingly intellectually defeated, has crept back to the centre stage of syllabus and research agenda. The question which must be asked is how has such a revanchism come about given the privileged position of criminology? For it is confronted, smack in the face by power and prejudice, backed by an inspiring intellectual tradition revolving around social constructionism, and, to top it all, where we all engage every day in a late modern world which valorizes human individualism and creativity and is increasingly pluralistic in its values?

The Hubris of Positivism

> Criminology has moved into an age of immense methodological sophis-
> tication. Given the expertise of criminologists in measurement, research
> design, and analysis, all that would seem to be required to collect 'large
> quantities of data on large representative samples of individuals' (Nagin
> and Tremblay, 2005, p. 918). Nor must we wait for rigorous science to
> show itself.' Of the 99 articles published in three volumes of *Criminology*
> (2001–4), 82% used statistical analysis of quantitative data, with 32%
> relying on nonlinear regression approaches, including HLM, trajectory
> analysis, negative binomial and tobit models (Bushway and Weisburd,
> 2006,1). (Hirschi and Gottfredson, 2008, p. 229)

Such an encroachment of positivistic method occurred, as my previous
examples have illustrated, throughout sociology in general and were
accurately predicted by Mills way back in the 1950s. But let me for a
moment continue to concentrate on the forces impinging upon criminology, holding in mind that criminal justice studies represents one of the
most fast-expanding sections of the social sciences and that there is a dramatically significant impact of positivist method and outlook in this area.

What is the reason for this revanchism? One does not have to look far
to identify the external, material forces which have transformed criminology. First of all there is the extraordinary burgeoning of the criminal
justice system, particularly, of course, in the United States, but also in the
majority of Western countries. This has involved massive expenditure on
prisons, police, treatment regimes and crime prevention devices, from
CCTV to DNA testing. It has been vastly augmented by the 'war' against
drugs and, more recently, against terrorism. The demand for consultancy
and evaluative research has, therefore, rocketed. Parallel to this, university teaching of criminology to train personnel, both practitioners and
researchers, has expanded exponentially so that criminal justice studies
has become the largest sector of social science teaching. Students who
once would have studied social policy and administration now study
criminal justice – a clear consequence of the movement from welfare to
criminal justice system interventions as the leading edge of social policy.
Further, the restricted funding available for higher education has led to
considerable pressure on faculty to bring in funding from research (see
Robinson, 2001). The crime control industry has, therefore, come to
exert, particularly in the United States, a near hegemonic influence upon
large sections of academic criminology. The war against crime, drugs,
terrorism, demands facts, numbers, quantitative incomes and outcomes –
it does *not* demand debates as to the very nature of these battles, it does
not want to question definition, rather it wants 'hard' facts and 'concrete'

evidence. The social basis for positivism is thus assured. Couple this with the ascendacy of neo-liberal thinking in the economic and political sphere, and the movement into a market society where market values have become the dominant ethos (Taylor, 1999; Hayward, 2004b) and you have the basis for the development of rational choice theory – a form, as I will argue later, of market positivism.

The response in the academy has been substantial and far-reaching. Research has begun to be dominated by statistical testing, theory has been downplayed, and 'soft' data eschewed (see Ferrell and Hamm, 1998). It takes a little reflection to realize that the dominant journal format of ill-developed theory, regression analysis and, usually, rather inconclusive results is, in fact, a relatively recent genre. Data which are in fact technically weak (because of the well-known difficulties inherent in the collection of statistics whether by the police, victimization studies, or self-report studies) and, which *in any case*, are by their very nature contested, blurred and ambiguous, and unsuited for quantification, are mindlessly churned through personal computers. The journals and the articles become myriad, yet their cogitation and pontification become more and more obscure – lost in a mess of figures, techno-speak and obfuscation. Meanwhile the ramifications within the academy involve a form of quasi-professionalization or bureaucratization. This is seen most blatantly in the PhD programmes. Here, induction into quantitative methodological techniques becomes a central part of academic training, qualitative methods take a more lowly position – and even here bizarre attempts are made to produce software which will enable the researcher to quantify the qualitative, to digitalize *verstehen*. Robert Park, you will remember, the great architect of the Chicago School admonished his students in 1927 to 'Go sit in the lounges of the luxury hotels and on the doorsteps of the flophouses; sit on the Gold Coast settees and on the slum shakedowns; sit in the Orchestral Hall and in the Star and Garter Burlesque. In short go out and get the seat of your pants dirty in real research.' Nowadays the distance between the world out there and the academy has become wider and wider. It is fenced in by numbers, sanitized by computer printouts. On top of this, the bureaucratization of the research process by overseeing academic committees has stultified the possible range and type of research. As Patricia and Peter Adler put it:

Beginning in the late 1970s, but not fully taking hold until the 1990s, Institutional Review Boards (IRBs) at most colleges and universities have made ethnographic work on criminal and deviant groups almost impossible to conduct. Even the new Code of Ethics of the American Sociological Association yields to the decisions of these boards, claiming that if projects are disapproved by these local agencies, the research, in the association's eyes, is unethical. Potentially gone, then, is any ethnographic research involving a covert role for the investigator (thus removing hidden populations further from view), any ethnographic research on minors that does not obtain parental consent (obviously problematic for youth involved in deviance or crime or who are victims of parental abuse), and any ethnographic research on vulnerable populations or sensitive (including criminal) issues without signed consent forms that explicitly indicate the researchers' inability to protect subjects' confidentiality. This approach puts governmental and institutional bureaucratic mandates ahead of the research bargains and confidences previously forged by fieldworkers, denigrating the impact of critical dimensions of fieldwork techniques such as reciprocity, trust, evolving relationships, depth, shifting roles, and the relative weighting of research loyalty (subjects versus society). (1998, pp. xiv–xv)

Between the iron cage of the Institutional Review Board and the gentle pulling and pushing of government funding, the discipline inevitably changes its form, its critical edge, and its direction.

But there is more to it than this, for the analysis so far is based on too much external pressure, financial or otherwise, as if this modern numerology were simply, and rather venally, coaxed out of the academy. But we must also, perhaps more importantly, explain the intellectual attractions of the scientific method. We must, in short, talk about conviction as much as about coercion.

I shall return to the attractions of positivism later in the book. But let me first note that the elective affinity between positivist criminology and the bureaucratic needs of the criminal justice system is not simply a question of the need for numbers and statistical functionaries willing to provide them. It is a question of shared notions of ontology and of social order, of world views which are coincident in their mapping of the social world and the place of the deviant within it, backed by common and more general anxieties with regard to social order. For the desire to place society in orderly and carefully delineated categories and the patterning of such order is not merely a useful accountancy device for the criminal justice system on the part of managers (which it is), or a scholarly desire to classify and seek regularity in the social universe. It is much more than that.

2

Measurement and the Sexologists

In April and May 1995 the columns of *The New York Review of Books* were subject to a remarkable and, some would say, acrimonious debate. It was an argument which was, to my mind, one of the most significant examples of academic whistle-blowing, wide ranging in its critique, apposite in its target and reasoning, timely and badly needed yet falling, as we shall see, on stony ground.

On one side of this skirmish was Richard Lewontin, Professor of Zoology at Harvard, a distinguished geneticist and epidemiologist, on the other a team of sociologists led by Edward Laumann and John Gagnon, from the University of Chicago, who had with others recently published *The Social Organisation of Sexuality* (1995a), and its popular companion volume *Sex in America: A Definitive Survey* (Michael et al., 1995). On the sides, chipping in with great gusto, was Richard Sennett, joint Professor of Sociology at the LSE and NYU – one of the foremost sociologists of our time.

This debate is of interest because it represents the direct confrontation of natural science with sociology or social science, as it is often hopefully and optimistically called. Such encounters are relatively rare and tend to occur when particularly politically distasteful findings are presented to the public as cast iron and embellished with the imprimatur of science. An example of this was Richard Herrnstein and Charles Murray's *The Bell Curve* (1994), accompanied by pages of statistical tables which purported to present the scientific evidence for the link between race, IQ and, indeed, crime. At that time many prominent scientists, including Steven Rose and Stephen Gould, were moved to intervene, but normally the walls between disciplines remain intact: indeed a collegial atmosphere of mutual respect coupled with lack of interest ensures that parallel and contradictory literatures about the same subject can occur in departments separated sometimes by a corridor or, more frequently, a faculty block. In the case of the natural and social sciences this is complicated by a unidirectional admiration – a one-sided love, one might say – or at least a state of acute physics envy – between the aspiring social scientist and the natural sciences. Be that as it may, a significant proportion of sociologists, the vast majority of psychologists and an increasing number of criminologists embrace, albeit with some doubt and hesitation, a positivistic path. Namely, that natural scientific methods can be applied to human action, that behaviour is causally determined, that incontestable objectivity is attainable and that precise quantitative measurement is possible, and indeed preferable. In the case of criminology, this entails the belief that the crimes of individuals can be predicted from risk factors and that rates of crime can be explained by the changes in the proportion of causal factors in the population.

Richard Lewontin sets out to review the two books. They arose on the back of the AIDS crisis and the need to understand the epidemiology of its spread. The survey was eventually well funded by the research foundations, was conducted by NORC, the premiere social survey research organization in North America. The project was initiated by the National Institute of Health on behalf of a coalition of Federal agencies concerned about AIDS. For a project which, as we shall see, was beset by problems of concealment, it is of ironic interest that, in the search for funding, the title of the project itself deliberately avoided mentioning sex, entitling itself: 'The National Health and Social Life Survey', while the original proposal issued by the National Institute of Health was entitled: 'Social and Behavioural Aspects of Fertility-Related Behaviour'. 'At very least', as Lewontin wryly comments, 'there is some anatomical confusion here' (p. 25). Despite this camouflage, funding was then refused by the First Bush Administration until eventually rescued by the Foundations.

The project involved a sample of 3,432 people representing 200 million post-pubertal Americans. Just for a minute let us think of the audacity of the sample survey – and this one more thorough than most – carrying with it the claim to generalize from such a small number to such a large population of individuals. Today we take for granted in public opinion polls, in market research, and in social scientific work, the facility of the social survey. These surveys are the staple of political debate and social commentary, yet their basis is much shakier than we often assume and it is for this reason that Lewontin's critique is of much greater purchase than a commentary on sex studies or criminology for that matter. Lewontin's criticism proceeds on two levels, one the problem of representativeness and two – and more substantially – the problem of truth. Let us first of all examine the problem of representation. An initial criticism is that the random sample was not actually from the total population. It is based on a sample of addresses drawn from the census, but it excluded households where there were no English speakers, nor anyone outside of the ages of 15–59. Most crucially it excludes the three per cent of Americans (some 7.5 million) who do not live in households because they live in institutions or are homeless. This latter point is, as Lewontin indicates, scarcely trivial in understanding the epidemiology of AIDS as it excludes the most vulnerable group in the population, including those likely to be victims of homosexual rape in prison, prostitution, reckless drug use, the sexually 'free' college-aged adolescents, and so on. The random sample is not, therefore, drawn from the population as a whole: a *very* atypical population is omitted and perversely it is of importance because it is atypical. Yet such a restriction in population sampled is a usual preliminary in survey research

However, once this somewhat restricted sample was made, the research team did not stint in their efforts to get as large a response rate as possible. After repeated visits, telephone calls and financial inducements ranging from $10 to $100, the result was a response rate of 79 per cent – of which they were duly pleased. Indeed, they declare themselves 'astonished' by this response rate which 'is even more remarkable because it includes as non-responders people who simply could not be found to be interviewed' (Michael et al., 1995, p. 33). Of course, as anyone who has ever conducted a social survey knows, finding the respondents is, to say the least, quite an important task! Yet, as Lewontin points out: 'It is almost always the case that those who do not respond are a non-random sample of those who are asked' (1995a, p. 28). In this case it could well be prudishness, but such equally non-random causes of non-responses occurs in other surveys. For example, in our own experience of over fifteen large-scale crime and victimization studies which we ran out of The Centre for Criminology, Middlesex University (see for example Jones et al., 1986; Crawford et al., 1990) we made considerable effort to reduce non-response but never managed better than 83 per cent. Indeed, criminal victimization surveys, as a whole, have between one fifth to a quarter of respondents whose victimization is unknown. As I remarked at the time, in the thick of quantitative research:

> It goes without saying that such a large unknown population could easily skew every finding we victimologists present. At the most obvious level, it probably includes a disproportionate number of transients, of lower working-class people hostile to officials with clipboards attempting to ask them about their lives, and of those who are most frightened to answer the door because of fear of crime. (Young, 1988, p. 169).

Even panel studies which follow a given population over time suffer from this problem. To take the famous Seattle Social Development Project as an example (see Farrington et al., 2003), which is a prospective longitudinal survey of 808 children. To begin with, these surveys are limited to the children/parents who consented to be included out of the population of 1,053 fifth-grade students targeted – that is, it has a 70 per cent response rate from the outset – with 30 per cent refusing consent. Secondly, youths dropped out over time so, for example, by the age of twelve the sample fell to 52 per cent. There is, of course, every reason to suspect that those who initially did not consent and those who fell out of the panel might have very different delinquency patterns to those who consented and remained within the panel.

Lewontin's first point – the problem of representativeness – is, therefore, clear and is as applicable to criminology as to other fields of sociology. Let me at this point remind the reader of Quetelet's warning. Adolphe Quetelet the founder of scientific statistics, and a pioneer in analysing the social and physical determinants of crime, introduced into academic discussion in the 1830s the problem of the unknown figure of crime. That is crime not revealed in the official statistics:

> This is also the place to examine a difficulty . . . it is that our observations can only refer to *a certain number of known and tried offenders out of the unknown sum total of crimes committed.* Since this sum total of crimes committed will probably ever continue unknown, all the reasoning of which it is the basis will be more or less defective. I do not hesitate to say, that all the knowledge which we possess on the statistics of crimes and offences will be of no utility whatsoever, unless we admit without question *that there is a ratio, nearly invariably the same, between known and tried offences and the unknown sum total of crimes committed.* This ratio is necessary, and if it did not really exist, everything which, until the present time, has been said on the statistical documents of crime, would be false and absurd.' (Quetelet, 1842, p. 82)

Quetelet's fixed ratios are, of course, a pipe dream, as unlikely as they would be convenient. His warning, written in 1835 (English translation 1842) has had echoes throughout the criminology academy for the last one hundred and seventy five years. If we do not know the true rate of crime all our theories are built on quicksand. They will be of 'no utility', 'false', and indeed 'absurd'. Legions of theorists from Robert K. Merton through to James Q. Wilson have committed the paradox of expressing their doubts about the accuracy of the data and then proceeding to use the crime figures with seeming abandon, particularly in recent years when the advent of sophisticated statistical analysis is, somehow, seen to grant permission to skate over the thin ice of insubstantiality (Giffen, 1965; Oosthoek, 1978). Others have put their faith in statistics generated by the social scientist, whether self-report studies or victimization surveys, as if Quetelet's warning no longer concerned them and the era of 'pre-scientific' data was over.

Indeed, Richard Sparks Senior and his associates, in the introduction to their groundbreaking London victimization study, summarized the decade of American research prior to their own with a note of jubilation: 'Within a decade ... some of the oldest problems of criminology have come at least within reach of a solution.' (Sparks et al., 1977, p. 1). As we have seen, the problem of non-response means that such a resolution of the age-old problem of measurement is not resolved. It would be so, of course, if the non-respondents were just – or almost – like the respondents and indeed such an excuse is often invoked with as much likelihood of validity as Quetelet's ratios. As it is, the atypicality of non-respondents is likely to overturn the significance levels of any probabilistic sampling. Richard Sparks was quite clear about this in his assessment of the potential of victimization studies. His initial excitement became tempered by considerable caution. Thus he writes, four years later:

> Much too much fuss is made, in practically all official NCS publications, about statistical significance (i.e. allowance for sampling variability). A variety of standard errors and confidence intervals for NCS data are now routinely quoted in those publications. Yet it is clear that *non*sampling error is of far greater magnitude in the NCS; adjustments ... may offset some of this nonsampling error, though only in a ballpark way, which makes questions of sampling variability virtually irrelevant. (1981, p. 44, n. 42)

Telling the Truth?

But let us go on to Lewontin's next criticism: the problem of truth. And here the problem is even more important and substantial than that of non-response and the hidden figure. This revolves around the key question of whether those who responded to the questionnaire were in fact telling the truth. That is, that social surveys may not only have hidden figures of non-respondents, but a hidden figure of non-response – and, indeed, sometimes 'over-response' – among the respondents themselves.

It is rare for surveys of attitude or self-reported behaviour to have any internal check as to validity. After all, if people say they would rather live by work than on welfare, if they profess liberal attitudes on racial matters, or if they tell you that they were assaulted twice last year, how is one to know that this is not true? One may have one's suspicions, of course, but there are few cast-iron checks. Every now and then, however, anomalies stare you in the face. In the case of the sexual behaviour survey there is a particularly blatant example. For the average number of het-erosexual partners reported by men over the last five years is 75 per cent greater than the average number reported by women. This is an obvious anomaly, it is, as Lewontin points out, like a violation of the only reliable law in economics: that the number of sales must be equal to the number of purchases. Furthermore it turns out that such discrepancies are well known in sex studies. For on the back of the panic over AIDS, parallel studies occurred across the Western world and all of them found a wide differential between the number of sexual partners reported by men and women. (For France see ACFS, 1992; for Sweden, Herlitz, 1990; for an insightful critical commentary, see Francome, 1993.) The controversy over sexual behaviour figures is reflected in the arguments between gay rights groups and researchers in Britain over the latter's claims that there are far fewer gay men than is usually assumed. Gay activists, quite cor-rectly, point to the likelihood of widespread concealment in the survey situation (see Katz, 1994).

Interestingly the gap is greater for some countries rather than others – French men, for example, would seem to have more discrepant claims than Americans or Britons. Such claims in numbers of sexual partners and frequency of sexual intercourse are very obviously a function of male boasting, female modesty and indeed different definitions as to what actually constitutes sexual intercourse. They tell us something about the differences between the sexes, something about different levels of double standards in various countries and over time, but only very obliquely and obscurely about different rates of sexual behaviour. Ironically, such discrepancies were well known to early sex researchers, such as Kinsey, who rather smugly the present researchers claim to have easily surpassed in their sophistication.

What is startling is that the researchers are well aware of this. Indeed the US researchers devote considerable time to debating which of several reasons might have caused this 'discrepancy' and conclude that the most likely explanation is that 'either men may exaggerate or women may underestimate'. As Lewontin remarks,

> So, in the single case where one can actually test the truth, the investigators themselves think it most likely that people are telling themselves and others enormous lies. If one takes the authors at their word, it would seem futile to take seriously the other results of the study. The report that 5.3 percent of conventional Protestants, 3.3 percent of fundamentalists, 2.8 percent of Catholics, and 10.7 percent of the non-religious have ever had a same-sex partner may show the effect of religion on practice or it may be nothing but hypocrisy. What is billed as a study of 'Sexual Practices in the United

States' is, after all, a study of an indissoluble jumble of practices, attitudes, personal myths, and posturing.' (1995a, p. 29)

What is of interest here is the awareness of thin ice, yet the ineluctable desire to keep on skating. Just as when the weakness of the statistics is plain to the researchers yet they continue to force-feed inadequate data into their personal computers, here the problem of lying, whether by exaggeration or concealment, does not stop the researchers, for more than a moment, in their scientific task. Of course, as a sociologist, such findings are not irrelevant: they inform you much about differences in male and female attitudes to sex – what they *don't* tell you is about differences in sexual behaviour. What Richard Lewontin is telling us is that the interview situation is a social relationship – that results are a product of a social interaction and will vary with the gender, class, and age of the interviewer and of the interviewee. But here we have it: it needs a Professor of Biology to tell sociologists to be sociologists. Thus, he concludes:

> The answer, surely, is to be less ambitious and stop trying to make sociology into a natural science although it is, indeed, the study of natural objects. There are some things in the world that we will never know and many that we will never know exactly. Each domain of phenomena has its characteristic grain of knowability. Biology is not physics, because organisms are such complex physical objects, and sociology is not biology because human societies are made by self-conscious organisms. By pretending to a kind of knowledge that it cannot achieve, social science can only engender the scorn of natural scientists and the cynicism of humanists. (1995a p. 29)

Of course this is not the end of it. Edward Laumann and his colleagues are outraged. They do not think it 'appropriate for a biologist 'to be reviewing their work, he does not have the right 'professional qualifications' – 'his review is a pastiche of ill-informed personal opinion that makes unfounded claims of relevant scientific authority and expertise' (1995b, p. 43).

Lewontin, in reply, notes caustically that it is understandable that the team

> would have preferred to have their own work reviewed by a member of their own school of sociology, someone sharing the same unexamined methodological assumptions. They could avoid the always unpleasant necessity of justifying the epistemic basis on which the entire structure of their work depends. (1995b, p. 43)

As to his incompetence with regard to statistical analysis, he points to being a bit disturbed to have to reveal his CV, but that he has a graduate degree in mathematical statistics which he has taught for forty years and this is the subject of about one-tenth of his publications including a textbook on statistics!

Lewontin returns to the strange belief that positivist sociologists have that there is no social relationship involved in the process of data collection:

> Is it really true that quantitative sociologists are so divorced from introspection and so insensitive to social interactions that they take such a naive view of human behavior? Do they really believe all those things they hear from the person on the next bar stool or the seat next to them in the airplane? The Yellow Kid, who made a living from fleecing the gullible, used to say that anyone who could not con a banker ought to go into another line of work. Maybe, but before giving up, they should try professors of sociology. Putting aside subjective questions, haven't they even read the voluminous literature on the sociology of fashion? It is ironic that a student of 'simple organisms' has to instruct those who inquire about human beings about the complexity of their objects of study.
>
> . . . people do not tell *themselves* the truth about their own lives. The need to create a satisfying narrative out of an inconsistent and often irrational and disappointing jumble of feelings and events leads each of us to write and rewrite our autobiographies inside our own heads, irrespective of whether anyone else is ever privy to the story. Second, those stories, which we then mistake for the truth, become the basis for further conscious manipulation and manufacture when we have exchanges with other human beings. If the investigators at NORC really do not care what strangers think of them, then they are possessed of an insouciance and hauteur otherwise unknown in Western society. It is precisely in the interaction with strangers who are not part of their social network, and who will never intersect their lives again, that people feel most free to embroider their life stories, because they will never be caught out. (1995b, p. 44)

And, of course, such a process of believing in the objectivity of data is fostered by the habit of researchers of *not* conducting their own interviews, of employing agencies such as NORC, or second hand, in terms of using older datasets or even a meta-analysis of past datasets. So the data arrive at their computers already punched, sanitized: they are a series of numbers with scientific-looking decimal points. Human contact is minimized and a barrier of printout and digits occurs between the researchers and human life.

But let us leave the last remarks of this section to Richard Sennett. He congratulates Lewontin on the brilliance of his analysis, he laments the current fashion of scientific sociology, and concurs with Lewontin's remark that, if work such as this is typical, then the discipline must be in 'deep trouble'. That's putting it mildly, suggests Sennett, 'American sociology has become a refuge for the academically challenged' (1995, p. 43). But he adds that mere stupidity itself cannot alone explain the analytic weakness of such studies for 'sociology in its dumbed-down condition is emblematic of a society that doesn't want to know much about itself' (1995).

Lessons for Criminology

But what has all of this to do with criminology? A great deal and more, for it is probably criminology, of all the branches of sociology and psychology, where the problem of unchecked positivism is greatest. The expansion of academic criminology, as we have seen, has been a consequence of the exponential increase in the size of the criminal justice system, just as the shift from students studying social policy/administration to criminology parallels the shift from governmental interventions through the welfare state to those utilizing criminal justice. The war on crime has been followed by the war on drugs and now the war on terror. This has been accompanied by an expansion in funding designed to evaluate and assess governmental interventions and programmes. The material basis for the revitalization of positivist criminology is considerable and, certainly within the United States, approaching hegemonic.

Let us examine some of the discrepant findings which have occurred in recent criminology.

Embarrassing Findings

Criminological research is replete with findings which range from the very unlikely to the ridiculous. I will give just a few examples:

The Education Effect

One of the most widely recognized anomalies is victimization research arising out of 'the education effect'. This is where higher reporting of victimization is linked to educational attainment and is, in Richard Sparks' (1981) estimation, one of the 'most serious' response biases. The education effect was first spotted by Biderman in his survey for the 1967 President's Commission (Biderman et al., 1967), it occurred in Sparks' and his colleagues London survey (Sparks, Genn and Dodd, 1977) and was found with regard to violence in *The British Crime Survey* (Hough, 1986. See commentaries in Skogan, 1986; Coleman and Moynihan, 1996).

It appears an obvious anomaly in the National Crime Survey where, for example, the 1977 report shows reported assault generally to rise with educational attainment so that, for example, for white respondents those with some college education had twice the rate of aggravated assault as those who had only completed eighth grade and for black respondents a similar pattern appeared. Middle-class people in general have a much greater intolerance of violence on survey responses of to variables which are linked to social class, in particular educational attainment. Sparks stresses the anomalous nature of such findings:

> 'Being a survey respondent' is, in many ways, a middle-class game; it requires a certain amount of verbal fluency and a capacity for abstract conceptualization, both of which are to some extent concomitants (if not consequences) of formal education. In a victimization survey, the tasks which a respondent must perform involve casting one's mind back over a particular period in one's past and fitting descriptions given by the interviewer's questions ('Did anyone break into your house?') to the events which may have occurred in that time. It would not be surprising to find that these classroom-like tasks would be better performed by those with more practice (in the classroom) at them; and there is increasing evidence that this is precisely what happens. (Sparks, 1981, p. 34)

This problem is universally acknowledged yet its solution peculiarly muted. More recently James Lynch, one of the most perspicacious and respected researchers working in this area, notes that the phenomenon is widespread and speculated that this may be due, among other things, to the fact: 'that minor violence is so ubiquitous among less educated respondents that they simply do not encode it in memory, whereas the infrequency of minor violence for higher-status respondents encourages them to encode these events' (2006, p. 237). Let us note, as an aside, that what this suggests is not merely a factor of memory or of ability to answer questionnaires but a much more significant cultural effect where upper middle-class people in general have a much greater intolerance of violence and therefore register minor acts of violence as more significant than those lower in the social structure. But more of this later. Lynch himself minimizes the problem pointing out that the education effect is not observed with more serious acts of violence where weapons are used: 'Consequently, while the education effect is not consistent with theory, it is a fairly localized problem for victimization surveys (restricted to minor assaults) and does not raise fundamental questions about the method more generally' (Lynch, 2006). (See also Cantor and Lynch, 2000.)

This is, of course, of great interest in that it concedes that there is a cultural problem of interpretation and evaluation for the mass of data which reduces with the seriousness of offence. After all we would expect to agree more about homicide being an act of violence than we would about a slap. But of course this would suggest that we would restrict our quantitative studies of violence to the minority of data deemed serious and even then we would have debate about the demarcation line. But Richard Sparks himself, after stressing how serious the anomaly is, goes much further than this, noting that such an education effect will in his words, 'infect' much of the survey data and, of course, let us add that this would be all the more insidious as no obvious anomaly could be observed in these presumably numerous instances:

> This bias is all the more serious in view of the strong associations which exist in contemporary American society between educational attainment and other demographic and social variables which are important both for criminological theory and for public policy concerning crime: that is, variables such as age, sex, race, income, area, and region of residence. Thus, for example, blacks, older persons, females, lower-income persons, southerners, and rural residents are, on average, less educated than their counterparts; the interrelations between these things, and the effects of those interrelations on educational attainment, may be extremely complicated. A response effect due to educational attainment is thus likely to infect pretty well any inference about victimization which might be made from NCS data. (Sparks, 1981, p. 34)

The Assault Rate on White Men
A similar finding for the above occurs in terms of assaults and ethnicity. The United States NCVS regularly comes up with results which show that the assault rate reported by white men is just about that of black men. For example, in 1999 the rate was 32.3 per 1,000 for whites compared to 31.0 per 1,000 for blacks. (Maguire and Pastore, 2001) This is totally against any evidence from homicide rates or other indices of violence which would suggest a much greater assault rate against black men (see Sparks, 1981, for similar earlier findings).

Rarity of Serious Crimes
Victimization studies consistently report levels of serious crime which are gross underestimations and are *freely admitted* as such. For example, the first British Crime Survey of England and Wales in 1982 found only one rape and that attempted (see Hough and Mayhew, 1983).

Variability of Findings with Different Instruments
If we take sensitive topics such as incidence of domestic violence, the range of figures are extraordinarily wide – and, in no doubt, underestimates. Thus in 1996 the percentage of women experiencing domestic violence, defined as physical assault with injury, was 0.5 per cent in

the police figures, one per cent in the British Crime Survey, and 2.2 per cent when Computer Assisted Self-Interviewing was used. An independent survey found a rate in the region of 8 per cent (see Mooney, 2000). Which figure in this range is one going to feed into one's PC? What sort of science is it where a variable varies sixteen-fold depending on the measuring instrument?

Self-Report Studies

These consistently come up with results showing that there is little variation between the levels of juvenile delinquency between the working class and the middle class, between black and white, and produce a considerably reduced gap between males and females. Hence Charles Tittle and his colleagues' (1978) extraordinary claim that there is no relationship between class and delinquency. What is even more remarkable is that influential theorists, particularly Travis Hirschi and his associates, have built theories around such a rank implausibility (see Gottfredson and Hirschi, 1990 in their grandly entitled *A General Theory of Crime*). As David Downes and Paul Rock point out: 'Since control theorists make so much of the strength of their case empirically, it is worth noting that in certain respects Hirschi's data strain credibility – a pleasant change from theories producing that effect' (1988, p. 237, n.).

There can be no better example of the fetishism of data than the rejection of the relationship between social class and conventional crime. If one is talking of *all* crime and includes corporate and white collar crimes this is, of course, a different matter, but this is not the primary focus of self-report studies nor the theories emanating from them (see Currie, 1985). All one can record about this surmise is John Braithwaite's pithy remark:

> it is hardly plausible that one can totally explain away the higher risks of being mugged and raped in lower-class areas as the consequence of the activities of middle-class people who come into the area to perpetrate such acts. (1981, p. 37)

Gottfredson and Hirschi's riposte to this is *far* from convincing:

> The most common device for 'clinching' the argument about social class and crime invites the disputee to park his car in a slum area or to walk the streets of lower-class sections of town and compare the experience with a similar walk in affluent areas. As a rhetorical device, this argument is effective, but it is not necessarily accurate (graveyards also exude fear, although there is some question about whether the people in them are especially dangerous) (1990, p. 80, n. 8)

Findings of the International Crime and Victimization Studies

The International Crime and Victimization Study (Van Kesteren et al., 2000) frequently finds rates of reported violence of nations which are almost the inverse of the homicide rates. In fact, I am surprised that no one has run a Pearson Rank Coefficient on their findings!

The Pluralism of the Hidden Figure

Until now we have discussed either technical problems of non-response or the more substantive problem of exaggeration or lying. I want now to turn to a third problem which generates even greater and more impenetrable barriers for scientific quantification. The first two problems – which Lewontin addresses – that of representativeness and truth, presume that there are objective data there to be registered. However, there is a profound difference between measurement in the natural world and in society, namely that the definitions of social phenomena are constructed by individuals and in this they will vary with the social constructs of the actors involved. If one hands out a dozen metre rules to students and asks them to measure the length of the seminar room, they will come to a common agreement with a little variation for accuracy. If one asks the room full of students to measure levels of violence they are, so to speak, already equipped with a dozen rules of different gauge and length. They will come out of the exercise with different amounts of violence because their definitions of violence will vary. And the same will be true of the respondents to a victimization study. All of us may agree that a stab wound is violence, but where along the continuum does violence begin: is it a shove (if so, how hard?), is it a tap (if so, how weighty?), or perhaps it is a harsh word, an obscenity, a threat? People vary in their definitions and tolerance of violence: there is a pluralism of measures. (See Hough, 1986; Young, 1988; Mooney, 2000), and this would vary by place and time. For, as Durkheim observed in *The Rules of Sociological Method* (1938), definitions vary with the social base, 'a society of saints' would not have less deviance, only a stricter definition of it.

Let us look at our 'anomalies' in this light. The peculiar results of the International Crime and Victimization Studies where the rates of violence reported approximate the inverse of the rates of violence occurring if we are to trust the homicide figures, may well be not only that reporting to strangers distorts the level of violence. It may well be that countries with low levels of violence may have low levels of tolerance of violence and thus report acts which other, more tolerant/violent nations, might ignore. Similarly the comparatively higher rates of violence against white compared to black men in the United States or the educated compared to the less educated may well reflect differences in definition of what constitutes 'real' violence.

Once we have acknowledged the pluralism of human definition, we can then return to the hidden figure with even greater doubts and trepidations. For the hidden figure will expand and contract not merely with the technical means we bring to it, but with the values of the respondents and indeed the categories of the interviewers. And the social rather than the merely technical permeates our measurement on all three levels: whether it is the respondents who refuse to talk to us, to those that in their relationship with a stranger (of class, gender, age, and perhaps ethnicity) will attempt to convey an impression of themselves (a product of their own personal narrative which they have woven around the 'facts' of their lives), to the values and meanings which the interviewee brings to the table.

Thus, to differential tolerance thresholds to violence, we must add different capacities in abstract thinking, a willingness to recall violence and to conceptualize what is often a blur of events as a series of events that can be conceptualized.

The Critique of Social Statistics

There are therefore three levels of critique with regard to social statistics which emerge from this analysis. The first is the problem of *representativeness*, the second, the problem of truth or what one might better call masquerading (because however untrue in its pretence it may be true in its consequences), and the third concerns questions of *interpretation and value*. Each of these presents different problems for social research, and each generates its own hidden figure.

Eysenck's Dilemma

It is important to stress how damaging such findings are for the positivist, for the scientific project of studying humanity. For positivism needs fixed categories, agreed measurements, objective and uncontested figures. The late Hans Eysenck, the doyen of psychological behaviourism, recognized this quite clearly in the last book he wrote on criminology with his colleague Gisli Gudjonsson. For, in *The Causes and Cures of Criminality* (1989) they begin by taking issue with the authors of *The*

New Criminology (Taylor et al., 1973) in our assertion that crime is not an objective category but a product of varying legal fiat. Eysenck and Gudjonsson quite clearly recognize this as an obstacle to science and get round the argument by differentiating two types of crime: victimless and victimful crime. Victimless crimes they concede – and they give examples from prostitution to anal sex – are subjectively and pluralistically defined. These are eliminated from the realm of objectivity and hence scientific study – but victimful crimes, and here they list such phenomena as theft, assault, murder, rape, are, they argue, universally condemned and, therefore, clearly in the sights of the objective. But this is obviously untrue: all of these crimes are subject to varying definitions – to talk of them having a fixed nature is to teeter on the brink of tautology. Rape is, of course, universally condemned because it is an illegal sexual attack, but what constitutes rape varies and, indeed, expands with time; witness the relatively recent acknowledgement of marital rape *as* rape. And assault, as we have seen, is greatly dependent on our tolerance of violence.

3

Amnesia and the Art of Skating on Thin Ice

Insider Sceptics

It is of interest that at the point of introduction of a new method of measurement, authors are often remarkably frank about the limitations of method: it is only later that doubts are expressed as an aside, a moment of hesitancy. Thus, both Richard Sparks Senior, the American pioneer of victimization research, and Mike Hough, the author of the first British Crime Survey (Hough and Mayhew, 1983) were remarkably candid about their research findings. Let us note at the outset that neither of these men were methodological radicals, both of them represent orthodoxy, both are diligent social scientists blessed with little epistemological doubt or theoretical wavering.

We have already seen how Sparks was sceptical about the use of tests of statistical significance as the non-response rates would easily skew any figures. But he goes much further than this, for he concludes his survey of victimization research with the ironic:

> At this point the reader may well wonder why this essay is subtitled 'an optimistic assessment'. Has it really been worthwhile to do fifteen years of extremely expensive research, merely to show that, Yes, Virginia, there really *is* a 'dark figure' or unrecorded crime? Is it worth continuing to spend money on a research technique with an error structure of unknown but possibly enormous proportions, which may be producing findings that are not only mistaken but downright misleading?
>
> (There are probably some people who have no difficulty in believing that the college educated are more at risk of aggravated assault than those with an eighth-grade education.) Is the victimization survey technique ever likely to provide information about crime that will be useful to researchers,

policy-makers, or administrators of the criminal justice system, and that could not be obtained in other (and less expensive) ways? (1981, p. 45)

Richard Sparks' answer to his question is, of course, yes, though he prefaces this with candour: 'At this point, I suppose I must declare an interest: I have invested about a decade of my professional career in this kind of research, and an investment of that magnitude is not calculated to make one condemn the method as worthless' (1981, p. 5). But his actual answer to the question is quite limited – gone is the scientific breakthrough which he had once heralded. He is left with a much more pragmatic approach. Victimization research reveals that there is a vast amount of criminal behaviour unknown; it puts police statistics and their limitations in perspective, it provides valuable information for policy-makers, etc. Here I think he is correct, particularly in terms of policy. For if we reject the notion of figures which can be used scientifically because of their precision and definitions, we can still use such survey research as baseline and ballpark figures. Let me give an example, where, because of problems of representativeness, truth and plurality of definition, though we can never produce figures which tell us what the rate of domestic violence is, we can still produce evidence of great social utility. We can produce figures which say, for example, that 15 per cent of the female population has, within the definition of violence suggested in the questionnaire, claimed that domestic violence has occurred against them – that this is no doubt an underestimate, is a composite of different interpretations of what constitutes such violence, yet is a large figure which demands that policy-makers take it seriously in terms of priorities and resources. This gives us figures, albeit vague and shadowy, which can be of great use to the policy-maker, but which have always to be interpreted, which are by their very nature blurred, which do not allow the refinement of decimal place, and are not the materials for statistical analysis but belong to a world of 'quite a lot', 'not much', or 'considerable' (see Mooney, 2000).

Let us turn to Mike Hough, writing in 1986, and reflecting on the findings of the pathbreaking first British Crime Survey, which he had recently co-directed. His remarks are extraordinarily insightful and serve to take us further in this critique. He points first of all to the various problems of under-reporting which we have already discussed, but he argues that he believes there is a clear distinction between the reliability of data about property crime and crimes of violence:

> These problems might be regarded by some simply as sources of measurement error – with the hope that methods can be refined in future. At their root, however is an insurmountable problem. There is not – and could probably never be – any degree of agreement between broad social groups

in defining assault, attacks, fights, etc. Critics of crime surveys sometimes argue that definitional problems vitiate the entire project of 'counting crime'. Definitions of particular crimes, the argument goes, are not absolute but vary across groups . . . This argument does not carry a great deal of weight so far as burglary goes, for instance, or car theft; one can assume extensive, though not total, agreement throughout the population about the sorts of incident which would qualify for a positive response to burglary 'screen' questions in a survey (. . .) But this is simply not so for most types of violent victimization. When does pushing, jostling and shoving become assault? And when does common assault turn into a more serious attack? Different people, and different groups of people, will apply different sets of criteria in answering 'screen questions' such as 'has anyone hit you or attacked you in any way?'. (1986, pp. 121–2)

Note then his notion of an 'insurmountable problem' with regards to violent crime, and his differentiation between types of statistics. His conclusion evokes an interesting parallel with medical statistics:

Whilst therefore a well-conducted crime survey may provide a better measure of the number of, e.g. burglaries in an area than do police records, it is hard to sustain the argument that either police records or survey statistics provide an adequate measure of violent offenses. A parallel with medical epidemiology can be usefully drawn. Some illnesses can be counted – with error, no doubt, but they can be counted so as to provide useful information. Thus, in England and Wales health statistics are collated about various forms of cancer, heart disease and the like. Some illnesses, however, cannot and could never be counted with anything approaching accuracy; the best examples come from mental health – depression, for example, schizophrenia or psychosis. It does not make sense to try to count the number of 'onsets' of these because there is no real agreement over their definitions. (1986, pp. 122–3)

They Know the Ice is Thin but Keep Skating on

What is remarkable is that the knowledge of the tenuous nature of the statistics is widespread, yet it does not seem to stop the would-be social scientist for more than a minute. Somewhere tucked into the text the authors admit the precariousness of their arguments, their scientific vulnerability, and yet continue on. It is as if the skater hesitates, notes the thin ice, yet skates blithely on. Let me give two examples out of the many; to do so is always invidious, but select we must:

Braine et al. Study of Desistance (2003)

> Laub and Sampson (2001: 9) indicate that many difficulties confronting the measurement of criminal desistance also confront the study of individual involvement in criminal activity more generally. This raises important and difficult issues about whether criminal desistance could be studied with official records or self-reports, the appropriate range of behaviors that fit within the concept of 'criminal behavior', and whether similar behaviors are interpreted consistently by different social and demographic groups (see e.g., Farrington and West 1995; Nagin et al., 1995; Uggen and Kruttschnitt 1998; Sommers et al., 1994; Warr 1998; Nielsen 1999; Benson 2001). Our objective in this paper is not to resolve these issues but rather to explore the implications of studying desistance through different analytical windows while assuming that the other difficulties in the study of criminal desistance are non-problematic. This approach allows us to focus our attention on variation in our results under different analytic frameworks while holding measurement issues constant. (Braine et al., 2003, p. 426, n. 6)

What is fascinating about this footnote is the thoroughness of the list of 'important and difficult issues' which they cite and which is backed by citing so many positivistic social scientists. It is resolved by assuming the difficulties to be 'non-problematic' and to proceed with the analysis – and note the pseudo-scientific language – 'while holding measurement issues constant'. They, in short, hold constant all the factors which could make their analysis a nonsense!

Myhill and Allen, Home Office Study of Rape (2002)

As we have seen, the first British Crime Survey found only one attempted rape in the whole of England and Wales. Extremely aware of the limitations of research into sexual victimization, and facing a barrage of criticism from feminist scholars, researchers at the Home Office in Britain set out to attempt to remedy this by the use of Computer Assisted Self-Interviewing techniques (CASI). The procedure in the 2000 sweep of the Survey was as follows: the majority of the crime victimization interviews are conducted as a face-to-face interview with the interviewer reading out the questions and instructions from his or her computer screen and inputting the results directly into their lap top computer. This is called Computer Assisted Personal Interviewing (CAPI). At the end of the CAPI interview, the respondents are invited to complete the self-completion section (two sections in the 2000 sweep on drugs and sexual victimization); the laptop is handed to them and the CASI interview begins. Thus the introduction of the supposedly anonymous technology is supposed to eliminate the embarrassment of the interview situation.

What can we make of this? First of all let us quickly skim over the usual problem of non-response (34 per cent in this instance), that there are differentials by age and class about ease and versatility in the use of computers, that in a minority of instances the interviewer assisted the interviewee, and that the presence of other people in the room – in many cases not only the interviewer – is bound to re-define the interview situation (see Mooney, 2000 for a critique of CASI with respect to domestic violence in the 1999 sweep of the BCS). Let us focus on the more substantive part of the problem, the screening question itself:

> Since age 16 has someone, either a stranger or someone you know used violence, threats or intimidation to force you to have sexual intercourse against your will? By sexual intercourse we mean either vaginal or anal penetration. (Myhill and Allen, 2002, p. 12)

It must be blatantly obvious that such a question will be subject to a multiplicity of interpretations and must of necessity be so. Indeed on the very next page they note, when trying to explain why the 1998 and 2000 surveys get the same result despite different screener questions:

> Perhaps the most interesting thing to note is that, despite wording changes, the prevalence rate derived from the 1998 and 2000 screener questions are virtually identical. Of course it is impossible to know the exact reasons for this. It does perhaps highlight, though, the problems associated with having one or two reasonably subjective screener questions acting as a filter for victims' experiences. *It is extremely difficult to guess with any accuracy exactly what types of incidents are being recorded, bearing in mind different people's perceptions and subjective interpretations of certain words and phrases.*' (2002, p. 13, italics mine)

But, of course, we know that rape is an extraordinarily contested area and, of course, the researchers being both well informed and meticulous are well aware of this. They note that the large proportion of rape between intimates makes women hesitate as to classification, they register Kate Painter's (1991) finding in her study of married women and rape that some victims were only willing to classify their experience as rape *retrospectively* after considerable hindsight, and she stresses that the concept of 'rape' may carry with it connotations with which women may not want to be associated. In short, they are aware of change, resistance, and contest surrounding the notion of what constitutes rape. Despite all of this the hubris of numbers overcomes this so that they can boldly state:

> the BCS estimates that 4.9 per cent of women have been raped since age 16 and that 9.7 per cent of women have suffered some sort of sexual

victimization since that age . . . The 2000 BCS estimates that 0.9 per cent of women suffered some form of sexual victimization during the last year and 0.4 per cent suffered rape . . . [it] estimates that there are approximately 754,000 females aged 16 to 59 in England and Wales who have been the victim of rape once or more since the age of 16. This includes approximately 61,000 victimized in the last year. (2002, pp. 17–19)

The above two examples are selected from the many: they are the stuff of footnotes or asides. Yet they nestle like dynamite in the book or article: they are the cautionary asides which, if read seriously, would destroy the main narrative, they are the momentary truth which in terms of their project should have never even been said. 'Normal science' in the terms of Thomas Kuhn, proceeds, of course, as usual – although it really isn't science: the articles mount up, the cross references are made, the careers develop and the knowledge – whatever one is to make of it – accumulates in the mountains of articles and monographs. What is of interest is the psychological mechanisms which permit this. Let us note at the outset they are very like the techniques of neutralization famously described by Matza and Sykes (1961), names the psychodynamics by which the delinquent loses his moral bonds with society, the excuses which permit delinquency, only in this case we are talking of processes by which a rational person is able to loosen his or her sense of reality and to metaphorically skate happily on thin ice.

Let us note that the hubris of positivism is not without a moment of hesitancy. The knowledge of gross scandal and injustice within the criminal justice system, the memories of college days and theories past, of constructionism, hidden figures and early excitement, the tedium of statistical manipulation, the phenomenal experience of everyday life with its pluralism, contest and shift in values all must undermine any serenity of belief. For the budding practitioners of positivism, science is inevitably a leap of faith. It is the following techniques of neutralization which help allay such fears and uncertainties.

The Fetishism of Numbers

First of all there is the fetishism of numbers, the illusion of precision, the promise of science. But the way in which extremely soft data become to be perceived as palpably hard data is facilitated by the increasing commodification of quantitative research in the social sciences. That is, it becomes rarer and rarer for the researchers to have contact with the researched. This is achieved by the following strategies:

- using 'objective' data without any need for survey, e.g. the relation-ship between homicide and deprivation internationally is simply carried out by correlating homicide rates (which are incorrectly seen as definitionally consistent between nations) and measures such as differences in income levels (despite the fact that relative deprivation involves the *subjective* assessment of deprivation which can, in fact, be greater when differences in income levels are narrower) e.g. Velez et al., 2003;
- by using existing datasets which obviate the need for primary research;
- by outsourcing the research to commercial survey organizations;
- by employing a research team who present the principal researchers with the neatly processed and coded data to investigate.

In all of these instances there is considerable distance between the sub-jects of research and the researcher. The hesitations, contradictions, passions, guesses of the human subject, the relationship inherent in the interview process, let alone the confusion and improvization of the coding room, are all shielded from the researcher. The social scientists encounter people as figures; as numbers on a printout or a screen. Finally the shift from the data to the written-up research report is granted an extraordinary autonomy from human interpretation, it is as if it is seen as a form of automatic writing. Yet anyone faced with a mountain of data knows that there are very many stories that could be written, although by the end of the report and its first presentation it takes on the shape of a singular and unchallenged tale. As Mills put it: ' If you have ever seriously studied for a year or two, some two thousand hour-long interviews, carefully coded and punched, you will have begun to see how very malleable the realm of "fact" may really be' (1959, p. 72).

The Autonomy of Numbers

Numbers once generated by research seem to gain a life of their own as they drift through cyberspace. It is as if their very detachment from the research agency gives them an extra validity. Indeed the extremely suspect data from the International Victimization Studies are cited willy-nilly whenever the need for international comparisons crops up. Thus even such distinguished scholars as Frank Zimring and Gordon Hawkins can describe the findings of such surveys on rates of violence in eighteen industrial countries as something of a revelation and then proceed to incorporate them as an essential part of their thesis that the United States is not exceptional in the extent of violence but only in the prevalence of guns. Thus they write:

> The major surprise for an American observer is the existence of reported rates of violent and non-violent crime in the United States that are quite close to those found in countries like Australia, Canada and New Zealand. There is certainly little ... that fits the average traveler's perception of danger or safety in the city streets of the reporting countries. Indeed, there is no strong statistical correlation between rates of reported violent crime in the eighteen nations and the homicide rates for the same countries. For those countries, then, the rates of violent crime reported by citizens is not a good predictor of their respective homicide rates. (1997, pp. 36–7).

Indeed they go on to point out that the correlation between the victim study rates and homicide rates for the reporting countries is a non-significant 0.37 and assault and homicide a mere 0.15. It does not seem to occur to them that it is the statistics that are flawed both in the representativeness of their samples and the ignoring of the basic fact of differing levels of tolerance of violence. Myself, I would be better guided by travellers' reports as to the dangers of violence in New Zealand and the United States than I would be by the International Victimization Studies.

The Normalization of Anomaly

Here the anomalies are seen as exceptions to the general reliability of the data. The researcher *knows* about them, *acknowledges* them but then deems them exceptional. Thus our discussion could be seen as a particular problem of the sociology of sex, or the 'education effect' could be a one-off, uncharacteristic entity. This is, of course, facilitated by the fact, as we have noted, that few survey results have built-in tests as to whether their findings are unlikely.

The recurrent problem that shaky and insubstantial data inevitably produce a wide range of contradictory results is countered by the magic of meta-analysis. Here a summary of research results is made, frequently involving the generation of actual averages, the assumption being made that the summation of variance and anomaly gives us some approximation of the truth rather than an amplification of error.

Such a denigration of the significance of unusual findings and the hasty attempts to fence off the black hole of anomaly conceals the widespread corruption of data that such perturbancies in the scheme of things represent. Thus, as Richard Sparks noted, the education effect will seriously disturb any categories where educational difference occurs (e.g. ethnicity, gender, locality, etc.).

The Technical Fix

Here it is admitted that there are problems of data but it is believed these will be solved as statistical techniques become more sophisticated and survey methods improve. Sometimes there is a belief that the sophistication of the statistics can make up for the woeful inadequacy of the data, sometimes as if the most recent innovations make up for the thin ice of the past. At times the research articles seem to lose themselves in the statistics, almost as if the innovation of technique, the equation, is the real focus.

The House of Cards

Abstracted empiricism is like a castle of playing cards with each card leaning upon each other. Just as quantitative techniques, with their array of numbers and decimal places, give some assurance of scientificity and solidity, the sheer *quantity* of research articles give a feeling of monumentality and science in progress. The references and cross-references proliferate and seem to prop up each sentence and bolster up each paragraph. The decline in grand narrative from sociology through to history necessitates a myriad of references and creates a denseness which hides the thinness of the text. As Phil Cohen amusingly points out:

> Volume 1 of *Das Kapital* is 800 pages long, and has only 200 bibliographic references, over half of which are to works outside the area of political economy. Freud's *Interpretation of Dreams* is 671 pages long and contains 310 references, of which over two-thirds are to works of art, literature or philosophy. In contrast, a 30-page article published in the journal *History Workshop* on 'Plebeian spiritualism, 1853–1913' contained 214 footnotes and even more references, none of which were drawn from outside its immediate research area. The fact that writers of case studies or monographs feel they have to authorize almost every sentence in this way is not I think just about a ritual display of scholarship; it speaks volumes about the kind of panic which can set in once the safety nets and guarantees hitherto furnished by grand narratives are taken away. (1997, p. 397)

The increase in the quantity of academic output (accelerated so successfully by the research assessment exercise in Britain and the general equation of CV length with academic productivity elsewhere) is complemented with this textual need for quantity. Indeed in many university departments articles become placed ahead of books in the status and weighting given to them: research 'findings' presumably being more important than providing the context to make sense of them.

The Loss of Subjectivity

The two strategies of positivism are to attempt to correlate material circumstances (economic conditions, family stability, opportunities for crime, etc.) to actual behaviour, or to relate attitudes to possible behaviour.

Let us briefly look at the first strategy: relationship of material circumstances to behaviour, or the move from an 'independent' to a dependent variable. Of course there can be no such thing as material circumstances which inevitably propel human beings in a pre-given direction. The 'same' material factor (whether unemployment, poverty, a broken home, etc.) can mean different things to different people at differing times and places. Yet the assumption of a narrative connecting a prior factor to present behaviour is commonplace. Indeed, as Herbert Blumer put it in his classic article, 'Sociological Analysis and the "Variable"':

> The indifference of variable analysis to the process of interpretation is based apparently on the tacit assumption that the independent variable predetermines its interpretation. This assumption has no foundation. The interpretation is not predetermined by the variable as if the variable emanated its own meaning. If there is anything we do know, it is that an object, event or situation in human experience does not carry its own meaning; the meaning is conferred on it. (1956, p. 688)

I will return to this later, but let us note that the 'tacit assumption' is complemented by the fact that to measure the subjective impact of such material factors at a particular time and place involves a considerably greater effort of research and data collection. It is a great deal simpler just to read the 'hard' statistics off the internet. Such a reading of the situation is suggested by the fact that often the material factors are accepted as raw data and not even scrutinized on a level of technical adequacy. Unemployment statistics are frequently used as 'hard data', for example, despite the well-known fact that they do not measure economic inactivity, including those who are discouraged from applying for jobs. I hesitate to say this, but there is a point at which positivism can be seen as the lazy option.

Passing the Attitude Test

Let us turn now to the attempt to relate attitudes to behaviour. Here all the previous strictures are of relevance – perhaps more so. Non-respondents will, in all probability, have attitudes which are atypical to those of respondents. But of respondents, themselves, measurement of attitudes is surely a most tenuous affair. Who, for example, is to admit to racism, to belief in the inequality of the sexes, to an aversion to work, to relishing violence? The attitudinal survey almost approximates an attitude test: what is the correct attitude to air publicly? It is thus an attitude to an attitude – a population schooled in multiple-choice questionnaires seeks the 'right' answer. Even more of a problem is when our attitude is held with hesitancy, uncertainty or contradiction. Many a strongly held but contradictory opinion has registered 3.5 on a 7 point Likert Scale. Further let us put all of this in the context of late modernity – there we have a situation of rapid attitude shift, of a media-saturated world where the correct attitudes to affairs of the day are widely and intensely debated. Here is a world of contradiction, of blurring, of boundary testing.

It should be noted that it is not just strictly attitudinal questions which suffer from such strictures but, as I have argued, behavioural questions. In fact behavioural questions are actually *attitude to behaviour* questions. It is worth noting that in the 1950s, when survey research was taking off, such criticisms were commonplace. Witness Thomas Rhys Williams' powerful article, 'A Critique of Some Assumptions of Social Survey Research', where he notes:

> The assumption that a reply by a respondent to a question is 'the answer' insofar as his social behavior is concerned is fallacious. This contention is by no means novel; Linton, La Piere, Merton and Deming, among many others, have pointed out that in most societies there exist institutionalized patterns of saying one thing and acting to the contrary. Anthropologists long since have discarded dependence on a response to an inquiry as a stable, ultimate datum in the study of human behavior, having learned that what people say they will do, or have done, may not correspond to their actual behavior. Linton has given a formal statement of this recognition in his discussions of the distinctions between the concepts of 'real' and 'ideal' social behavior. In the course of clinical research, psychologists have recognized this practice as a fundamental and regular attribute of human mental processes; it is designated currently as the 'process of rationalization'. (1959, p. 57)

He adds:

One cannot ignore easily the fact that many survey researchers, aware or not of the differences between real and ideal social behavior, have shown a consistent tendency to present reports that read as if survey responses were the ultimate data to be gained in studies of human social behavior . . . It is difficult not to infer that the assumption of the validity of a survey response as a social datum has become a mechanism by which survey students can turn from the always complex, often bewildering, and usually laborious task of describing human behavior in exact detail. (1959, p. 57)

It is often at the beginning of the expansion of a research methodology that the doubts are expressed most openly, witness the parallel examples in the use of victimization research which I have already mentioned. But the first caveats, like the awareness of thin ice, are soon forgotten. But let us investigate a little further the findings of La Piere.

Whoever Remembers La Piere?

Irwin Deutscher, in his remarkable book *What We Say/What We Do* (1973) presents this gap between attitude and behaviour as a problem which is palpably obvious, which is at the very heart of social research, but which is astonishingly glossed over in methodology textbooks and in research articles and reports. There are, he writes:

> . . . three avenues through which social scientists can seek to understand human behavior: (1) we can observe it in process; (2) we can view the records men leave behind – written or otherwise artifactual; and (3) we can ask questions and listen to answers. There are different techniques for implementing these approaches and they may be employed in various combinations. Among sociologists, it is the last – the verbal approach – which is most commonly used. We interview; we survey; we poll; we converse; we eavesdrop. Although we are often constrained to use verbal elicitation techniques, we are sometimes as interested in behavior or action as we are in verbalizations. Assuming the old-fashioned textbook definition of attitudes as 'tendencies to act', we frequently proceed to draw conclusions about the behavior of people on the basis of what they tell us. We assume that verbal responses reflect behavioral tendencies. (Deutscher, 1973, p. 12)

He cites the wonderfully pragmatic, the astonishingly optimistic, comment of the psychologist P. E Vernon:

> Words are actions in miniature. Hence by the use of questions and answers we can obtain information about a vast number of actions in a short

space of time, the actual observation and measurement of which would be impracticable. (Deutscher, 1973, p. 12)

There we have it, attitude research is this practical, it is economic, the verbal elides with the behavioural *and* the controversy which boils up every now and then is soon forgotten. It is, as Deutscher put it, 'a problem found and lost'. Deutscher's gnawing doubt about the conventional basis of social research started with the findings of Richard La Piere. It was while La Piere was attending a seminar of Bronislaw Malinowski at the London School of Economics in 1927 that he encountered the notion of the difference between the 'verbalization' of customs of preliterate people and their actual customs which were so palpably obvious to anthropologists. He was working at the time on a comparative study of racial prejudice in France and England, pivoting around the attitudes of hotel proprietors. He asked the attitudes of the proprietors towards black people, yet he was concerned with the problems of 'verbalization' so he supplemented his questions with a behavioural question. Nothing he thought could be more practical and direct than asking the proprietor: 'Do you permit members of the Negro race to stay here?' (1934, p. 131). The results he found of attitudes and self-report behaviour were concordant and his doubts were for a while allayed. But they remained, perhaps, he wondered the evidence he had gleaned from his study was not a direct comparison of attitudes or behaviour, but the self-report answers were themselves still a "verbalized" reaction to a symbolic situation' (1934, p. 131). A few years later something occurred which reawakened his doubts. Let me put it in his own words:

> Beginning in 1930 and continuing for two years thereafter, I had the good fortune to travel rather extensively with a young Chinese student and his wife. Both were personable, charming, and quick to win the admiration and respect of those they had the opportunity to become intimate with. But they were foreign-born Chinese, a fact that could not be disguised. Knowing the general 'attitude' of Americans towards the Chinese as indicated by the 'social distance' studies which have been made, it was with considerable trepidation that I first approached a hotel clerk in their company. Perhaps the clerk's eyebrows lifted slightly, but he accommodated us without a show of hesitation. And this in the 'best' hotel in a small town noted for its narrow and bigoted 'attitude' towards Orientals. Two months later I passed that way again, phoned the hotel and asked if they would accommodate 'an important Chinese gentleman'. The reply was an unequivocal 'No'. That aroused my curiosity and led to this study. (1934, p. 232).

La Piere then set about constructing a carefully controlled experiment which took two years and necessitated over ten thousand miles of driving twice across the United States and up and down the Pacific coast. This involved observing the treatment the Chinese couple received in hotels, auto-camps, tourist homes and restaurants. As it was, of the 251 establishments approached, only one, an auto-camp, refused to accommodate them. Six months later he would write a letter to each of these establishments asking: 'Will you accept members of the Chinese race as guests in your establishment?' Over 90 per cent replied no, there was only one yes response with the remainder undecided. Thus the first, the overt reaction, and second symbolic one, contradicted each other. As Deutscher put it, 'not only was there no relationship between what people say and what they do, but under some conditions there may be an inverse relationship between the two' (1973, p. 14).

Subsequently Allan Wicker, in 1969, published a review of 31 studies of the consistency between attitudes and behaviour and concluded that there was little or perhaps no relationship, while in 1989 Terry Dockery and Arthur Bedeian meticulously considered the various criticisms of the study and concluded that the findings of La Piere remained vindicated. Let us leave it to La Piere himself to spell out the implications of his work for attitude research:

> The questionnaire is cheap, easy, and mechanical. The study of human behavior is time consuming, intellectually fatiguing, and depends for its success upon the ability of the investigator. The former method gives quantitative results, the latter mainly qualitative. Quantitative measurements are quantitatively accurate; qualitative evaluations are always subject to the errors of human judgment. Yet it would seem far more worthwhile to make a shrewd guess regarding which is essential than to accurately measure that which is likely to prove quite irrelevant. (Cited in Deutscher, 1973, p. 21)

Voting Dry and Drinking Wet

Deutscher himself, in *What We Say/What We Do*, amasses a wealth of studies which undermine the conventional wisdom of sociologists, market researchers, pollsters and behavioural psychologists. Charles Warriner's (1958) wonderful study of drinking in a small rural community in Kansas, for instance, which has direct resonance with the findings of our sexologists. For in this temperance village the public morality was that the drinking of alcoholic beverages was wrong and in several thousand events Warriner found no public violation or rejection of this morality. Yet from his first visit to the community onwards he found leaders of the community in private, consuming alcoholic drinks, indeed even some members of the Women's Christian Temperance Union drank and served alcohol in their homes. As one informant said: 'this town is full of hypocrites; they vote dry and drink wet' (1958, p. 165).

This phenomenon of voting dry and drinking wet encapsulates the difference between attitudes and behaviour and, even more importantly, public and private *behaviour*. Criminology and the sociology of deviance has, of course, a particular interest in this discrepancy, for much of the behaviour it studies is covert and subterranean; by its very nature it is not the way one acts publicly and not what one would admit publicly, whether in discussion with strangers or answering questionnaires.

Of course, it is not an either/or, both attitudes and behaviour are aspects of understanding individuals or groups. As we have seen, the different beliefs (or boasts) as to the number of sexual partners between men and women and between, say, the British and the French, is of interest in itself. But this does not allow us to discount La Piere's critique. For the problem is where attitudes are seen as behaviour, where attitudes to male sexuality are seen as an index of sexual activity, where attitudes to race are identical with actual racist behaviour, and where, to use criminological examples, attitudes to fear of crime become elided with avoidance behaviour, where the fashionability of particular drugs at particular times shape the responses to self-reported drug taking and, most importantly, where attitudes to domestic violence serve to conceal reported rates *as well as* shaping what the respondents think of as domestic violence.

The Doubts of Merton and Mills

About the same time as La Piere was publishing his findings, Robert K. Merton and C. Wright Mills were pondering the implications of the attitude/behaviour gap and, as Irwin Deutscher points out, both attempt to link such divergences to wider structural factors. This was a time when both these pre-eminent sociologists were at the beginning of their careers and shared *for this period at least* both methodological doubts and left leaning politics (see Gouldner, 1973; Young, 2010). They had a steady exchange of letters about the new methodology of questionnaires and social surveys or 'opinionnaires' as Merton referred to them. Thus, in a paper given at the 1938 meeting of the American Sociological Society (subsequently published in 1940) Merton examined sceptically the findings of 'opinionnaires' on group differences in judgements about African-Americans. In this he was particularly concerned with religious and regional differences (e.g. the possibility that Northerners treat Negroes less 'favorably' than they talk about them and that Southerners talk about Negroes less "favorably" than they treat them' (1940, pp. 21–2) He stridently dismisses the currently popular Thurstone Attitude Scale with its linear continuum of attitudes favourable and unfavourable to African-Americans. As he pointed out, the scale is not really linear, many individuals endorse attitudes at contrary points of the scale and adding up the attitudes listed to give a numerical score is therefore meaningless. He is intensely critical that sociological and psychological insights are subjugated to mathematical concerns. Logical consistency is assumed, for example, to be 'normal' in human attitudes and behaviour. Thus he writes: 'But in making this assumption, the investigator is playing the role of logician rather than psychologist or sociologist. He is in effect, tacitly assuming that these presumably incompatible assertions *should not* be endorsed by the same persons . . . In making this assumption the investigator is using *norms* of logic, not facts of sociology . . . To assume, as Thurstone does, that persons hold rigorously consistent social opinions is to fly in the face of a store of clinical observations by psychologists, sociologists, anthropologists and John Doe himself' (Merton, 1940, p. 20)

An Open Season on Numbers?

Am I suggesting an open season on numbers? Not quite: there are obviously – as Sennett points out in the *Sex in America* debate – numbers which are indispensable to sociological analysis. Figures of infant mortality, age, marriage, common economic indicators are cases in point as are, for example, numbers of police, imprisonment rates and homicide incidences in criminology. Others, such as income, unemployment, or ethnicity, are of great utility but must be used with caution. General trends, such as a long-term rise and fall of crime rates, can be deduced, although with none of the crisp definition usually assumed. Indeed, in Chapter 6, in analysing the remarkable drop in crime in the US and Britain, I will do precisely that. There are things in the social landscape which are distinct, definite and measurable, there are things which are shadow figures, approximates like those that occur frequently in the biological sciences, which are the best we can do in the circumstances, there are many others that are blurred because we do not know them – some because we are unlikely ever to know them, others, more importantly, which are blurred because it is their nature to be blurred. Precision must be constantly eyed with suspicion, decimal points with raised eyebrows. There are very many cases where statistical testing is inappropriate because the data are technically weak – it will simply not bear the weight of such analysis. There are many other instances where the data are blurred and contested and where such testing is simply wrong.

Will this mean an end to quantitative work? No, far from it, it is more a question of setting rules and limits, of discriminating between the solid and the subjective, of determining where statistical testing is useful and where it is a distraction, of differentiating where numbers are fixed entities and where they are *naturally* blurred and in flux. It is directed against abstracted empiricism and the particular genre of positivism which has taken root in numerous journals and in the mindset of many academics; it is not directed against the domain of numbers *per se*. It would, it is true, restrict statistical testing to those instances where the data are reasonably distinct and objective, and where the technical problems of non-response are either tackled or non-applicable. This would be a considerable reduction, but numbers are signs to be interpreted within specific cultural contexts, figures in themselves do not have any magical objectivity. In this way the balance between numbers and conceptualization shifts, instead of numbers dominating and concepts atrophying, theory and conceptualization take centre stage and numbers find their place, wherever appropriate, fully situated and contextualized. It is not more and fancier statistical testing that will solve the problems of numbers in the social sciences, rather it is theory and conceptualization, an imaginative understudy of culture and context, that will give numbers relevance, utility and their place.

The Critique of Social Statistics

There are thus three levels of critique with regard to social statistics which emerge from the analysis in Chapter 2. The first is the problem of *representativeness*, the second, what I will call *masquerading*, and the third concerns questions of *interpretation and value*. Each of these presents different problems for social research, and each generates its own hidden figure(s).

As we shall see sociology shares the technical problem of representatives with measurement in the natural sciences. The problem of representativeness particularly and the decisions as to what to include in the population occur both prior to sample and during the survey itself. As we have seen in the research of Edward Laumann and his team, this involved the exclusion of households where there were no English speakers or anyone outside of the ages 15–59 and, perhaps most significantly, those who do not live in regular households, e.g. students, prisoners, homeless. Most frequently this is simply a problem of economics, the cost of inclusion of 'exceptional' groups within the sampling frame agreed with the survey agency is prohibitive or, more mundanely, the cost of each extra household surveyed rises as one hits the more difficult to access households or interview-resistant individuals. In the latter, and most common instance, the magic mantra of probability sampling is invoked with its extremely doubtful premise of a uniform population where the respondents and non-respondents are presumed fairly similar. Such an ingenuous and taken-for-granted attitude to social surveys has arisen concomitant with the massive use of survey methods in consumer research and opinion polls. It is evident that in such abstracted empiricism the limits of inclusion within the sampling frame and the notion of a 'good' response rate, where one-fifth to one-quarter of the population are routinely excluded, has been relegated to a mere technical problem. Such a situation is institutionalized in that the survey itself is usually outsourced to survey research firms. The research bureaucrats that Mills described are now well ensconced in the day-to-day practice of the academy.

But not all of the problems of representativeness in social science are restricted to the simply technical. The fluidity of conceptions of the subject matter, the lack of fixed definitions of what constitutes the phenomenon to be surveyed, make for rapid changes in the potential population. It can, for example, double in a short space of time. A study of rapists, for example, would, over the last two decades, shift its coverage *quite reasonably and necessarily* to include date rape and rape in marriage. A study of zebras or foxes, hydrogen atoms or C_2H_5OH molecules would not. Representativeness is thus largely, although not totally, a problem on a technical level and it should be stressed that it is a potential weakness in the social sciences, but a problem of the natural sciences as well. It is only too often forgotten that the measurement of the natural world outside of the laboratory is fraught with difficulties and abounds with hazy figures and guesstimates. How many butterflies are there in the forest? How many foxes in the shire? To take the latter instance, in the bitter debate about the hunting of foxes in Britain, the argument revolved, at least on the overt rationalistic level, around whether fox-hunting did indeed control the number of foxes. Questionnaire studies asking farmers and landowners their estimates of the number of foxes killed suggested overestimates in the region of 7–12 times (Heyden and Reynolds, 2000). The outright ban on hunting for nearly a year in 2001, due to an outbreak of foot-and-mouth disease, provided a unique opportunity to quantify the impact of hunting. A team from Bristol University (Baker et al., 2002a; 2002b) constructed a meticulous study measuring fox abundance in terms of faecal counts before and after the ban. This was achieved by measuring levels of fox faeces along the transects of 160, 1km squares, following linear features (hedgerows, fences, riverbanks, tracks, etc. –

along which foxes usually move), randomly selected throughout Britain. Needless to say, such a method has all sorts of problems: the faeces had to be new, to be from foxes, to not disappear due to decomposition; the landowners sometimes refused a second survey, the accurate delineation of hunted and non-hunted areas, the intensity of hunting, etc. All of this is not, thank goodness, a detour into the fox-hunting debate (the results showed hunting had little impact on fox numbers, incidentally), but simply to illustrate that measurement in the natural sciences, outside of the laboratory, is difficult, intricate, imprecise, and often messy.

Even the more pressing questions of our time, on which vast sums of money and, indeed, human destiny hang, are beset with problems of not merely accurate, but approximate measurement. The answer, for example, to whether there is global warming is dependent on measurement across a time series involving markedly different instrumentation – and earlier on no instrument at all. Controversies arise with regard to the varying location of thermometers in different periods. Today, for instance, readings are frequently in urban areas with warmer sub climates ('urban heat islands'), hence sampling may be different, and a built-in bias occurs (Houghton, 2001). And the same is true of the debate as to how large the world's oil reserves are, where figures range from the overly optimistic to the distinctly catastrophic (Vidal, 2005), or indeed the size of the population of meteors greater than 1km in diameter, which have some likelihood of impacting upon us (NASA, 2004). In the latter instance, NASA, as part of its Near Earth Object Program, has a Congressional Mandate to catalogue at least 90 per cent of all meteors of this size by 2008. By April 2009 between 60 and 80 per cent of these objects had been traced – it depends on how many they actually are, and this is controversial. The estimation of the population of meteors in the lower range of 50m to 1km, which can merely cause local or regional rather than global disaster, remains a task for the future!

My intention here is to point to the fact that natural science, so valorized by positivist sociology, is scarcely an idyll of exactitude and precision. To criticize the social sciences, and the level of representativeness, is not to abandon quantitative measure *tout court*, but to realize the difficulties even at this level and to advocate imaginative and non-doctrinaire means of achieving this goal. It is not, for example, to condemn approximation; much of the natural sciences – biological research springs immediately to mind – relies on approximation; the number of faeces per square metre, the number of butterflies in the forest, etc. A scattergram of dots, has scarcely the precision of an *in vitro* laboratory experiment. But approximation should not be confused with vagueness and precision is not the same as truth. The very worst data are those whose very precision occludes the truth.

I would argue that on a purely technical level, many of the databases in the social sciences are palpably inadequate. There is simply not enough scepticism and too much acquiescence to social pressures while the complexity of data collection is unacknowledged. Thus, even if the social did not differ in its nature from the physical world, even if a science called criminology were possible, the actual practice of the true believers in positivism is often spectacularly inadequate. What are we to make of a gigantic enterprise of measurement such as the International Criminal Victimization Survey now in its twentieth year and its sweep with samples drawn for New York to Phnom Penh, from Mozambique to New Zealand? What are we to make of data which are based on response rates in the national surveys which average out at 51 per cent and range from 27 per cent in the USA to 33 per cent in Norway to 83 per cent in Bulgaria? Which had an 18 per cent response rate in Warsaw yet claimed a 96 per cent response rate in Phnom Penh and Lima?

Unfortunately the very reverse occurs in present-day abstracted empiricism, measurement in the social sciences is seen as simple, and complexity is somewhat conveniently allocated to the statistical analysis *after* the data have been collected. In *The Exclusive Society* (1999) I argued against the notion of *the social as simple*: the idea that the natural world demands rocket science, while the social world in terms of everything from measurement to intervention is some sort of doddle. As we have seen, estimating crime rates, or indeed actual levels of unemployment or numbers of single mothers for that matter, is scarcely simple, whereas social and political intervention, from drug 'wars' to those intent on establishing democracy in Iraq, are fraught with difficulties and counterproductive outcomes.

Measuring the natural world or measuring society, then, has frequently at base considerable problems with regard to the interpretation of data. The pragmatic solution, here, is to look at the congruence of different measures so as to triangulate results, to talk frequently in ballpark figures and to be satisfied, at times, with statements such as 'it is at least', 'it is certainly more than', etc. Above all, we need always to be aware of the precariousness of the data, yet to be well aware that some things are much more easily measurable than others. The failing with positivism in the social sciences at this level is compounded by the fact that its adherents view the problems of research as restricted to this level; indeed, as we have seen, its practitioners often underestimate the troubles that natural scientists, from biologists to astro-physicists, have in terms of measuring the physical world. But, as Richard Lewontin pointed out, the social world is even more complex than this.

Let us turn now to *the problem of masquerading*. By this I mean that human beings form a relationship with the researcher, however distanced and formal this may be, which involves taking up a role: the interview is a performance, a masquerade of pretence and presentation. In contrast, in the physical sciences, H_2 molecule does not purposely conceal itself from the researcher, or pretend to be a molecule of argon or helium. Human beings are more than reactive or adaptive but reflexive, creative and interpretative. It should immediately be obvious that the research relationship, the *narrative* between researched and researcher, is of particular interest to the human subject, whose very essence is the creation of a series of narratives about themselves and others.

Yet positivists view the problem of the social sciences as how can we most effectively transfer information from the subject of inquiry A to the observer B. Good research facilities are well-designed questionnaires, sophisticated sampling techniques, adroit statistical manipulation and sympathetic interviews and are like a well-constructed telecommunications cable transmitting the data along the line, from a distant and unmet A to point B where academics peer at the assembled dataset on their PC or roll of printout. But how different an actual interview is from this! To start with, it is a social relationship, not an inert line of communication, and it is a relationship which is very often between unequals. And as such it generates answers which are structured with everything from suspicion (e.g. attitudes to work, estimates of income, figures for personal drug or alcohol use) to desire to project oneself as a 'good' and educated citizen. Here what is the *correct* answer becomes paramount, greatly encouraged, I daresay, by an education involving multiple-choice questionnaires and the art of ticking the right boxes. The good and educated citizen, for example, will eschew racist responses, knowing from the mass media and from school that these are the *wrong* answers. The actual racist attitudes of those questioned may only be evident in the conversations between intimate friends and family or revealed every now and then in the anonymity of the ballot box. They exist under the radar of public debate. Contradiction, hesitation, uncertainty are ironed out by the rigid categories of questionnaire and the belief of the interviewee that the 'educated' person has *definite* opinions; indeed this is a hallmark of personal rationality. The interview is a sterling scenario for presenting a consistent narrative, the very unusualness of someone listening patiently and respectfully to you (how different from one's friends with their rude interruptions and disagreements!) (see Bourdieu, 1999). The taking up of the role of interviewee, and all the Goffmanesque performance that this entails (foreground: attentiveness, rationality, coherence; background: suspicion, defensiveness, perhaps resentment) only encourages the taking up of attitudes. So particularly in the media-saturated world of late modernity, the appropriate attitudes are always there to be plucked out of the ether. Such a *relativism of reply* must underscore any reading that we have of interview, from unstructured to questionnaire-based, that presents itself as seemingly objective data.

Lastly, let us briefly examine the *problem of interpretation and value*. Here we enter the thorny area of relativism and objectivity. It is one stage beyond the masquerade, because here there is at least an indication that behind the performance, the role taking, the pretence and deception, there is an objectivity, truth and reality. Thus, as far as measurement is concerned, lying, concealment, exaggeration, all suggest that there is a true figure. That we simply have a further problem here of a hidden figure falsely illuminated. Here we consider the fact that the figure itself may be contested and indistinct. Here is a step beyond Lewontin's critique – a third level problem. But the fundamental discovery of the labelling school, in its initial excursus into constructionism, was that the same sequences of behaviour are evaluated differently from various perspectives in the social structure. Reality is, in short, contested.

The impact of late modernity on measurement

In the introduction to this chapter I noted how in late modernity the causes of crime become loosened from their fixed structural moorings. That the 'same' circumstances become imbued with different meanings. The causes of crime, in the sense of a narrative leading from personal circumstances to crime committed, are more varied; they are in less of a fixed relationship. We have seen in our discussion of measurement how the effects – the outcome of such a narrative, are subject also to differential interpretations. They are part of this constructed narrative of meaning, both of the actor in the course of his or her life and in the present context of their relationship, to the interviewer in the act of measurement. But here again such a social construction is also subject in late modernity to greater contest and pluralism of definition. So the hidden figure expands and contracts with the values we bring to it. In a pluralist society it is no longer possible to talk of a hidden figure x with which we can attempt to measure, but a whole series of hidden figures x, y, z, etc.

How can we have a notion of fixed objective measurement when all the definitions are in flux? How can we possibly have an objective figure of a phenomenon whose nature and parameters are so fiercely contested, whether in the courtroom, chat show, or public debate? The distinction from the physical sciences is quite clear. As I have said, an atom of hydrogen is an atom of hydrogen, two litres of gas are two litres, H_2 is H_2 give or take isotopes. Atoms do not discuss with each other which element they are, they do not disagree with the chemist, they cannot conflict or be unsure of each other and themselves.

4

The Bogus of Positivism

In the following pages [in a book on schizophrenia] we shall be concerned specifically with people who experience themselves as automata, as robots, as bits of machinery, or even as animals. Such persons are rightly regarded as crazy. Yet why do we not regard a theory that seeks to transmute persons into automata or animals as equally crazy?

(Laing, 1965, p. 23)

Thus Ronnie Laing describes patients coming into his surgery believing that they are animals or things, exhibiting all the traits of advanced and chronic determinism. Yet the model human condition proffered by psychologists like Hans Eysenck, or B. F. Skinner, or innumerable sociological determinists, is what people usually refer to as being mad. How then does this further madness, that of believing that human behaviour can be encapsulated in a formula or captured in an equation, come about?

And it is even more paradoxical than this. Because, as I have mentioned earlier, it is necessary to ask the question: how can it be, in a hyperpluralistic world where creativity and self-invention is a priority, where the solidity of the world is increasingly shaky, and where reflexivity is the order of the day, that such a mechanistic ideology can flourish?

It is the need to explain this madness, to resolve this paradox, that I will turn to in this chapter.

The Identity Crisis and the Attractions of Essentialism

Late modern societies offer two alternatives: the possibility of an opening up of the human condition, of a liberative disenchantment with the taken-for-granted world, and the very opposite, a flight to the solid, the secure and the seemingly unchanging. On one side, you have the self-constructions, identity and subculture: the spin-off of the consumer society is the market in *lifestyles*. On the other hand, both in work and in leisure, there has been a disembeddedness. That is, identity is no longer secure; it is fragmentary and transitional – all of which is underscored by a culture of reflexivity which no longer takes the world for granted. The identity crisis permeates our society. As the security of the lifelong job, as the comfort of stability in marriage and relationship fade, as geographical mobility makes community a phantasmagoria where each unit of the structure stays in place, but each individual occupant regularly moves, where the structure itself expands and transforms and where the habit of reflexivity itself makes choice part of everyday life and problematizes the taken for granted – all of these things call into question the notion of a fixed, solid sense of self. Essentialism offers a panacea for this sense of disembeddedness.

In *The Exclusive Society* (1999) I discuss the attractions of essentialism to the ontologically insecure and denigrated. To believe that one's culture, 'race', gender or community has a fixed essence which is valorized and unchanging is, of course, by its very nature the answer to a feeling that the human condition is one of shifting sands, and that the social order is feckless and arbitrary. To essentialize oneself successfully it is of great purchase to essentialize others negatively. That is to ascribe to the *other* either features which *lack* one's own values (and solidity) or which are an *inversion* of one's own cherished beliefs about one's self. To seek identity for oneself, in an essentialist fashion, inevitably involves denying or denigrating the identity of others.

Liberal and Conservative Othering

In a later book, *The Vertigo of Late Modernity* (2007), I was concerned with this process of creating clear delineation between groups, despite the fact that cultural globalization and hybridism actually blurred the values and boundaries of the late modern world. That is, the tendency to set up a fixed notion of the self and one's group against that of an Other, clearly delineated and different. I distinguished two forms of Othering. Firstly, conservative othering which, by its nature, is a form of demonization. It is an inversion, a projection onto other groups of negative attributes, qualities of evil and depravity, which are set against the solid virtues of one's self and one's own kind. This is the most frequently encountered in the literature: it is characterized by the anthropological work on purity and danger (see Douglas, 1978). Zygmunt Bauman's (1995) descriptions of ethnic exclusion and genocide, in David Sibley's

(1995) graphic 'geographies of exclusion', where gypsies, blacks and homosexuals are set up as alien others, and in Kai Erikson's (1966) famous analysis of witchcraft in Puritan New England, where the 'shapes of the devil' are inversions of the 'true' Christian morality and behaviour. Over against these dramatic creations of folk devils I contrasted a less blatant, less explored, probably more widespread and certainly more insidious form of exclusion and projection: namely, that of liberal othering.

Liberal othering is characterized by diminishing and distancing. The deviant group is seen as distinct from us because of their lacking. They would conversely be *just like us* if they had the benefits of our material circumstances and social upbringing. They are not alien, but uneducated, uncivilized, irrational. They lack control: at worse they are wanton, at best somewhat infantile. The benign gaze of the colonial administrator of the past, or the concerned social worker of today, looking into the inner city or to the sink estates or banlieues on the perimeter views the poor as in moral and social deficit and fundamentally detached from the economic structure.

And this diminishing is coupled with distancing. These people are separate from us, they are not connected to us either economically or socially. In the First World they are cast as a residuum, an underclass no longer part of the class structure: they are, in Tony Blair's cold and ironic phrase, a 'workless class'. Their supposed disconnectedness underscores the middle-class sense of solipsis. The magical way in which the comfortably off feel that they exist outside of relationships of class (see Ehrenreich, 2001).

The poor, in our society, are not recognized for the work they contribute, despite miserable wages and conditions; rather they are stereotyped as the unemployed and the unemployable, outside of the economic circuits. Yet they are not invisible: as a stereotypical underclass they are portrayed as feckless, anti-social and criminal: they are the other half of the binary of the responsible, honest, law-abiding citizen. Ontological insecurity gives rise to a desire for clear-cut delineations, and for othering: it generates a binary of those in society and those without it, which is seen to correspond to the normal, on the one side, and the deviant and criminal on the other. The existence of such a binary, pivoted as it is on crime and deviance, has obvious attractions for the criminologist.

The Binaries of Social Exclusion

Society at Large	The Underclass
The Unproblematic	The Problem
Community	Disorganization
Employment	The Workless/Workshy
Independence	Welfare Dependency
Stable Family	Single Mothers/The Dysfunctional
The Natives	The Immigrants
Drug Free	Illicit Drug Use
Victims	Criminals
The Responsible Citizen	The Anti-Social

(from *The Vertigo of Late Modernity*, 2007)

Hiatus in Society, Hiatus in Method

Such a philosophy of hiatus and clear-cut difference is seen in the rise of a fundamentalist positivism in the social sciences which attempts to generate a fake objectivity by postulating a yawning gap between the observer and the observed. Such a distancing is unique in the annals of othering. It is usually – although not always – underpinned by the notion of deficit – but as it aspires to a scientific rendering of reality, it conceives of such an othering in a numerical fashion. Notably, it attempts to project onto human reality an underlay of numbers, a quantifiable frame on which human action is seen to hang. Further it claims that such a depiction in number and equation, in graph and in Greek symbolism gets down to the heart of the matter – portrays the true nature of what is actually going on in human conduct. With this in mind, Gilbert Geis (1991) in his well-argued 'The Case Study Method in Sociological Criminology', highlights the pretentiousness yet insignificance of much quantitative sociology. He cites Clive Entwistle who, in a memorable passage, wrote:

> The sociologist likes to think of himself as a 'scientist' in the sense that a physicist or a chemist is a scientist. Indeed, in his anxiety to assume that authoritative role, he has proved himself most willing to jettison every unquantifiable element in the field of human studies. He does not throw out the baby *with* the bath water – he throws out the baby and keeps the bath water for hard chromatographic analysis. The baby is held to be described by the results. (1987, p. 19)

This process of quantitative othering is facilitated by portraying the major problems of research as being technical, to whit the problems of reaching out across the gulf and collecting a representative sample – indeed, where sampling procedures are seen to generate the very reverse of othering. What is omitted in this discussion is that so-called technical problems such as non-response or 'incorrect' responses (whether by concealment, minimization, or exaggeration) are, in fact, social in their nature and reflect the social relationships of the observer/observed, scientist/object of study, interviewer/interviewee, etc. The kid in the classroom filling in a self-report delinquency schedule, the lower-class individual ticking the boxes of a personality test purportedly measuring 'self-control', the man or woman talking to the middle-class person with a clipboard standing at their front door, or the officious yet solicitous voice on the telephone teasing out the answers, represent in the majority of instances relationships of subordination. To take one example out of many, what are we to make of a NORC interviewer sitting in the living room of a respondent in a desperately poor area of Chicago, part of the celebrated Urban Poverty and Family Life Survey, asking their respondents their attitudes to work? 'Would they prefer a job to aid?', 'Is plain hard work important to getting ahead?', 'Do they think people have the right to receive aid without working?' (see Wilson, 1996). Sociological investigation occurs in a world which is stratified by class, gender, age, race and ethnicity. It is about these divisions but it also occurs across such inequalities. At the very least it frequently involves relationships of class. The poor are not some inhabitants of a distant island, they are an integral part of our (middle-class) material existence. They perform all the menial jobs from childcare through dishwashing, cleaning, support staff in health and education, to waiting table and filling shelves which make our lives possible, they are, further, part of our ideological reality – their othering is manifestly functional to our feelings of social contentment in this 'best of all possible worlds', while their values are irretrievably intertwined with ours. What are we to make of the invisibility of the working poor? All the more extraordinary in that they are not a small part of the social order, but a sizeable and intrinsic part of the economic circuit. What is surprising is that they are cast as a residuum: as the long-term unemployed, or those only spasmodically in work

Rarely do social investigators write reflectively about their respondents and their attitudes to the interview and the interviewer. Contrast this with the reflectiveness of Richard Sennett and Jonathan Cobb in their eloquent *The Hidden Injuries of Class*. Thus they write of Frank Rissarro:

> [He] did not so much grant an interview as give a confession. The interviewer began by asking a neutral question, something about what Rissarro remembered of Boston while he was growing up. He replied by talking with

little interruption for more than three hours about intimate feelings and experiences to this stranger whom he had never met before. Rissarro talked to the interviewer in a peculiar way: he treated him as an emissary from a different way of life, as a representative of a higher, more educated class, before whom he spread a justification of his entire life. At various points where he spoke of situations where he felt powerless and the interviewer sympathized, Rissarro would suddenly respond to him as simply a human being, not as an emissary sent in judgment; but then, as he returned to the story of his life, which he seemed to live through again as he described it, the interviewer once again became a representative of a class of people who could do what they wanted and who made him feel inadequate. It was Rissarro's chief concern throughout to show why circumstances had not permitted him to take care of his life in the same way. (1993, p. 24)

Sennett and Cobb are concerned with the class relationship of their inter-view, indeed one of the hidden injuries of class concerns the problems of the presentation of self of those low in the social structure towards the more educated interlopers in their life. This becomes even more clear when they attempt something which no NORC investigator would ever condone, asking interviewees whether they would like to be interviewers. The reply they received is greatly revealing:

> The staff of this project consisted of people with backgrounds similar to our own. Initially, a few of the people interviewed were asked if they would like to work as interviewers in turn, but most said they thought it would make them uncomfortable, because they would feel they were sitting in judgment. When we would then ask if they thought *we* were sitting in judgment, that characteristic break would occur – they told us not to take it personally, they liked us. (1993, p. 42)

Now 'sitting in judgement' is very distant from the scientific ideal of neu-trality, yet it accurately underscores the situation of interview, whether it is about juvenile delinquency, attitudes to work or welfare, incidence of violence against women or, as we shall see later in this book, claims with regard to number of sexual partners.

The prevalent image of survey research is rather like that of a biolo-gist scooping a sample of marine life out of a pond. He or she leans over, looks into the murky pond, puts in the gauze sieve, and drains out a selection of creatures. They've never been scooped before, they are a 'new' sample, they are unreflective creatures sometimes difficult to get hold of yet a hitherto untouched group whose quantitative breakdown can simply be analysed into clear and unambiguous categories. Yet, in fact, there is no such thing as a new sample. In a way the questions have already been asked and in the tumult of chat shows, news programmes and newspaper columns, the answers have already been rehearsed. It is the constant theme of 'effects research' in mass media studies where there is the mass media message on one hand and the audience on the other when, in reality, the social world is saturated with media imagery and mutual reflective parts that any conception of before and after is derisory. Once again there is no simple before and after: in a world of mirrors reflecting mirrors, no opinion is pristine. In the case, for example, of welfare and work, the whole panoply of Reagan and Clinton administrations, the pontification of experts and columnists, the 'vox pop' opinions of John and Jayne Public all have been presented before us. Public discourse is already structured in terms of the dominant hegemony and the 'correct' answer is available to the respondent a long time before the interviewer turns up in his or her sitting room. Yet, of course, reality is much more difficult than that: attitudes are contradictory, nuanced, ambiguous, but such a complexity is not what survey research is about – it is concerned with the easily codeable, the clearcut, the reproducible.

Disorderly Populations, Disorderly Knowledge

David Sibley, in his fascinating book *Geographies of Exclusion* (1995), notes the parallel between social exclusion in our society, the exclusion of certain types of knowledge: of dangerous classes and of dangerous knowledge, if you like. I am suggesting a parallel process, but one which, stresses the isomorphy between the categories of conventional patterns of exclusion, particularly liberal othering, and positivist categories of truth and knowledge. I want, in short, to suggest that the elective affinity between essentialist currents of popular social thought and positivism is close, intimate and interdependent. Conversely, methods which suggest the blurring, overlap and contest of social categories and social groups appear as disorderly both in the public sphere and within the academy. For this reason the intellectual arguments against positivism are very obviously linked to the views of society with which they are associated.

The arguments against positivism are well rehearsed: I had my own shot against the natural scientific approach to crime quite a few years ago (see, for example, the first two chapters of *The New Criminology*, Taylor et al., 1973). Let me, therefore, just briefly look upon this widespread attempt to create a natural science of society, and of crime in particular. The fundamental driving force is the demands of science itself. What I want to argue is that the demands of science mesh very closely with a particular view of society and that it is only if such a society actually exists that a social science is possible. Furthermore, that this view of society is fundamentally flawed and particularly so in our present period of late modernity.

This perspective on social order is well known to us all: it is the 'orthodox', the 'conventional', the 'taken-for-granted' world carried by mass media, implicit in the pronouncements of politicians and social commentators, reflected in much public opinion, grounded in the fears and anxieties of many. Namely, society is conceived of as monolithically consensual, where deviance is seen as a minority and marginal category, where the criminal and the deviant are seen as clearly delineated and distinctly different from the 'normal', and where such a majority/minority binary revolves around the division between those who are endowed with rationality and free will, and those who are determined. That the very idea of a social *science* necessitates such a cosmology.

In reality, the active nature of human action, the creative basis of human cultures, and the pluralism of values which manifestly surround us both in terms of direct and virtual experience, is manifestly at odds with this. Further, this is particularly accentuated in the present period where human creativity and reinvention is a social ideal and pluralism (or what I will call hyperpluralism, see Chapter 5) surrounds us like a cacophony of voices. Indeed, as I will argue, the very attraction of the consensual image of society, in part, stems from the ontological insecurities which such a hyperpluralistic late modern society engenders. Thus the needs of social science mesh with widespread popular currents of thought and the structure of thinking represents something of a defence against the insecurities of the modern world.

Determinism and the Denial of Human Creativity

> . . . just as in a given volume of water, at a given temperature, we find the solution of a fixed quantity of any chemical substance, not an atom more or less, so in a given social environment, in certain defined physical conditions of the individual, we find the commission of a fixed number of crimes. (Ferri, 1895, p. 75)

Thus we had Enrico Ferri's famous 'law of criminal saturation', at the beginning of the positivist revolution at the turn of the twentieth century. For there to be scientific laws of crime there must be a determinism of human behaviour. Human creativity, the ability to choose to act differently in the 'same' circumstances undermines such certainty: it generates unpredictability, it subverts generalization. But the fundamental human characteristic is to chose interpretation, albeit in circumstances very often

not of one's own choosing. Even the bound and blindfolded man await-
ing the bullet heading towards his forehead at an execution can interpret
his fate either as a pitiful tragedy or a glorious martyrdom. Even the
tyrant, Saddam Hussein, standing with a noose around his neck in Camp
Justice prison, can mock his Shi'ite hecklers for their lack of manliness as
they condemn him to hell while he reads his prayers asking for salvation.
The problem of determinism is that it involves a paper-thin narrative
of cause and effect, the human narrative which binds circumstances to
action is invariably missing. The subjectivity of human beings is such
that, as David Matza argues, it cannot be reduced to the adaptability of
organism or the reactivity of the material world. Which is not to say that
people do not act as if there were no choice ('what choice did I have?'),
or believe themselves trapped, say by heroin or alcohol molecules, into
creatures of determinism. Thus:

> Capable of creating and assigning meaning, able to contemplate his sur-
> roundings and even his own condition, given to anticipation, planning and
> projecting man – the subject – stands in a different and more complex rela-
> tion to circumstances. This distinctively human capacity in no way denies
> that human existence frequently displays itself in ways characteristic of
> lower levels. Frequently man is wholly adaptable, *as if* he were just organic
> being. And sometimes though very rarely, he is wholly reactive, *as if* a mere
> object. But mere reactivity or adaptation should not be confused with the
> distinctively human condition. They are better seen as an alienation or
> exhaustion of that condition. A subject actively addresses or encounters
> his circumstance; accordingly, his distinctive capacity is to reshape, strive
> toward creating, and actually transcend circumstance. (Matza, 1969, pp.
> 92–3)

But let us go a little further and do a double-take on this. For the very act
of choosing a determining role can be a creative act, however demeaning
and denaturing, which gets people out of awkward situations and feelings of guilt and responsibility. Or, it can be an act of bad faith or false
consciousness.

On a public level, such belief in determination is seen in the phenomenon of essentialization, whether of one/s self or of others. That is, the
notion that one's being, or the being of others, is an essence, a prewritten
script which merely unfolds, rather than being a product of human culture
and creativity. Such essentialism may be linked to the idea of addiction or
some posited personal pathology, but on a wider scale is associated with
notions of race, gender, class, nation or religion as determining essences
which explain behaviour outside of human agency, or, so to speak, take
over human consciousness. Such essences can be mobilized to explain
human weaknesses as well as inherent superiority or inferiority (see

Young, 1999, pp. 103–4). For example, in the case of gender, the notion of machismo can be used to explain the supposed masculine propensity to violence, infidelity, or the innate superiority of the male of the species and, in this process, this is counterposed to an essential female other, a femininity which is its very opposite (see de Beauvoir, 1953). In the case of race, racist notions of inbuilt superiority or inferiority, personal characteristics and destiny are, of course, widespread and insidious. It is important here to note that public prejudice and 'scientific' findings interact and feed upon each other. The early work of Cesare Lombroso (1896), one of the fathers of scientific positivism at the turn of the twentieth century, was in part motivated by the widespread prejudice against the influx of the more dark-skinned Southern Italians into the North of Italy. These immigrants – like so many immigrant groups today – were seen to have a predisposition to criminality. Indeed, Lombroso 'scientifically' took this prejudice further by famously postulating that criminality was a form of *atavism*, an evolutionary throwback.

Such scientific racism persists, one may even say flourishes, today. One need only note the widespread publicity for Richard Herrnstein and Charles Murray's *The Bell Curve* (1994), one of the best-selling social-science books of the last twenty years, which purported to show the statistical and genetic basis for racial differences in intelligence; and lack of intelligence, it was argued, was a paramount cause of criminality.

It is important, therefore, to consider how the othering of the deviant (whether criminal, dope addict, sexual pervert, or indeed immigrant, single mother, underclass, etc.) involves a positivism of hiatus and of binaries. That is *We*, the Otherers, are seen as possessed of free will, detachment, and subjectivity, whereas We and They, the Othered, are seen as determined creatures, objects of intervention and investigation. The world is divided in two and there is a distance between them and us. Human creativity is, thus, apportioned to the 'normal majority', and determinism to the deviant and the marginal.

Objectivity, Neutrality and Consensus

For science to occur there must be a vantage point which is neutral in its gaze and which is free from bias or prejudice. It must be a position from where all rational individuals would concur in their perceptions and where definitions of objects to be studied are agreed upon. A horse must be a horse and not a zebra, a planet a planet and not a star. Events in the social world are, of course, categorized by its participants. In the case of crime, for example, a rape is defined by statute and by common sentiment, murder, fraud, theft likewise. There is a consensus, or so it goes, an agreed definition existing within society. Social science, criminology in this instance, needs this consensus, it cannot abide with a situation of relativism, it needs social consensus in order to make a vantage point of objectivity possible.

But here again social reality subverts the project of a natural science of society. Because definitions of reality in a plural society are myriad, and to privilege one over another would probably lead to taking the point of view of power and privilege. For some people, then, rape is a rare occurrence, whereas for others it is a commonplace of marriage and of dating. Definitions and tolerance of violence vary widely throughout the population: where one part of the population views 'spare the rod and spoil the child' as a useful guide to childrearing and another views the physical hitting of children as rampant child abuse. Thus the same behavioural acts are defined differently by different people. This was, after all, the revolutionary principle of labelling theory which shook the solid basis of a science of society. But here in the social world some horses are zebras, and some zebras horses, some stars rendered planets and some planets shine as stars. The social world is a social construction and in pluralist society is characterized by constant contest and change in definitions.

Quantification

> ... suicides do not form, as might be thought, a wholly distinct group, an isolated class of monstrous phenomena, unrelated to other forms of conduct, but rather are related to them by a continuous series of intermediate cases. They are merely the exaggerated form of common practices. Suicide, we say, exists indeed when the victim at the moment he commits the act destined to be fatal, knows the normal result of it with certainty. This certainty, however, may be greater or less. Introduce a few doubts, and you have a new fact, not suicide but closely akin to it, since only a difference of degree exists between them. Doubtless, a man exposing himself knowingly for another's sake but without the certainty of a fatal result is not a suicide, even if he should die, any more than the daredevil who intentionally toys with death while seeking to avoid it, or the man of apathetic temperament who, having no vital interest in anything, takes no care of health and so imperils it by neglect. Yet these different ways of acting are not radically distinct from true suicide. They result from similar states of mind, since they also entail mortal risks not unknown to the agent, and the prospect of these is no deterrent; the sole difference is a lesser chance of death. ... For suicide appears quite another matter, once its unbroken connection is recognized with acts, on the one hand, of courage and devotion, on the other of imprudence and clear neglect. (Émile Durkheim, 1952/1897, pp. 45–6)

Here, in the introduction to *Suicide*, Durkheim adroitly recognizes the way in which concepts in sociology blur into each other, although he famously, then, proceeds to ignore his own admonitions. For here he demonstrably breaks the ice before skating upon it: international suicide figures from France, Prussia, Saxony, Bavaria, England, etc. are paraded together as if there were some obvious comparability. All of this is a well-trodden track, the literature abounds with doubts and commentary (e.g. Douglas, 1967). Can there be a better example of unrepresentativeness (than the hidden figure in Catholic compared to Protestant countries, of masquerading: the person who intends to commit suicide and the 'cry for help' coupled with the irony of those who intended to die but survived and those who died without intending it) and interpretation and value: the idiosyncratic interpretations of coroner and witness? Suicides blur into other forms of behaviour: and, as David Matza pointed out in *Becoming Deviant* (1969), they overlap, ironically, with the most meretricious of behaviour.

In order to have scientific laws we must have quantification, in order to have numbers we must have discrete and similar entities: lions, zebras, hydrogen atoms, C_2H_5OH molecules. But we do not have this in the social world, *or do we*? In order to tackle ontological insecurity people look for fixed categories and essences, definitions of themselves and, very importantly, in order to validate these definitions, clear images of others, delineated from themselves. Thus the popular need, in late modernity, for clear-cut identities meshes with a science that needs precise delineations. This is in a world where identities blur and fade, and where high definition, crisply demarcated others are in short supply. Witness the concept of drug addiction and abuse in a society where the same drug can be used medically or illegally (e.g. Ritalin), where the most prestigious sports are the most drug infested, and where psychoactive drug use (Prozac, Valium, beta-blockers, as well as alcohol, caffeine and nicotine) are part of everyday life.

The Nomothetic Impulse

Drug abuse leads to crime, poverty is criminogenic, surveillance is effective against anti-social behaviour . . .

Nomothetic approaches to criminology conjure up universal generalization arising out of studies in one particular time and place delineating causes of crime and good practice in its control. The nomothetic impulse is at the heart of positivism: the search for generalization which is independent of nation or of locality. You can catch a whiff of this when examining the equation by which I introduced Chapter 1 of this book. They are asking, *literally*, what 'dose' of policing do you need to 'treat' drug dealing in 'nuisance bars'. This process of generalization is dominated by American research (see Edwards and Hughes, 2005): it is very largely based on studies carried out by American criminologists within the United States. The fact of this dominance is rarely commented upon (see Willis et al., 1999), yet the predeliction with work within the United States is exceptional and perhaps surprising. For example, the extensive studies of citations in major journals and textbooks indicate a remarkable focus. (e.g. Cohn and Farrington, 1994, 1998; Wright and Cohn, 1996). In David Fabianic's (1999) summation of the literature, he identifies eighty-nine most-cited scholars – only four of whom are not North American. One of these is Australian (John Braithwaite) and three are European. Of the Europeans one is dead – Émile Durkheim, and the two living are myself and David Farrington. This finding fills me with nothing but dismay, a plethora of scholarship around the world is ignored, it exists under the radar of the American academy. Of course there is a circularity in this: the most well-known journals and textbooks are American and Americans do tend to cite Americans.

The distinction between nomothetic and idiographic approaches was first coined by the Kantian philosopher Wilhelm Windelbaud (1845–1915), it was subsequently developed in sociology by Piotr Sztompka (1990) with regard to the use of the comparative method. The nomothetic approach to the comparative methods looks for, as we have seen, universal patterns of behaviour, whereas the idiographic looks at the unique cultural circumstances of a behaviour or practice and forgoes generalization. Let us note, for a moment, that most nomothetic work is not based on research which is comparative in the sense of cross-cultural but is, as I have indicated, based largely on studies within the United States. There is something of an ingenuousness about such positivism. It seems to argue that just as studies of the natural world would say of gravity or of electromagnetism or of viscosity that they can occur anywhere and the results be exported and promulgated, why not in the social sciences? Let us ignore the fact that this is not true: environmental factors will obviously influence such studies and, anyway, natural science usually produces generalizations based on 'closed' systems in the laboratory where outside factors are held constant, whereas 'open' systems where external factors impinge are a much more difficult arena (see Sayer, 1992). To believe you can simply transport generalizations which work in Pittsburgh to St Petersburg and translate 'best practices' willy-nilly is another matter. You would have to believe cultural influences are merely a thin patina over the hard core of basic human behaviour. But, of course, such a denial of culture and meaning is the central current of positivism.

The nomothetic method is, then, one of abstraction, one that brackets out or minimizes cultural differences, yet which fixes its source and fulcrum of generalization in the criminological institutes of university courses, firmly in the United States and, in a minority of those in Europe. Here again we see the 'scientific' approach of positivism has a great deal of elective affinity with popular notions of the nature of the social world girded, as it were, with anxieties and ontological uncertainties. The idea of the United States, the major world superpower, being the centre of the world, of America being the pivot of the modern cosmology and the arbiter of progress and objectivity is a widespread popular sentiment propagated by everything from Hollywood to military muscle. It makes Europeans blanch but, then again, on behalf of the First World they duplicate such a stance towards developing nations. The nomothetic method, therefore, is grounded in a taken-for-granted popular attitude to what is 'normal' reality. But let me restate even within the First World there is widespread evidence that variation in culture and material predicament change the basis of generalization and the ability to export and transplant theories. As C. L. Willis and his associates put it:

> American theories of crime, by and large, have been born and bred in American society and essentially apply within the unique political, cultural, and social context of the American experience. The ethnocentrism of American criminology limits its generalizability to other political, social, and cultural settings. (1999, p. 230)

Indeed Adam Edwards and Gordon Hughes (2005) detail a wide range of cultural differences which undermine such universalism and studies of the actual impact of American policies, and in this case in its 'nearest' cultural neighbour the United Kingdom suggest that transposition rather than translation is occurring (see Jones and Newburn, 2002; Newburn, T, 2002).

Further it is apparent that nomothetic theory, witness, for example, Gottfredson and Hirschi's *A General Theory of Crime* (1990) can be criticized for its over-emphasis on individualism (see Pavarini, 1994). For, as Edwards and Hughes put it: 'what masquerades as universal, "unbiased", knowledge in American criminology is actually the projection of American culture and political-economic values of individualism.' (2005, p. 348). Perhaps even more telling is that all attempts at such nomothetic generalization would seem to proceed by abstracting culture from behaviour. In doing this they descend quite automatically into tautology and banality. The three most well-known examples of this are Travis Hirschi's 'social control theory', Edwin Sutherland's Differential Association Theory and Alfred Lindesmith's General Theory of Addiction.

Despite several generations of criticism the nomothetic method has reached a near hegemonic position in American criminology reaching from establishment-oriented work to some areas of critical criminology. Against this one should point to the existence of strong yet minority currents which simultaneously exist, albeit surrounded by the mêlée of scientific positivism and the strange fact that such a preponderant position does not occur in any of the other criminologies of the First World. The most stark contrast is between criminology in the United States and the United Kingdom, particularly as the latter country is the most similar to the United States in having a large research base and teaching both on an undergraduate and a postgraduate level, which rivals all other branches of sociology. It is not that abstracted empiricism does not occur in Britain, indeed it certainly does, but that it occupies more of a minority of the criminological academy as one glance at, say, *Criminology* (the American Society of Criminology journal) compared with the *British Journal of Criminology* will assure you. And this in itself is a peculiar turn of events, for one has to ask oneself about the maturity of a discipline where two countries with similar intellectual infrastructures and a common language can produce a different canon of theory. If the positivists are correct, this is scarcely a 'normal science', in T. S. Kuhn's (1970) famous formulation where theory is agreed within the worldwide academy and the focus is on fitting empirical findings into an accepted explanatory framework. Yet to many in American criminology, the theoretical battle is over and the days of normal science are upon us. To give one example of many, Malcolm Holmes and William Taggart (1990) set out to test whether criminal justice studies have reached the scientific maturity of criminology proper – a subject of some heated debate in certain circles. They start with the assumption that maturity is indicated by emphasis on statistical manipulation, multivariate analysis, the elaboration of causal relationships, and less on the definitions of problems, literature reviews and historical analysis associated with the 'early stages' of criminology. They look at criminology and criminal justice journals and find a coming together of the latter with the former, presumably more mature discipline. Furthermore, this process is occurring in a 'progressive' direction. Thus:

> The journals are dominated by inductive empiricism, which we defined to include work that attempts to generalize from a set of observations. Indeed, approximately two-thirds of the articles in each journal have this methodological orientation. Literature reviews are next most common, followed by studies employing descriptive and historical interpretive methodologies. The disproportionate emphasis on nomothetic research suggests that both disciplines accept work formulated so as to address specific, comparatively narrow questions.

This pattern becomes even more evident when the data for 1975–83 and for 1984–88 are compared. In the recent data, inductive empiricism becomes more common in *Criminology* (from 66.7% to 81.7%) and in the *Journal of Criminal Justice* (66.5% to 71.7%). We found a corresponding decrease in other orientations, especially literature reviews (21.6% to 10.4% and 20.1% to 17.6% respectively). (1990, p. 430)

It is in such a context that the downward shift in status of books and articles in books as measures of academic 'productivity' can be understood. For now that the theoretical debate is over, the journal with its reporting of research findings, so to speak, from the forefront of scientific investigation becomes the major forum of the discipline and pinnacle of academic achievement. Further, although it would be invidious to name names, several criminology courses in the United States have dropped theory from their curriculum and many have made theory an elective.

The Problem of Specificity

Positivism seeks generalizations which are independent of culture. A discussion of whether maternal deprivation leads to crime or if beat policing is effective, would be typical endeavours. And it makes assumptions, of course, unemployment leads to crime; it is self-evident that a recession has led to the rise in heroin use among young people, etc. Such a mechanistic relationship between objective conditions and human behaviour is absurd. It is central to a critical position that objective conditions are interpreted through the specific subcultures of groups involved. This is the nature of human experience and social action. Generalization is possible, but only given specific cultural conditions and social understandings. Thus, absolute deprivation (poverty, unemployment, etc.) is no guide to the genesis of crime. This is a central failure of sociological positivism, both in its aetiology and its policy-making. It is much more likely that relative deprivation and experienced injustice in certain limited political situations is at the root cause of crime.

Positivism, furthermore, suffers from the problem of undifferentiated categories. It attempts to relate, in our example, unemployment to crime, as if both sides of the equation consisted of homogeneous entities. Unemployment can be the prerogative of the idle rich, the temporary movement between jobs, the sudden redundancy of those who have worked all their lives, the structural unemployment of those who have known nothing else, and so on. And its experience is mediated by age, class, gender and race within particular subcultures, located spatially in areas with totally different experiences of unemployment. So-called hard facts must be constantly unpacked into the varied specifics of lived realities. And crime itself is far from a unitary phenomenon. It can involve insider dealing, various crimes of the workplace, white-collar infractions, interpersonal violence, ranging from domestic violence to armed robbery, property crimes of every sort, shape and variety. Even when we focus on a seemingly homogeneous phenomenon such as burglary, we are melding together behaviour with totally different actors, motivations and targets – witness the contrast between the 'opportunistic' burglary by youngsters on the street and the calculated break-in of the professional burglar.

The utter vacuity of the general 'law': unemployment leads to crime, is displayed when one considers the majority of the human race: women, who have a very high rate of unemployment (in terms of non-domestic labour) and extremely low crime rates. But unemployment does give rise to crime in certain circumstances. The failure of such positivism is seen in the Home Office study of the relationship between race and crime (Stevens and Willis, 1979). Here they found there to be a positive correlation between white unemployment and the white rate of crime. But for blacks, the relationship was puzzling: for there was a negative correlation between black unemployment and certain sorts of black crime and 'somewhat surprisingly' the *white* unemployment rate was found to correlate highly with the *black* crime rate. 'A plausible interpretation', the authors note, 'seems hard to find' (p. 23). For, from the point of view of positivism, it is as if one pushed one table and the table next to it moved! But as John Lea and I have argued elsewhere, such a finding is by no means strange:

> As we have argued, there are no direct relationships between objective factors and behaviour. The experience of blacks in areas of high white unemployment may well be that of racial discrimination and scapegoating. Such an alienated subculture would have a considerable reason to break its lawful bonds with the wider society; it might also experience the demoralization which is the basis of much criminality. In areas where there is massive black unemployment, there may be less basis for a comparison with whites and thus a relative lack of the frustration that leads to criminality. (1984, p. 160)

Such an analysis can be applied to generalization in a wide variety of areas. For example, in the field of drugs research I have argued for a socio-pharmacological approach. This rejects both the notion that the effects of drugs and the moral careers of drug users can be read, so to speak, positivistically from the pages of a pharmacopoeia or relativistically, that drug use is a mere function of culture alone. Rather, specific drugs have effects in particular cultural set-ups: the psychotropic nature of the drug both structures and is structured by the culture (Young, 1971b). Similarly, in the field of subcultural theory, Ward and Kassebaum, in their pioneering study of women's prisons (1966), cut through the debate around whether inmate subculture is transmitted from the outside pre-prison culture of the prisoners, or is a functional product of 'the pains of imprisonment' experienced while within the prison. By adding the crucial variable of gender to the discussion they have shown how the way in which the pains of imprisonment are experienced is a function of the gendered subculture of the inmates. The 'same' prison conditions produce widely different subcultural solutions dependent upon the subjective assessment of the inmates.

As we have seen, if we are to be wary about sociological generalizations within one nation at one time, then we should be all the more wary about general laws which attempt to cross historical periods and jump from examples in one country to another. A classic illustration of this is Andrew Scull's decarceration thesis (1977) which empirically assumed that all forms of deviancy involving incarceration would pass through the same sequence (as if the reactions of the powerful would not vary with the specific deviance) and, even more oddly, that the British figures, which did not fully substantiate his thesis, were simply 'lagging behind' those of the United States (see also Cohen, 1988). Here we see not only a generalization from one social country to another, but from one category to another.

Thus, to be more precise, the problem of specificity refers to generalizing about crime, law or victimization from one country or one social group and assuming that one's conclusions apply to all countries or social groups. It is being unable to see how general variables come together in a very specific form in any particular situation. This results in work which is not only inadequate as a generalization, but is lacking in its ability to cope with what is special about the precise constellation of factors which delineate any particular situation. Specificity is a heuristic failure, both on the level of the general and the particular.

The three major problems of specificity which have dominated criminological thinking have operated on the level of both social category and nationality. The first is obviously the fashion in which male, working-class crime has been used to depict all criminality. The impact, first of all, of radical and then feminist criminology has been to sharply dislodge such thinking. The consequences for theory have been enormous. The new empirical dimensions have not yet worked themselves out throughout the maze of conventional theory.

The second, which we have already encountered, is how the depiction of crime in advanced industrial countries is used to describe crime in general. Colin Sumner, in a brilliant essay on crime and under-development (1982) rightly castigates those authors, such as Clinard and Abbott (1973), who see crime in poor countries as just a replay of that which has occurred in the West, and their general economic development as just a delayed natural evolution. He points to the way in which all the traditional criminological generalizations become overturned when one begins to look at police behaviour, crimes of the powerful, crimes of the poor and of political oppositionists within the context of global imperialism. Such work has only just begun, but it is of utmost importance that radical criminology makes a committed attempt to tackle the problems. No one else will. Positivism never did it and indeed sees itself as producing control generalizations which will apply anywhere, from the country estates of England to the streets of Soweto.

The third problem of specificity is a relatively recent phenomenon occurring in the post-1945 period, that is the Americanization of criminology. It is important to realize the significance of the domination of American criminology on the criminologies of the rest of the world. The central paradox is that the vast output of this country – often involving the most innovative work in the field – emerges from a country which is extremely atypical in terms of the majority of advanced industrial countries. The homicide rate, for example, is over three times higher in New York City than in London, and if we are to look for countries which have similar rates of violence to the United States it would be to Latin America, rather than any other industrial country, East or West: it is four times that of England and Wales, over six times that of Germany. There are a series of atypical characteristics of the United States which may well relate to its exceptional crime rate. For example, its lack of social democratic politics, its meagre welfare state, its extremely high commitment to the American Dream version of meritocracy, its high emphasis on formal legal equality as an ideal, its remarkable ethnic pluralism, the extent and range of organized crime, the extent of ghettoization, etc. (see E. Currie, 1985; 1998). All of these factors are likely to have a profound effect on the theory generated in such a society. The theory of differential association, Mertonian anomie theory, neo-Chicagoan labelling theory, social control theory, are all illuminated if we begin to think how they fit so well such an exceptional state. This is not an argument for theoretical isolationism. There is no doubt that the United States has, in the twentieth century, produced many important developments in theoretical criminology. It is to argue, however, that these theories cannot be merely transplanted to, say, a European context; they have to be transposed *carefully*.

The contradiction, then, is that *the* most influential work in criminology stems from one of the most atypical advanced industrial societies. The extent of this paradox can, perhaps, be illustrated if we imagine that Japan became in the 1990s the leading producer of criminological work. Japan is, of course, an extremely atypical capitalist society – and in the area of crime it is the absolute opposite of the United States. Even by European standards the changes in the crime rate are remarkable. For example, from 1948 to 1982 the crime rate in Japan declined by 36 per cent compared to a rise of 348 per cent in England and Wales over the same period. And this was despite dramatic changes occurring in Japanese society; massive industrialization, vast internal movements of population, urbanization and general social upheaval (Government of Japan, 1983). It would not be difficult to imagine the types of criminological theory which would emerge from Japan if it indeed dominated the field of criminology. At the bottom line one can imagine quite 'reasonable' theories which linked a rise in the standards of living with a drop in crime. And one can visualize, perhaps with a certain *Schadenfreude,* criminologists in Berkeley or New York trying to fit the evidence of their own country in the new dominant paradigm.

Or to take a more recent controversy it has been assumed by many positivist criminologists that there is a constant relationship between age and homicide committed by men. That it is assumed to occur 'everywhere and all times the same' (Gottfredson and Hirschi, 1990, p. 124). Namely that homicide in males rises to a peak in the 19/20 age range and declines thereafter. It is easy to imagine non-sociological explanations being grafted to such a supposedly universal finding say testosterone production) and the attraction of this to criminologists who yearn for reductionist 'scientific' explanations. Such a finding has been contested using historical evidence (See Greenberg, 1985, Monkkonen, 1978) but the contemporary Japanese evidence is even more striking. Here homicide peaks with men in their forties (decline in testosterone!) and David Johnson (2008) points to a similar profile in South Korea and posits the existence of an East Asian model of homicide rather like the East Asian models of economic development forced economists to revise their conventional accounts of political economy.

To argue for specificity is not to argue against empirical generalization. It is to say that generalization is possible within particular social orders concerning particular groups. Nor is it to argue that cross-cultural theories of crime are impossible – it is to say firmly that these theories find their result in specific societies. For example, the notion of relative deprivation as a theory of discontent which results in crime in certain social and political circumstances, is one of great heuristic value. But there is a big jump between how the form and content of relative deprivation is experienced among boys in the Lower East Side of Manhattan, to how it is structured in terms of girls in Florence, Japanese youth in Tokyo or corporate criminals in Switzerland.

The Bogus of Positivism

The positivist dream of a scientific sociology of crime, which attempts objectively to relate cause and effect, becomes all the more impossible in late modernity. As we have seen, both the causes of crime and the definitions of crime, that is the outcome or effects, become problematized. That is, social predicaments give rise to much more pluralistic vocabularies of motive ('causes') while the meanings of the outcomes ('effects') are fiercely contested. To move from, say, unemployment to crime, or deprivation to crime, you need narratives; correlation alone cannot assure causality, it is only the narratives which link factors to outcomes that can do this. People turn 'factors' into narratives – they are even capable, as we shall see, of turning such factors on their heads. Furthermore, what is crime itself is part of this narrative. It is a variable dependent on subcultural definition and assessment.

The bogus of positivism is that it only *seemed* to work when the world was reasonably static, where vocabularies of motive were apparently organically linked to points in the social structure and where definitions of crime were consensual and unproblematized. The loosening of moorings in late modernity, and the multiple problematization consequent on pluralism destroys this illusion. As Martin Nicolaus exclaimed in his famous article in *Antioch Review* so many years ago, 'What kind of science is this, which holds true only when men hold still?' (1969, p. 387).

5

Loosening the Moorings: The Emergence of Cultural Criminology

Taking the Hum out of Humdrum

In November 2003, John Laub, in his presidential address to the American Society of Criminology's annual meeting in Denver, Colorado, commented:

> When I entered the field as a graduate student in the 1970s, criminology was an exciting field because people were passionate about ideas. Today 'career concerns' are center-stage in the field – for example, publication counts, citation counts, the amount of external funding generated, departmental rankings and so forth are the new measures of intellectual impact and scholarship. (2004, p. 3)

He talked about 'the Golden Age of Theory' and then added, almost *sotto voce*, in a footnote: 'One can ask in all seriousness. Why is so much of criminology today boring?'

Here was a distinguished criminologist, active in research and eminently knowledgeable about the development of criminology, bravely admitting that there is something amiss in the discipline. I sometimes conjecture that much of orthodox criminology has what one might call an Anti-Midas touch – an ability to turn gold into gravel. Here we have a topic which is the subject of heated conversation in the workplace and at the bus stop, which is one of the major foci of cinema and television, the stuff of video games, the staple diet of the media and the central theme of a multitude of genres within popular literature, from crime thriller to serial killing. Furthermore, the act itself is frequently loaded with malice, thrill and fear – it not unusually galvanizes the offender and traumatizes the victim. Yet both the phenomenology of crime and the fascination of the spectator are somehow lost in the scholarly literature. Indeed sometimes, this is the intention. Marcus Felson (2002), for example, enjoins us to accept that the majority of crime has precious little drama and indeed is 'not much of a story' (p. 3). Indeed he positively seems to celebrate the mundane. He sees it rather like all the other mass of events in everyday life. Yet Felson seems to forget that everyday life is, in fact, a site of frequent drama, tragedy and joy and that even the dullness of habit and routine is often a site of great intensity, an escape from the existential fears of the world, a place of reassurance and solace. The human condition is very much a story of stoic restraint, anger, pleasure and resistance with every now and then what only can be described as incandescent moments, people fall in love, a glance at a child across the room, the Saturday night out when all at once everything seems to click, a phrase, a tune, an electric guitar; whomever the person, whatever the life. Vertiginous it is, sometimes frightening, often joyful: humdrum it is not.

Cultural criminology is of importance because it captures the phenomenology of crime – its adrenaline, its pleasure and panic, its excitement, and its anger, rage and humiliation, its desperation and its edgework. I wish to argue that cultural criminology not only grasps the phenomenology of crime but is also much more attuned to the phenomenology of everyday life in general in the late modern era, both the search for excitement and the retreat into the tedium and tension of conformity. We are confronted at this moment with an orthodox criminology which is denatured and desiccated. Its actors inhabit an arid planet where they are either driven into crime by social and psychological deficits or make opportunistic choices in the marketplace of crime. They are either miserable or mundane: they are digital creatures of quantity, they obey probabilistic laws of deviancy – they can be represented by the statistical symbolism of lambda, chi and sigma, their behaviour can be captured in the intricacies of regression analysis and equation.

The structure of my argument is that, given human beings are culture-creating beings and are endowed with free will, albeit in circumstances not of their own making, then the *verstehen* of human meaning is, by definition, a necessity in any explanation of human activity, criminal or otherwise (see Ferrell, 1997). It is in late modernity that such creativity and reflexivity becomes all the more apparent yet, and here is the irony: it is precisely at the time of the cultural turn that a fundamentalist positivism occurs within the social 'sciences' with increasing strength and attempts at hegemony. But, before we examine the nature of the close fit between cultural criminology and late modernity, let us first look at the antecedents of cultural criminology in subcultural theory and the cultural turn of the 1960s.

The Nature of Culture

Crucial to the understanding of cultural criminology is its interpretation of the 'cultural', itself a subject of controversy and contest. First of all it is not positivism. That is, it does not see culture as a simple function of material situations or structural positions. Culture is *not* a dependent variable of structure. Yet, and here there are differences with the 'new American cultural sociology' (see Smith, 1998; Alexander and Smith, 2002), for culture is certainly not an *independent* variable. It is in no way autonomous of the patterns of inequality and power or the material predicaments of the actors. The history of its antecedents in subcultural theory, both the early American work on the subcultures of prisons and delinquency and the subsequent Marxist-inspired studies in Britain on youth cultures and moral panics, belie this. Witness the Gramscian concern with class and power in the work of the Birmingham School (e.g. Hall and Jefferson, 1975; Hall et al., 1978) which the cultural sociologists dismiss as 'unduly restrictive' and a 'presuppositional commitment to a power-based frame of analysis' (Smith, 1998; Sherwood et al., 1993).

Thus the cultural hegemony of the powerful and the subcultures of acquiescence and resistance of the less powerful are scarcely independent of class and power. The earliest subcultural work on total institutions particularly Goffman's *Asylums* (1961) can be seen as exemplars of resistance to power (far more radical than Foucault's later work as Marshall Berman was to point out in *All That's Solid Melts Into Air*, 1983). As for the immediate material predicament of social actors, the very early subcultural work on 'the pains of imprisonment' demonstrated a dialectical relationship between conditions and culture. Namely, although all inmates experienced the pains of imprisonment, the extent and the nature of these pains were dependent on the culture they brought to the prison (e.g. in terms of class and gender) just as 'the pains' in turn shaped the particular inmate culture that arose to attempt to surmount the privations of a prison life (see Young, 1999, pp. 89–90). The totalitarian nature of the prison, the regulation and surveillance of life in the finest detail is experienced very differently whether the inmates are male or female (see Giallombardo 1966; Ward and Kassebaum, 1966), whether they have a previous experience of institutional living, say in the army or youth corrections, are middle or working class or whether. In a more dreadful instance, survival in the concentration camps of the National Socialists, in the most extreme and inhuman circumstances, was dependent on the culture of the inmates – whether they were Jehovah's

Witnesses, political prisoners, or middle-class people who had believed in the benign nature of authority all their lives (Bettelheim, 1943).

Secondly, and related to the first, cultural criminology is not a cultural positivism where crime or deviance is ascribed to the simple acting out of the culture of a group. Thus it would take issue with the famous subcultural formulation of Walter Miller (1958) where crime is simply the enactment of lower-working-class values. Nor is it in the tradition of cultural conflict theory although there is a tendency to interpret it as such. This position originally formulated by Thorstein Sellin (1938) argued that much crime and delinquency was merely the result of cultural conflict between the values of immigrant groups and those of the host society. For example, the ideas of honour, vengeance and vendetta among Sicilian immigrants, which led to conflicts with American values. This has clear echoes today in the supposition that multiculturalism generates a sense of inevitable collisions of norms, most particularly that between Muslim and Western values (see Bovenkerk and Yesilgoz, 2004). Such collisions do occur but cultures are not static, they are not an essence waiting to be enacted, rather they are heterogeneous, they blur, change, cross boundaries and hybridize. To talk, for example, of proclivities to crime in relationship to ethnic cultures – say Jewish or Jamaican – is a pointless essentialism, stereotypical in its notion of fixity and stasis and of no explanatory value whatsoever.

Two Notions of Culture

Zygmunt Bauman, in *Culture as Praxis*, distinguishes two discourses about culture, longstanding and seemingly diametrically opposed:

> To put it in a nutshell: one discourse generated the idea of culture as the activity of the free roaming spirit, the site of creativity, invention, self-critique and self-transcendence; another discourse posited culture as a tool of routinization and continuity – a handmaiden of social order.
>
> The product of the first discourse was the notion of culture as the capacity to resist the norm and rise above the ordinary . . . It stood for what the most daring, the least compliant and conformist spirits were assumed to be distinguished by: irreverence to tradition, the courage to break well-drawn horizons, to step beyond closely guarded boundaries . . .
>
> The product of the second discourse was the notion of culture formed and applied in orthodox anthropology. There, 'culture' stood for regularity and pattern – with freedom cast under the rubric of 'norm-breaking' and 'deviation'. . . .
>
> The two notions of culture stood in stark opposition to each other. One denied what the other proclaimed; one focused on the aspects of human reality which the other presented as impossible or, at best, as abnormal-

ity . . . The first was the story of human freedom, of the randomness and contingency of all man-made forms of life; the second assigned to freedom and contingency a role akin to aetiological myths, concentrating instead on the ways in which their order-disrupting potency is defused and devoid of consequence. (1999, pp. xvi–xvii)

Culture of the second sort is the province of traditional social anthropology and of Parsonian Functionalism. Culture is the stuff of cohesion, the glue of society, the preservative of predictability, the uncritical support of social structure. Culture of the first sort fits much more readily within the subcultural tradition; it is culture as praxis, the culture of transgression, of resistance, of human creativity. And if for this discourse transgression signals creativity, cultural creation for the first, it is the very opposite: transgression is the very *absence* of culture. Yet the two discourses are not irreconcilable. Of course, the notion of culture as somehow outside of human creation, as an unreflexive prop of social structure, a mysterious functional creation of the social organism, is preposterous. But the *belief* in tradition, the embracing of stasis and conformity, the mobilization of rigid stereotype and fundamental values is, of course, a fact in itself and a fact of considerable impact and reality.

Thus a sociology which foregrounds human creativity does not entail the ignoring of those cultures and actions which involve its renunciation. As we have seen, human beings have always the feasibility, the capacity to transcend even the direst circumstances but they have also the possibility of acting 'as if' they were a cultural puppet or an inanimate artifice. Thus, if we are, in Dwight Conquergood's (1991) wonderful phrase, to view culture as a verb rather than as a noun, then we must remember that this verb is cast both in a passive and an active tense. Culture may well be a performance, but it can be as much an act of acquiescence as of rebellion.

The Concept of Subculture

Let me briefly outline the idea of a subculture, for it is out of the tradition of subcultural theory that cultural criminology evolved. The concept of subculture is clearly linked to the notion of culture developed within social anthropology. David Downes (1966), in his study of working-class delinquency in the East End of London, invokes the definition of culture formulated by C. S. Ford, namely: 'learned problem solutions'. That is, subcultural responses are jointly elaborated solutions to collectively experienced problems. Deviant behaviour from this perspective is viewed as being a meaningful attempt to solve the problems faced by a group or an isolated individual – it is not a meaningless pathology. It is necessary, therefore, to explore and understand the subjective experience of the actor. Thus Downes writes: 'Whatever factors and circumstances combine to produce a problem derive from the individual's frame of reference – the way he looks at the world – or the situation he confronts' (1966, p. 6). To achieve this aim it is necessary to delineate how new situations – and with them new problems – are assessed from the point of view of the culture that the individuals *already* embrace. In short: subcultures emerge from the moral springboard of already existing cultures and are the solutions to problems perceived within the framework of these initial cultures.

Culture is seen, in this anthropological sense, as the ways people have evolved to tackle the problems which face them in everyday life. It includes language, ways of dress, moral standards, political institutions, art forms, work norms, modes of sexuality – in sum all human behaviour. That is, people find themselves in particular structural positions in the world and, in order to solve the problems which such positions engender, evolve certain subcultural 'solutions' to attempt to tackle them. Thus people in each particular structural position evolve their own *subculture*. And, of course, the major structural axes are those of age, class, ethnicity and gender. These shape people's lives in the context of the particular space they occupy (for example, whether they are in the inner city or rural areas), the particular work and leisure activities in which they are involved, and the specific time and country we are talking about. The structural predicaments which give rise to problems of particular groups are varied and stratified throughout society. Subcultures, of course, overlap, they are not distinct normative ghettos: the subculture of young black working-class men will overlap a great deal with their female counterparts. But there will also be distinct differences stemming from the predicaments of gender. And, of course, people in the same structural position can evolve different subcultures and these will change over time. For example, in terms of youth culture: mods, rockers, skinheads, teds, punks, may all be varieties of attempts by working-class youth to deal with roughly similar problems. For subcultures are human creations and can vary as widely as the imagination of the participants involved. All human beings create their own subcultural forms and although we often tend to use the term for the young and the deviant, it is important to note how this is just a matter of focus. Police officers, social workers, academics, for example, form their own subcultures which are, in their way, as developed and exotic as those existing in the world of crime or youth culture.

Human beings are storytelling animals, they create stories of themselves and about others. They devise narratives about themselves, they talk to their peers about these narratives, they tell stories of other people as exemplars, as contrasts, as positives and negatives and sometimes as saints, sometimes as folk devils. Subcultures are bundles of narratives within which the social world hums, subcultures talking about themselves and subcultures talking about subcultures.

Subcultural theory attempts to deal with the fundamental problems of social analysis: how to relate the subjective meanings of actions to an objective assessment of their situation, how to relate the individual actions to the values of his or her group, how to relate the macrostructure of society to the microcosm of human action, how to tackle problems of rationality and irrationality, of social organization and disorganization and how to relate the past to the present social predicament of the actors. Such an approach closely parallels and fleshes out C. Wright Mills' notion of the sociological imagination. That is it places the individual in a given structural position, it relates the social dynamics of the system to the psychodynamics of the individual and back again (the dialectics of structure and agency), it relates social values to subcultural values and it places the individual in a subculture in flux, that changes over time in response to changing material conditions and the reactions of others. It even goes so far as to suggest that self-blame, the belief that one's predicament is detached from the general problems of the system is a specific response of certain self-deluding subcultures, itself a typical product of the First World or American Dream – of which more shortly.

The Culture of Discontent

In subcultural theory deviant subcultures are viewed not as pathological groupings of maladjusted individuals who lack culture, but rather as consisting of individuals who collectively evolve meaningful attempts to solve problems faced by the individuals concerned. Whether it is juvenile vandalism or the latest teenage style, cultural responses are meaningful rather than meaningless. Yet a whole series of terms have evolved, both in orthodox criminology and in the wider public discourse, which, rather than explaining deviant behaviour, in fact attempt to *explain it away*. Terms like mob, psychopath, undersocialized, hyperactive, primitive, animal, mindless (as in 'mindless' violence), immature, mad – all serve one purpose. They take the observer's values as obvious and 'normal' and they castigate other people's values as not meaningful alternatives, but a lack of value, meaning and rationality. In contrast, subcultural theory argues that human behaviour is fundamentally meaningful and differences in behaviour represent the *different* problems and solutions to these problems which particular subcultures have evolved.

A riot, for instance, is not a situation where a mob of people have taken leave of their senses, but a response understandable in terms of the subculture concerned. This is not to say that it is necessarily the most effective method of achieving the aims of the individuals, but rather it makes sense given their limitations and their understanding of the situation. It is, in fact, a common method of voicing protest by relatively powerless groups. As the social historian Eric Hobsbawm commented:

> No other European country has so strong a tradition of rioting as Britain and none which persisted well past the middle of the nineteenth century. The riot, as a normal part of collective campaigning, was well-established in the eighteenth century. (1964, p. 379)

Indeed, subcultural theory from the 1950s onwards exercises itself by demonstrating how behaviours which are viewed as unacceptable and irrational to the 'normal' decent citizen are, in fact, attempted solutions to particular problems experienced by people at certain points of the social structure. And here it echoes, of course the anthropological conundrum about the functions of cannibalism, seemingly bizarre and undecipherable tribal customs: unspeakable kinship rituals, strange taboos and fetishes, cargo cults, etc., etc. In criminology it involves a move away from the simple, utilitarian, Mertonian belief that crime is merely another route to monetary success goals, to that of focusing on behaviour which is on the face of it self-defeating and implausible. Thus Albert Cohen, in his classic subcultural text *Delinquent Boys: The Culture of the Gang* (1955), starts off from the recognition that most delinquency is not the means to access desired goods, but rather is 'non-utilitarian, malicious and negativistic'. He gives examples from the literature: the stealing of goods which are almost immediately disregarded and discarded, the breaking of milk bottles, terrifying 'good' children in the playground, putting glue in a keyhole, banging on doors and running away; while at school: 'The teacher and her rules are not merely something onerous to be evaded. They are to be *flouted*' (1955, p. 28). Their behaviour is 'anti-social' in the sense of being against the social rules of those in authority, but it is in its very nature social in its creative mischief, it is at core *transgressive*. Cohen does not relegate this behaviour to mischievousness or the normal high spirits of childhood, but first of all points to the structural locus of such delinquency as being low in the social structure. It is male, it is young, it is lower working class: these are the kids in every school who make trouble, these are the malcontents in the mall, these are the children who oversubscribe to the juvenile delinquency statistics. He does not rule out delinquency among middle-class kids, nor among girls, but this is the focus. What is it, he asked, about 'growing up in a class system'? Cohen's answer to this is well known and has influenced countless subsequent studies. Namely, that at school, children are judged in terms of performance and personality by middle-class standards, standards by which lower-working-class children are poorly socialized into achieving. Such an experience of status deprivation and humiliation is avoided by reacting strongly against middle-class values, by negating and inverting them. A reaction formation, a process of energy and intensity, *cultural work*, where middle-class values are inverted and status reasserted by such a rebellion. Similarly, over twenty years later, the Marxist subcultural theorist Paul Willis, in *Learning to Labour* (1977), analyses how the lower stream of the class – 'the Lads' – realize that they are destined for low-skilled jobs where academic achievement is irrelevant. Their structural problem is that they are being asked to compete against middle-class standards for which their own background ill prepares them, in order to achieve academic qualifications irrelevant to their future jobs. They culturally 'solve' the problem by playing up in the classroom, rejecting the teacher's discipline, by despising 'swots' – 'ear'oles' – while at the same time evolving a subculture which gives high status to manliness and physical toughness. That is, they begin to evolve a culture which rejects standards which threaten their self-esteem and more relevantly fits their future work as labourers. They turn their misfortune into a virtue. Similarly, Ken Pryce, in *Endless Pressure* (1979), his study of young blacks in Bristol, notes how a proportion reject 'shit work' – they evolve a leisure culture which helps them survive unemployment and racism and enables them to avoid the few and menial jobs available to them.

Thus explanations of classroom behaviour which reduce the activities of youth to the defects and failings of individuals are rejected. These can be, and of course often are, phrased in quasi-scientific language (for example, 'hyperactivity', 'underachievement', 'low IQ') and they can be at times associated with progressive, caring views (for example lead poisoning in the inner cities). None of this makes them, from a subcultural point of view, any the less suspect. In all these instances subcultural theorists, instead of viewing deviant behaviour as pathological, irrational or lacking in meaning, are interpreting it as a cultural response with a definite meaningful rationality. To start with, the theorist is seeing the problem through the eyes of the people in the subculture. That is, he or she is granting the group being analysed a subjectivity instead of invoking spurious 'objective' notions of pathology or sickness unrelated to their interpretations of their situation. But this does not imply a rejection of an objective assessment of the situation. Rather it is to disagree with much of what passes as objective accounts – they are in fact most often attempts to belittle subcultures of discontent. By denying the culture, meaning and reason, one is unable to encompass the vital component of human subjectivity necessary in the explanation of human behaviour in contrast to explanations of animal behaviour or inanimate movement.

Reflexivity and Tenability

All of the above being said, it is quite possible for actors to accept such negative and pathological definition of themselves and for these to enter the narratives of their lives and to be part and parcel of the subcultures they live in. They may for example exist in a subculture which has come to believe in the American Dream and thus understand their 'failure' in life, as their own fault, as the result of some weakness or defect. After all this is precisely how Robert Merton saw the Dream, namely as a cultural 'sop' which reduced the chances of rebellion against a system which systematically produced low rates of social mobility (see Merton, 1938; Young, 2010). Subcultures can carry narratives of mystification and recipes for disaster. For subcultural solutions are not necessarily a correct reading of the situation and they are not, as Matza pointed out, of necessity *tenable*, they may not work, they may make things worse. To criticize explanations of deviancy as a pathology is not to deny that some people do act *as if* they were suffering from a pathology while to believe that all subcultures are equally tenable in their solutions for living is to engage in romanticism. For subcultures with their narratives of life may be liberatory but they can also be self-defeating (see Maruna, 2001).

Let us now examine the remarkable changes that have occurred in the recent period before we describe more fully the fit between cultural criminology and late modernity.

The Journey into Late Modernity

In *The Exclusive Society*, I argued that the last third of the twentieth century and the beginning of the twenty-first has witnessed a remarkable transformation in the lives of citizens living in advanced industrial societies. The Golden Age of the post-war settlement with high employment, stable family structures, and consensual values underpinned by the safety net of the welfare state has been replaced by a world of structural unemployment, economic precariousness, a systematic cutting of welfare provisions and the growing instability of family life and interpersonal relations. And where there once was a consensus of value, there is now a burgeoning pluralism and individualism (see Hobsbawm, 1994). A world of material and ontological security from cradle to grave is replaced by precariousness and uncertainty and where social commentators of the 1950s and 1960s berated the complacency of a comfortable 'never had it so good' generation, those of today talk of a risk society where social change becomes the central dynamo of existence and where anything might happen. Such a change has been brought about by market forces which have systematically transformed both the sphere of production and of consumption. This shift from Fordism to Post-Fordism involves the unravelling of the world of work where the primary labour market of secure employment and 'safe' careers shrinks, the secondary labour market of short-term contracts, flexibility and insecurity increases, as does the growth of a so-called 'underclass', working at near poverty level wages on the margins of employment and unemployment. Secondly, the world of leisure is transformed from one of mass basic consumption, to one where choice and preference is elevated to a major ideal and where the constant stress on immediacy, hedonism and self-actualization has had a profound effect on late modern sensibilities (see Campbell, 1987; Featherstone, 1985).

The late modern period is characterized by disruption of employment, of marital stability, of greater spatial mobility, by a pluralism of contested values, by the emergence of mediated virtual realities and reference points, and by the rise of mass consumerism. It embodies two fundamental contradictions: firstly a heightened emphasis on identity in a time when lack of social disembeddedness serves to undermine ontological security and, secondly, by a stress on expressivity, excitement, and immediacy, yet at a time where the commodification of leisure and the rationalization of work mitigates against this. This is a world where narratives are constantly broken and rewritten, where values are contested, and where reflexivity is the order of the day. This is a new world where a personal narrative of development is an ideal, where virtual narratives abound in the media and on the net, yet where narratives are constantly broken and are disembedded from work, family and the community. For all of these reasons a criminology which stresses the existential, which is focused upon subcultures of creativity and style, which emphasize the adrenalized excitement of human action, on one hand, and the tedium and commodification on the other, goes with the grain of everyday life. Moreover, and counter to claims to the contrary (see Garland, 2001), neo-liberal theories such as those of rational choice and routine activities theory do not fully mirror the texture of our time, but only one part of it: the mundane, the denatured, the mediocre. Let us start by looking at the situation of late modernity.

The Loosening of the Moorings

This process of boundaries dissolving and boundaries being built up like children's sandcastles on a beach is characteristic of late modernity. At the same time there becomes an increasing awareness of the social construction of boundaries and their contested nature. That is, any sense of the absolute, the reified, the natural, becomes exceedingly precarious. In this process people become more cognizant of their own role as actors in society. For, although the existential condition and the creation of human meaning has always been part of what we mean by social, this certainty becomes all the more apparent in late modernity. Why is this?

Voluntarism

On the back of the movement towards flexible labour and the modern consumer society with its myriad choices, an individualistic society arises where choice, expressivity, meaningful work and leisure become ideals. The American Dream of the post-war period, with its stress on the taken-for-granted ends of material comfort becomes overtaken by a new First World Dream, where meaning and expression are paramount and where lifestyles do not so much beckon as are there to be created. Finding yourself becomes more important than arriving.

Disembeddedness

The flexibility and mobility of labour and the increased instability of the family result in people's lives becoming disembedded from work, family and community. Their identity does not immediately and consistently present itself with a taken-for-granted and unreflective naturalness. The irony, then, is that just as there is a greater stress on creating one's identity, the building blocks of identity become less substantial. Furthermore, in a lifetime of broken narratives, constant re-invention becomes a central life task.

Mass Media and Virtual Realities

In late modernity the mass media expands in terms of the percentage of time of a person's life that it takes up – in England and Wales, for example, television and radio alone take up an extraordinary 40 per cent of the average person's waking life, or 60 per cent of the free time of those in work. The media overall becomes more multi-mediated, diversifying and relating to wider audiences (see McRobbie and Thornton, 1995). As the physical community declines, the virtual community arises, carrying with it virtual realities with new and emerging role models, subcultures of value, vocabularies of motive and narratives both fictional and 'factional'. In particular, the two 'others' are polarized: positively the celebrity, and negatively various 'others', particularly around the notion of an underclass. Powerful positive and negative orientation points are thus available, various and particular, for the mass of people whose personal narratives have constantly to be rewritten and reinvented. In between, a whole host of identities parade themselves from characters in soap operas to 'ordinary citizens' who pop up in everyday news items. These identities are there like costumes on a clothes rail to be worn tailor made, to be readjusted and transformed, to be disliked or desired. Thus at the same time as secure identity is destabilized, choices and reference points are on offer in plenty.

Vertical and Horizontal Media:

Media of communication are usually thought of as vertical, a monologue downwards: thus the mass media involves the few talking to the many. The late modern period begins to reverse this; with the rise of e-mail and the cell phone, there is now a vast media network which facilitates horizontal communication between friends, family and peers, which exponentially expands the facilities of the fixed telephone links which preceded it. At the same time the traditional vertical media – television, film and radio proliferate both in the quantity of outlets and the new media, such as the internet, with an increased undercurrent of dialogue and feedback – commentaries and blogs.

The effect of this is to expose the individual to a considerable variety of values, vocabularies of motive, possible personal narratives and identities while allowing the plurality of subcultures – both already established and emerging lifestyles – to develop and survive. In short it both presents and fosters pluralism and between these two moments greatly engenders a hybridity of culture where bits and pieces of value and behaviour are bricolaged together.

Mass Migration

The demands for labour, first of all in manufacturing and then later in the service industries, the enticements of affluence aided and abetted by the images transmitted by a global media, the opening of borders as part of neo-liberal policies, the breaching of borders elsewhere, all combine to encourage the mass movement of populations into the developed world. This process is most clearly seen in Europe. Previously relatively homogenous populations have now become manifestly multicultural. Such a mass immigration is, of course, scarcely new to settler societies such as the United States and Australia. In 1900, for example, the immigrant population of New York City was possibly higher, although it was largely from one rather than four continents as it is today.

The Shock of the Plural

The pluralism of values available through the mass media is thus greatly supplemented by the increase in immigration. This creates a world which is more varied in its values and is considerably augmented by the plurality of lifestyles generated by the new individualism. People are, therefore, presented with a social world where values are contested and where there are very many alternatives of appropriate behaviour and aspiration. The sheer variety of cultures adjacent and interacting is a new phenomenon characteristic of late modernity. They involve changes in the media of communication and changes in the city; they involve changes in actual physical movement and in virtual and mediated transportations; they involve a proximity of plural values both on a global and on an immediate level. The shock of the plural is experienced at the turn of a switch and in walking down the street, it is global in its reach and local in its basis.

Hyperpluralism and Hybridism
Hyperpluralism is the daily exposure to a very high number of cultures and subcultures, of definitions of the situation, of what is normality and of what is deviant. It is a scenario not consisting of a segregated, mosaic of cultures (rather like Amitai Etzioni's ideal communitarianism), but one where there is a constant overlap, contest and hybridity. It is a situation where one is no longer sure what it is to be normal, where the opaque window of the taken-for-granted world is fragmented, where light distorts and constantly changes colour with each refraction and change in angle of vision. It is one where the perceptive observers of the social world whether sociologists, psychologists, anthropologists, social historians and whoever, begin to perceive themselves not as the 'natural eye' of the social majority, but rather as if they were themselves a particular, perhaps rather unusual, ethnic group with strange customs, lifestyles and (usually liberal) politics.

HYPERPLURALISM:

A Majority of Minorities:	there is no majority population in terms of the subdivision of ethnicity, class, age or gender
Plurality of Cultures:	there is a large plurality of cultures from all continents, across the world
Lack of Binaries:	there is neither a majority contrasting a small minority nor a more sizeable binary division
High Proportion of First Generation Immigrants:	a large part of the population were not born locally and probably not in the 'host' country
Hybridization and Porosity:	cultures are relatively open, hybridism is frequent, transnational consciousness is common

The Hyperplural City

Urban geographers are amazed by the sheer diversity of some of the most iconic cities of the Western world. London, for example, has over 30 per cent of its population born abroad, coming from fifteen or more countries; New York over 33 per cent, Toronto over 45 per cent (see Gordon et al., 2007). And these percentages are obviously underestimates because of illegal immigration. They call them the alpha cities: New York, Toronto, Los Angeles, London, Sydney, Miami, Melbourne, Amsterdam and Vancouver with the beta cities of Paris, Montreal and San Francisco not far behind. They refer to them as being *hyperdiverse* characterized both by their quantity of immigrants and the quality or variety of cultures (see Benton-Short et al., 2005). They point to four characteristics: a high percentage of the population is foreign born, there is a high absolute number of immigrants, a heterogeneity where no one group represents over 25 per cent of the immigrant population, and immigrants should have arrived from all over the world rather than largely from an adjacent country. To this one might add that they have arrived on a fairly permanent basis rather than being temporary workers; in order to separate out cities such as Dubai and Muscat, hyperpluralism takes hyperdiversity one step further by adding some sociology to this geographical insight. And to these effects of migration should, of course, be added the endogenous accent on subculture and the building of new lifestyles.

The quantity of stimuli referred to by Georg Simmel (1903/50), when he evoked *'the rapid crowding of changing images, the sharp discontinuity in the grasp of a single glance, and the unexpectedness of onrushing impressions'* in his characterization of urban life in Berlin at the beginning of the twentieth century, is far surpassed in the modern metropolis. The heterogeneity of class and status which Louis Wirth (1938) discerned in the Chicago of the 1930s, is far overtaken in the hyperplural city of the present.

The ethnographer should, George Marcus argues, experience *defamiliarization* when finishing his or her research. That is, not only should they see the world they have investigated with clear and questioning eyes, they should return home to find their own world questionable. The day-to-day routines, the most obvious 'natural' things that appear, as they are, unnatural, contingent, a product of human creativity at a particular place and time. Such a defamiliarization is a regular occurrence for the immigrant, one of nature's ethnographers, for him or her, caught between two worlds, home loses its certainty even before immigration – in everywhere from the Dominican Republic to Poland images of the developed world permeate consciousness – and afterwards nothing ever seems obvious again. For example, in the old days on the west coast of Ireland people used to hold American wakes for family and friends emigrating to the United States, because they would be unlikely to see them ever again. Today traffic back and forward is commonplace, communications are cheap, the media fill in all the details before you leave and a transnational consciousness develops stretching across borders, continents and oceans. In hyperpluralism something even more dramatic occurs, for the indigenous population itself begins to find its citadels of symbolic security porous and insecure. The world turns inside out upon itself.

The Narcissism of Minor Differences

Freud, in *Civilisation and its Discontents* (1929), was concerned with how minor differences between people frequently caused more discomfort than considerable differences. Writers such as Michael Ignatieff and Anton Blok (1998) have taken this idea and transferred it to understanding cultural conflicts. Ignatieff, for example, in *Warrior's Honor* (1999) views the conflicts in the former Yugoslavia and Northern Ireland with this lens. Without needing to adopt a Freudian metaphysic (as Ignatieff does), it is possible to take the nub of the idea and interpret it quite simply in terms of human reflexivity. Cultures which are dramatically different do not present themselves as possible choices to guide our own behaviour and are much easier to be viewed as the accoutrements of people who are essentially different from us. Cultures which are of minor or slight difference present themselves as possible choices, they represent a disquieting possibility that our own cultural choices are incorrect and, at the very least, not simply the natural behaviour which any 'normal' person would exhibit (see Young, 1999, pp. 180–2).

Cultural globalization via the mass media and mass tourism brings cultures together, narrowing differences both between nations and within nations. Paradoxically the narcissism of minor differences becomes all the more apparent in the late modern world and generates not only a sense of choice rather than determination and inevitability, but also as cultures experience cross-over and hybridization, a blurring of categories rather than a separateness.

The Market in Worlds

Thus, Zygmunt Bauman contrasts the post-war modern world with the late modern world of liquid modernity. In the former there were:

> patterns, codes and rules to which one could conform, which one could select as stable orientation points and by which one could subsequently let oneself be guided, that are nowadays in increasingly short supply. It does not mean our contemporaries are guided solely by their own imagination

and resolve and are free to construct their mode of life from scratch and at will, or that they are no longer dependent on society for the building materials and design blueprints. But it does mean that we are presently moving from an era of pre-allocated 'reference groups' into an epoch of 'universal comparison', in which the destination of individual self-constructing labours is endemically and incurably underdetermined, is not given in advance, and tends to undergo numerous and profound changes before such labours reach their only genuine end: that is, the end of the individual's life.

These days patterns and configurations are no longer 'given', let alone 'self-evident'; there are just too many of them, clashing with each other and contradicting one another's commandments, so that each one is stripped of a good deal of compelling, constraining powers. (2000b, p. 7).

It is in such an era that the taken-for-granted world which Alfred Schutz depicts as the '*epoché* of the natural attitude' (1962) changes to one of reflexivity, what I have termed a phenomenological *epoché* (1999, pp. 97–8), where the social construction of the world becomes apparent, where social reality is up for grabs and reinterpreted from a myriad standpoints, where contest, blurring and change is the order of the day. For we live, as the sociologist of religion, Helmut Schelsky (1957) observed, in a world of 'permanent reflectiveness'; indeed he talks of 'a market in worlds'. This, then, is a world of pluralism, of choice, of difference – although some-times of a minor nature – a world where human subcultures are in flux. The cultural turn, therefore, follows subcultural theory in viewing culture in the anthropological sense as attempts to solve the problems which people face at particular points of the social structure and emphasizes the creative nature of culture. It holds with Bauman the stress on culture's 'endemic restlessness and inborn inclination to transcendence' (Bauman and Tester, 2001, p. 33), and stresses the particularly restless and creative nature of late modernity. But, of course, this is not all of the story. As I have documented elsewhere (1999, 2007), the insecure and disembedded nature of identity formation in the present period can easily lead to choices of bad faith. That is, embracing identities grounded in fundamentalism, in gender, or 'race', in nation and in traditional culture, which are con-ceived of as fixed and determined essences. For, as we have seen, in liquid modernity boundaries dissolve only to be re-erected again. Yet for all their reaction against the voluntarism and change of later modernity, even these adaptations – the most lowly and least controversial being the embrac-ing of habit, of creating a cocoon of unquestioning regularity in one's life (what Merton termed 'ritualism') – these too are choices and social inventions.

Such changes accompanying the cultural turn have extraordinary implications for sociology, particularly for explanation, but also for measurement and research practice. Further there are, as we have seen, strong parallels between the certainty and 'objectivity' demanded by positivist methodologies and the security offered by social fundamentalism and, dare I say it, the practice of 'skating on thin ice' which I have documented has more than a hint of a similar bad faith coupled with the constant neurosis that the ice will fail and that history will deem it folly rather than scholarship.

The Flux of Identity in Late Modernity

Let us note at this juncture the significantly changed circumstances of identity formation and with it the vocabulary of motives associated with given roles and structural positions. For the combination of the ideal of choice, disembeddedness and pluralism engenders a situation where vocabularies of motives begin to lose their fixed moorings in particular parts of the social structure and in specific social circumstances. That is, the old rigid moorings of Fordism, the demarcations of class, age and gender, the concentric demarcations of the Chicago model of space in the city begin to dissolve. Vocabularies of motive become loose and are cast adrift from their structural sites; they can shift and be fixed elsewhere. This is not randomly: there obviously has to be some fit between structural predicament and subcultural solution, but the level of determination and predictability diminishes. Furthermore, they can be bricolaged elsewhere in the system: they can be reinterpreted, transposed and hybridized. And, finally, and most crucially of course, they can be changed and innovated sometimes dramatically.

Let us, for a moment, look at the relationship between material and social predicaments, identity, vocabularies of motive and social action, taking crime as an example, although we could as well focus, say, on educational achievement or sexual behaviour. There is an extraordinary tendency to suggest that the motive to commit crime springs fully fledged out of certain material predicaments (e.g. poverty, unemployment) or social circumstances (e.g. lack of control) or biological characteristics (e.g. youth and masculinity), almost as if no connecting narrative or human subjectivity were necessary (see Katz, 2002). In reality, as we have seen, a situation like poverty will result in totally different assessments and responses dependent on the narratives which the subjects use to interpret their predicament – indeed the very assessment of whether one is poor or not will depend on social interpretation. There can be no causality in society without reference to meaning, and even high correlations – as all the methods textbooks tell us – do not necessitate causality (see Sayer, 1992). What is necessary is to understand that we live in a situation where such meanings change rapidly and do not adhere fixedly to particular social roles, or material predicaments. We can separate out two facets of this process: liquidity and change.

Identities carrying with them vocabulary of motives, ideals, reference groups, frustrations; pride and grievance can unravel more readily across society and space. Thus, reference groups can be distant – even virtual – and, more importantly, increasingly universal in their providence. For example, as Tony Bottoms and Paul Wiles posit, youth in Britain can have as reference points beach life in Sydney, or as Donna Gaines found out in *Teenage Wasteland* (1998), her study of teenagers in New Jersey, the vocabulary of motives and lifestyle surrounding dropouts from school could travel across class and have as key references heavy metal groups. Some like the British group Led Zeppelin, were not only orientation points from across the Atlantic, but 'retro' in time. Indeed, studies of middle-class delinquency frequently show how working-class norms spread up the structure (see H. and J. Schwendinger, 1985). The paradigm case of this is, of course, the rise of hip hop music and rap lyrics from the black ghettos, with its rhetoric of respect, rejection, and challenged masculinity having huge audiences among white youth of all class backgrounds. On a different level, the universal values of feminism, arising originally from middle-class white feminists, have now a purchase which resonates across the world: from Iran to Benin, from Birmingham, England to Birmingham, Alabama and whose parameters of freedom and equality become a key benchmark in so many women's lives. In the realm of crime, motivation, style and even modus operandi are globally connected: a serial killer from Singapore gains narrative from American novels, a Yardie in Brixton, London, picks up notions of gangsterdom from *The Godfather*, as indeed do the American Mafiosi themselves. All of these concepts travel across time and place, structure and space, disseminated widely by a prolific and insistent media, yet, of course, all change in the process: hybridize and cross over as they are transposed between groups. But the close fit between motives and structure, the more localized and specific responses, become weakened with the extraordinary power of the mass media, coupled with the undercutting of embeddedness in locality and the mass nature of cultures characteristic of the recent period.

Secondly, let us look at change. Late modernity has been characterized by extraordinary changes in the major social sites of class, youth, gender, and ethnicity. Concepts of what it is to be young, what it is to be female, what pleasures we should expect, our attitudes to work, sexuality, and leisure have all been dramatically recast. I will concentrate on a few selected examples of such change – but first of all let me point out what is perhaps – *or should be* – the obvious. None of these changes were predictable from the social, economic and cultural 'variables' present before these fundamental roles and values were reinvented. They are understandable, in retrospect, in terms of responses to material and social change, but they were re-fashioned by human actors who simply re-wrote their narratives.

Edward Shorter, in his magisterial *The Making of the Modern Family* (1977), points to the two major transformations in the late modern family being the greater freedom of women and the loss of control over adolescents. The advances and acceptance of contraception, plus the extension of life span, changed the historical role of women dominated by childbirth and childcare throughout their adult lives. This allowed the development of working lives and gave rise to perhaps the most important structural change of late modern times, the entry of women into the labour force and greater female independence. This resulted, he argues, in much greater levels of family instability and rise in divorce rates. To this one might add: that this fundamental structural change generated second wave feminism, one of the most influential intellectual currents on a global scale of the late modern world, the evolution of the concept of the dual role and of equality. Furthermore, of immediate interest is that the movement of women out of the family gave rise to a feminization of the public sphere, a rising intolerance of violence in all spheres of life. It has involved characteristically a growth of intolerance of violence in public life and the widespread denunciation of violence in private life (e.g. wife battering, child abuse, rape and sexual abuse).

As for adolescents, Shorter agues that the availability of work or of extended education enables their intensive socialization outside of the family particularly by their peer group. Let us add to this such a movement of youth into the public sphere, paralleling the greater autonomy of women, allows for a group with some degree of financial independence, complemented with greater sexual freedom because of contraception, often frustrated in their desires for material goods and expressive freedoms, to enter the arena in terms of a new creation: the dissatisfied and often rebellious teenager. And, of course, the teenage 'revolution' was one of the great changes of the late twentieth century – something so dramatic that, as so often with such sweeping changes, we can scarcely realise now that it is a recent phenomenon.

Here again let me restate the obvious. No one knew what youth was going to do with its new position and status. If, for example, you were attempting to predict crime rates from the 'variables' which seemed to explain crime rates in the 1950s, one would have talked about inequalities, employment levels, educational achievement, percentage of adolescent males in the population, divorce rates, etc. But even the most sophisticated statistical analysis (very unlikely at that time) could not have predicted the extent of youth crime – and the reason for this is palpably simple: you could not have anticipated what was to happen to 'youth'.

Before I turn to a brief outline of cultural criminology, let me repeat the structure of my argument. First, I have noted how the social and meaningful nature of human action makes positivistic methods inappropriate, secondly I stress how the particular conditions of late modernity heighten such a situation of creativity and reflexivity. Lastly, to reiterate, the irony is that positivist methods expand precisely in the period when they are palpably less tenable.

Cultural Criminology

Let us begin by considering what is this phenomenon called 'cultural criminology'. It is above all the placing of crime and its control in the context of culture. That is, of viewing both crime and the agencies of control as cultural products: as creative constructs. As such they must be read in terms of the meanings which they carry. Furthermore, to highlight the interaction between the two: the relationship and the interaction between constructions upwards and constructions downwards – the continuous generation of meaning around interaction. Rules created, rules broken, a constant interplay of moral entrepreneurship, moral innovation and transgression.

But to go further than this, to place this interplay deep within the vast proliferation of media images of crime and deviance where every facet of offending is reflected in a vast hall of mirrors (see Ferrell, 1999), where the street scripts the screen and the screen scripts the street, and where there is no linear sequence so the line between the real and the virtual is profoundly and irrevocably blurred.

All of these attributes: the cultural nature of crime and control, their interaction in an interplay of constructions, and the mediation through fact and fiction, news and literature, have occurred throughout history and are a necessary basis for any criminology which claims to be naturalistic. But what makes cultural criminology quintessentially late modern is twofold: the extraordinary emphasis on creativity, individualism and generation of lifestyle in the present period, coupled with a mass media which has expanded and proliferated so as to transform human subjectivity. The virtual community becomes as real as the community outside one's door – reference groups, vocabularies of motive, identities become global in their demesne. And it was at the beginning of the late modern period that the antecedents of cultural criminology emerged. For it was in the mid 1960s that the cultural turn occurred within the social sciences. Paramount here is the work of Clifford Geertz, whose symbolic anthropology has had influence across disciplines from history through literature and political science to labour history (see, for example, Berlanstein, 1993). Here the emphasis is on understanding social action in terms of the deep reading of culture. Thus Geertz wrote:

> The concept of culture I espouse . . . is essentially a semiotic one. Believing with Max Weber, that man is an animal suspended in webs of significance he himself has spun, I take culture to be these webs, and the analysis of it to be therefore not an experimental science in search of law but an interpretative one in search of meaning. (1973, p. 5; see commentary in Harcourt, 2001, pp. 109–21)

Explicit in this endeavour is a stress on the interpretative rather than the mechanistic, the positivistic. Thus both a reduction of human action to a reflex of the material situation or a positivistic enactment of a pre-given culture are ruled out of court. Rather, an interpretative analysis focusing on the way in which human actors generate meaning becomes paramount.

Parallel to this cultural shift, which resonated throughout the social sciences, but less well known and most probably independently, arose a similar agenda, cultural in its focus and post-modernist in its sensibility, within the sociology of deviance. On this process of deconstruction there were two major influences: subcultural theory and labelling theory. I have detailed how subcultural theory gave meaning to deviant behaviour. This was supplemented by the radical phenomenological tradition of Becker, Kitsuse and Lemert, backed by the work of writers such as Peter Berger and Thomas Luckmann, This was extraordinarily influential, involving, as it did, the existential sense of freedom confronting and curtailed by the labels and essentialization of the powerful. Both strands were social constructionist; subcultural theory revealed how subcultural narratives and behaviour arose to tackle the problems facing particular groups, labelling theory how such meanings were denied, subverted and transformed by the narratives imposed from above whether of penality or of therapy. One was how meaning was constructed from below, the other how meaning was constructed from above.

By the mid 1980s such a humanistic sociology, buttressed by strong critiques of positivistic methods was a major force within criminology and the sociology of deviance. Since then, however, as we have seen, there was been a palpable shift back to positivism. It is in this context that cultural criminology seeks to retrace its roots and move on into the twenty-first century.

Let us now examine the major tenets of cultural criminology.

The Pulse of Energy

Two approaches to crime dominate contemporary sociological theory: rational choice theory and positivism – the first stresses the mundane, the second the measurable. Both have very simple rational/instrumental narratives. In the first, crime occurs because of choice – depicted as an availability of opportunity and low levels of social control, particularly where individuals are impulsive and short-term oriented (see Felson, 2002). Curiously (or perhaps not), every intellectual attempt is made to distance crime from structural inequalities and social injustice. Rather, we have one-dimensional, calculative individuals committing crime where it is possible, coupled with putative victims who, as likely targets are in turn attempting to calculate their optimum security strategies. In sociological positivism, inequality, lack of work, community breakdown, lack of social capital, are recognized, but the jump from deprivation to crime, particularly violent crime, is scarcely attempted, rather it is assumed (see Katz, 2002). It is a desperately thin narrative, a rationality of choice where intensity of motivation, feelings of humiliation, anger and rage – as well as love and solidarity – are foresworn. If the first is the criminology of neo-liberalism, the second is that of social democracy – but in truth there is little to choose between them. Even in terms of determinism: rational choice theory might be better renamed market positivism, for between the determinants of poor character and opportunity for crime there is only a small space for the most pallid of market choices.

Against these two abstractions – the rational calculator and the mechanistic actor – cultural criminology counterposes a naturalness. The actual experience of committing crime, the actual outcome of the criminal act bears little relationship to these narrow essentialisms. Rather, the adrenaline rush of crime, that place, as Jeff Ferrell put it, between 'pleasure and panic', the various feelings of anger, humiliation, exuberance, excitement, fear, do not fit these abstractions. They are not mundane and frequently not miserable. Nor do they have the instrumental payoffs that rational choice theory would suggest, nor the adjustments for the deficit of inequality that sociological positivism would pinpoint as the major mechanism. The armed robber could make more money as a day labourer, as the ex-con John McVicar (1979) remarked, the juvenile delinquent; as we have seen, does not pursue utilitarian goals; he spends much of his time making mischief and mayhem while in school. Yet rational choice theory would seem to believe that the delinquent inhabits the same sphere of rationality as an actuary or a financial advisor. In fact the only sort of criminal who acts like a financial advisor is, in all probability, a financial advisor.

Jack Katz in his seminal *Seductions of Crime* (1988), pointed to just this, how the sensual, visceral, bodily nature of crime is ignored in the orthodox academic depictions of criminality – in remarkable contrast, of course to the accounts of offenders or indeed of much crime fiction. Furthermore, such a feeling of energy and intensity extends throughout the whole process of crime and its depiction: from the offender, to the intense gutted feelings of the victim, to the thrill of the car chase, to the drama of the dock, to the trauma of imprisonment. And behind this, the outrage of the citizen, the moral panics of the media, the fears of urban dwellers, whether in the streets or at home. As Jeff Ferrell puts it:

> Adrenalin and excitement, terror and pleasure seem to flow not just through the experience of criminality . . . but through the many capillaries connecting crime, crime victimization and criminal justice. And as these terrors and pleasures circulate, they form an experiential and emotional current that illuminates the everyday meanings of crime and crime control. (1998, p. 38)

Here we have a naturalistic and an existential position (see Morrison, 1995) which contrasts with the denatured essentialism of rational choice theory and sociological positivism.

The Two Cities

Jonathan Raban, in his book *Soft City* (1974), contrasts two images of the city. On the one hand the conventional depiction of the city as mass planning, rationalized consumption and production, the urban grid of neighbourhoods and zones, an iron cage where humanity is channelled and pummelled, to the soft city where all sorts of possibilities are on offer, a theatre of dreams, an encyclopaedia of subculture and style. Similarly, Michel de Certeau (1984) depicts the city of planners, of rationalistic discourse, of quantitative data and demographics, with the 'experiential' city, the street level interaction that occurs beneath the interstices of plans and maps (see Hayward 2004a). And there is close parallel between this and Mikhail Bakhtin's notion of the 'second life of the people' (1984), which is, as Mike Presdee puts it, 'the only true site for the expression of one's true feelings for life. It is where the irrational laughs and mocks the rational – where truth can be told against the cold-hearted lies of rational, scientific modernity.' (2000, p. 8)

This dual city, not of spatial segregation and division within the city – although these, of course, occur – but of an 'underlife' of the city, runs throughout cultural criminology and is a key concept. It is reminiscent of the insights of the sociology of deviance, where deviance is not marginal but a world bubbling up just under the surface of appearances (a place where ethnography can go, but social surveys merely reflect the surfaces) –

or Goffman's 'underlife' of institutions. It is not that the soft city is the only reality. Far from it, the bureaucratic rationalistic world impinges increasingly on every aspect of human existence. It is that this world by itself is an imaginary of planners, politicians, and official spokespersons. It does not grasp the existential fears, hopes, joys, resentments, terrors of everyday existence – and such a pronouncement is evident, of course, way outside the questions of crime or delinquency. This is the world where transgression occurs, where rigidity is fudged, where rules are bent, and lives are lived.

It is the world upon which the imaginary of the powerful impacts upon the citizen. As Presdee puts it: 'The second life is lived in the cracks and holes of the structures of official society. It searches for and finds the unpunishable while official society seeks to dam up the holes, and fill the cracks, criminalizing as it does and making punishable the previously unpunishable' (2000, p. 9).

It is this struggle between the forces of rationalization and that of existential possibility and lived lives which is central to cultural criminology. It is seen in Ferrell's work on boredom, and in Keith Hayward and Mike Presdee's work on the commodification of culture. It is not, therefore, that rational choice theory or sociological positivism (with its images of planning and inclusion) fails to touch upon the reality of crime, these theories are precisely those which create the iron cage of rationalization. And any notion that a future utopia can be achieved by increasing levels of security and situational crime prevention, or by simply including the excluded in a world of work and commodified consumption, is profoundly in error. It presents the problem as the solution.

Furthermore, it is precisely such a struggle that occurs within the academy. For it is the forces of 'professionalization', the bureaucratization of research through Institutional Review Boards, the structuring of funding, the sanitization of quantitative methods, which seek to distance the criminologist from his or her object of study.

The Transgressive Subject

Crime is an act of rule breaking, it involves an attitude to rules, assessment of their justness and appropriateness, and a motivation to break them whether by outright transgression or by neutralization. It is not, as in positivism, a situation where the actor is mechanistically propelled towards desiderata and on the way happens to cross the rules. It is not, as in rational choice theory, a scenario where the actor merely seeks the holes in the net of social control and ducks and dives his or her way through them. Rather, in cultural criminology, the act of transgression has itself attractions, it is through rule-breaking that subcultural problems attempt solution.

Important here is the stress in cultural criminology on the foreground of experience, the existential psychodynamics of the actor, as well as, the background factors of traditional positivism (e.g. unemployment, poverty, poor neighbourhoods). In this it follows Katz but is critical of his position which tends to dismiss any focus on social background as a mistaken materialism and irretrievably positivistic. Thus Jeff Ferrell, in his review of *Seductions of Crime*, where he writes that despite Katz's critique:

> the disjunctions between Katz's criminology and certain aspects of left criminology are not insurmountable; much can in fact be learned from the intersection of the two. If, for example, we understand social and economic inequality to be a cause, or at least a primary context, for crime, we can also understand that this inequality is mediated and expressed through the situational dynamics, the symbolism and style, of criminal events. To speak of a criminal 'event', then, is to talk about the act and actions of the criminal the unfolding interactional dynamics of the crime, and the patterns of inequality and injustice embedded in the thoughts, words, and actions of those involved. In a criminal event, as in other moments of everyday life, structures of social class or ethnicity intertwine with situational decisions, personal style, and symbolic references. Thus, while we cannot make sense of crime without analyzing structures of inequality, we cannot make sense of crime by *only* analyzing these structures, either. The esthetics of criminal events interlocks with the political economic of criminality. (Ferrell, 2000, pp. 118–19; see also Young, 2003b)

This relationship between foreground and background can be rephrased in terms of the instrumental and the expressive. As we have seen, sociological positivism would translate background factors of deprivation into a simple foreground narrative of experienced deficit with crime as the relief of such deprivation. Rational choice theory would dispense with social background and have a foreground dominated by an equally simple and abstract narrative of taking the available opportunities to acquire desirable goods, etc. Cultural criminology in contrast would point to the way poverty, for example, is perceived in an affluent society as an act of exclusion, the ultimate humiliation in a consumer society. It is an *intense* experience, not merely of material deprivation, but of a sense of injustice and of ontological insecurity. But to go further than, that late modernity, as described earlier, represents a shift in consciousness, so that individualism, expressivity, identity become paramount and material deprivation, however important, is powerfully supplemented by a widespread sense of ontological deprivation. That is, there is a crisis of being: in a society where self-fulfilment, expression, and immediacy are paramount values, yet the possibilities of realizing such dreams are strictly curtailed by the increasing bureaucratization of work (its so-called McDonaldization) and the commodification of leisure. Crime and transgression in this new context can be seen as a breaking through of restraints, a realization of immediacy and a reassertion of identity and ontology. In this fashion, identity becomes woven into the rules broken.

An extraordinary example of this is the work of Stephen Lyng and his associates on edgework (Lyng, 1990; 1998). Here Lyng studies the way in which individuals engaging in such acts of extreme risk-taking as base jumping, joy-riding, sky-diving, motor-bike racing, push themselves to the edge of danger in a search for control. Like a metaphor for reality, they lose control only to take control.

The Attentive Gaze

Jeff Ferrell and Mark Hamm talk of the methodology of attentiveness, of a criminological *verstehen* where the researcher is immersed within a culture. The phrase 'attentiveness' reminds me of David Matza's (1969) 'naturalism', the invocation to be true to subject – without either romanticism or the generation of pathology. It is also reminiscent of the work of their heroes, James Agee and Walker Evans who, in *Let Us Now Praise Famous Men* (1960/1941), write and photograph with such a sensitivity, respect, and feeling the lives of Southern sharecroppers during the depression.

This is an ethnography which is immersed in the production of 'the thick description' of Geertz, which is interested in lifestyle, the symbolic, the aesthetic, the causal. Its attitude to quantitative data invokes Feyerabend's (1978) methodological injunction 'anything goes'. But quantitative data analysis must be dislodged from its present claims of scientific objectivity, precision and certainty. They must be reconceptualized as imperfect human constructions and carefully situated in time and place (Ferrell and Sanders, 1995). And, in a significant inversion of orthodoxy, it is noted that 'they can perhaps sketch a faint outline of [deviance and criminality] but they can never fill that outline with essential dimensions of meaningful understanding' (Ferrell and Hamm, 1998, p. 11).

We must therefore substitute 'a sociology of skin for a sociology of correlation' and this must be associated with a high level of reflexivity. And here, once again, one finds echoes of Clifford Geertz, for the criminologist, like the anthropologist, comes to his or her research with a heavy luggage of culture and preconception. We need, therefore, an ethnography of ethnography, a double awareness of the process of research.

But let us pause for a moment before we examine the possibilities and problems of critical ethnography and focus for one chapter on the most recent and gross failure of positivism; that is the inability to explain the fall in the crime rate. For here we can see quite plainly the limitations of a method which deals in supposedly solid demographic variables rather than meaningful social relationships and which seeks universal generalizations based on the suppression of cultural differences.

6

Giuliani and the New York Miracle

We live in a time of rapid change. In these times, rather than the variables determining the change, it is almost as if the change occurs and the factors seem to scuttle after them. Prediction of real-life events of any consequence has always been a lamentable failure in the 'social sciences', just think of the collapse of communism and look at the writings of political scientists prior to the days of glasnost or the recent inability of the most 'sophisticated' econometricians to predict the financial crisis and the collapse of the bubble. In criminology we have witnessed in our lifetimes two dramatic changes completely contrary to our scientific predictions. First of all, in the period from the 1960s onwards, the crime rate increased remorselessly in the majority of industrial countries, despite the fact that all the factors which had been identified as reducing crime were on the increase (e.g. wealth, education, employment, housing). Elsewhere I have termed this the 'aetiological crisis' in criminological theory (1994), which was followed by a crisis in penality as imprisonment rates and policing numbers grew, yet the crime rate doggedly continued to grow. It was this that set in motion an intense debate among criminologists and is in part the basis for the extraordinary plethora of theories that have occurred in the last thirty years. But having spent the whole of our professional lives researching why crime should almost inexorably go up (whether because of relative deprivation, broken homes, social disorganization, breakdown of controls, labelling, etc.), we find ourselves in the infuriating position of the crime rate in very many industrial countries (including the US and the UK) beginning to go down, against all predictions that I know of. Here we have a double trauma, or whammy, if you want. So here we are at the beginning of the twenty-first century facing the second aetiological crisis, not even sure how long this one will last but searching once more for an explanation.

The Crime Drop in America and the Crisis of Positivism

On 16 November 2000, in San Francisco, a packed meeting of the American Society of Criminology gathered together to discuss a most extraordinary happening in the world of crime. For, from 1991 onwards, violent crime in the United States, which had led the developed world by far in rates of murder and robbery, had begun to fall. Homicide dropped by 35.7 per cent from 1991 to 1998 (from 9.3 to 6.3 per 100,000) (Blumstein and Wallman, 2000). Al Blumstein, of the National Consortium on Violence Research, had brought together a dazzling array of experts: demographers, economists, sociologists and criminologists, all contributing their views on the change with graphic charts and probing statistical analysis. I listened with fascination to how they factored each of the developments over the period to explain the phenomenon, from changes in the distribution of handguns, the extraordinary prison expansion, zero-tolerance policing, down to changes in crack-culture and technology. At the end of the session they asked for comments from the audience, no doubt expecting some detailed remark about policing levels or the influence of handgun availability, or such like: some finesse in factoring, but the first question, from a Canadian colleague, was something of a revelation. She pointed out, ironically, how Canadians were supposed to be condemned to lag behind their American cousins culturally, but that they too had had a drop in violence, despite the fact that they had not experienced such a period of rapid prison expansion, that zero-tolerance policing was not *de rigueur* and that Canada had only a small problem of crack-cocaine (see commentary in Ouimet, 2002). She was followed by a Spanish woman, who said something very similar about her country. And, in fact, there was a crime drop in thirteen out of twenty-one industrial countries during 1997–8 (Barclay et al., 2001). Furthermore, England and Wales has experienced a prolonged crime drop and despite a shared language and ease of access to data this has been largely ignored by American criminologists.

Blumstein's team focused on the relationship between variable changes and the drop in violence. Once international data are examined, one must seriously question whether they were looking at the correct variables. Furthermore, to cap it all, they traced their line of correlation between these variables and the level of violence when, in fact, property crimes were also declining. The most immediate explanation of this is that we are encountering 'spurious causality'. That is, Blumstein's team had taken somewhat instinctively 'American' variables and unbeknowingly ignored the likely causes of the drop occurring at the same time in more than one country. Here again we have an instance of wide-scale awareness of the practice of moving from correlation to causation, coupled with an undue haste to move on over it in the interest of science. As Andrew Sayer puts it in *Method in Social Science*, his classic account of realist methodology:

> To a certain extent, the limitations of 'statistical explanations' are well known and teachers of statistical methods usually have their favourite example of a 'spurious correlation' such as that discovered between the birth rate and the number of storks in different regions of Sweden. The problem is usually acknowledged in a token fashion by placing the terms 'statistical explanation' and 'causal' in square quotes, but the use of statistical analysis is often intended to *suggest* that the quantitative relations so discovered are causal. Regression equations, for example, say nothing in themselves about causal or conditional relations, yet there is a widespread assumption that 'causal analysis' and regression analysis are virtually synonymous. (1992, p. 193; see also Goertzel, 2002).

But the enigma of the crime drop takes us far beyond the world of technical mistakes. The usual procedure in such analysis is to take the demographics and other factors which correlate with crime in the past and attempt to explain the present or predict the future levels of crime in terms of changes in these variables. That is, it assumes that there is a fixed and ahistorical relationship between them and crime (and whatever other item the social scientist would wish to explain) which is independent of time and culture. The problem here is that people (and young people in particular) might well change independently of these variables. And in this instance, the factors manifestly do not add up and the social scientists begin to have to admit the ghost in the machine. Thus, Richard Rosenfeld, of Blumstein's team, writes perhaps a little ruefully:

> If the church is the last refuge of scoundrels, 'culture' is the final recourse of social scientists in search of explanations when existing economic, social and political theories have been exhausted. (2000, p. 157)

So, there we have it, culture becomes the final refuge of scoundrels! And Rosenfeld comments, 'It is possible that American adults are becoming, in a word, civilized' (2000, p. 156). For a moment let us leave aside the ethnocentrism, given that such a civilizing effect seems to be gaining momentum worldwide and concentrate on the American commentators. Thus Andrew Karmen, in his meticulous analysis of the New York crime drop – *New York Murder Mystery* (2000) – casts his eyes across all the various explanations judiciously giving them various explanatory weightings, but at the end of the book talks of 'the final demographic factor which might be the most important of all' (2000, p. 249). But then, he reflects, 'the shift is not even strictly demographic in nature:

it is attitudinal and behavioral as well as generational' (2000, p. 249). And, he adds, 'Unfortunately the existence of this suspected evolution in subcultural values defies precise statistical measurement. It is not clear what kind of evidence and statistics could prove or disprove it.' Karmen points to the possibility of profound changes in the norms of urban youth culture. And here he refers to the pioneering work of Ric Curtis, the New York urban anthropologist who talks of the 'little brother syndrome'. That is, where younger children, having witnessed the devastating effects of hard drugs, gun culture, and intensive predatory crime on their older brethren, decide that these things are not for them, they are no longer hip or cool – the culture evolves and turns its face against the past. This observation has ready resonance with, for example, any attempt to understand changes in the extent of drug use and the drug of choice in terms of the impact of the 'war' against drugs. The pressures of the criminal justice system can it seems change the price of drugs, the level of cutting and adulteration and perhaps the mode of administration but, however many dollars, pounds or euros are thrown at the problem, it cannot explain the attractions of particular drugs at any time and the shifts from one drug of preference to another. This seems to relate to changes in fashion – although this is perhaps too light a word for it – changes in subcultural project would probably be more fitting.

Curtis relates these changes closely to the development of late modernity, to the loosening of the moorings to which I referred in the last chapter. Thus, he writes: 'The postmodern global economy is one in which identity formation is less dependent upon the influence of family, neighborhoods, race/ethnicity, nationality and history, and more than anywhere else the inner city is an empty canvas, an open frontier where new structures, institutions and conventions are waiting to be built' (1998, p. 1276).

The Problem of American Ethnocentrism

The discussion of the crime drop has by and large been characterized by an American ethnocentrism and similar puzzling declines elsewhere have been largely ignored; it is as if not only has American criminological theory cast off from the rest of the world but its empirical base has been fastened securely to the United States. Remarkable changes in crime rates of this sort involving an unexpected downturn across a varied set of offences for a length of time and reflected both in victimization and police figures, however ragged and approximate in their nature, demand explanations which involve general patterns of structural and cultural change as well as specific social change and interventions in particular locations. They involve both generality *and* specificity. It is of some interest, for example, to find that the decline in America is led by a decrease in black crime, as Barry Latzer (2008) has pointed out, but it would be preposterous to think that American race relations can be invoked to understand the somewhat parallel changes in Canada, let alone England and Wales. There is no doubt whatsoever that the extraordinary situation of the African-American population must be taken to account, but the coincidence of change suggests something more general happening at the bottom of the class structure of both countries.

Frank Zimring and *The Great American Crime Decline*

Frank Zimring in *The Great American Crime Decline* (2007) rises to this challenge; he attempts to engage in a comparative analysis of the crime drop, albeit largely in two countries: the United States and its neighbour Canada. Other countries are mentioned but almost all the discussion is restricted to the US and its close neighbour, with the exception of an appendix on the debate about the effects of abortion on the crime rate. Zimring's approach is systematic; he goes one by one through all the usual suspect variables: levels of imprisonment, the demographics of youth, the fluctuations of the economy. It is an extraordinarily thorough piece of work, but its conclusions are surprisingly inconclusive. He notes the extraordinary parallels between the decline in crime both in magnitude and in range of crimes between the two contiguous nations. Yet, while the good news is, of course, the decline in crime 'the bad news is that leading indicators of crime rates in the United States have little predictive value' (Zimring, 2007, p. 179). And, although Canada showed 'a perfect temporal fit with trends in the States ... Many of the factors believed to be important in the US decline – a decade-long economic boom, an explosive expansion of incarceration, added police – didn't happen in Canada' (2007, p. 200). As he nears the end of the book, he delivers a bombshell of a cautionary warning which would have been perhaps more fitting at the beginning: 'Between 1985 and 1990, the prison population grew at the greatest rate in history, the youth population declined, the economy boomed and life-threatening crime in the United States went up. Since all these macro-trends had failed to predict even the direction of the crime rate in the late 1980s it did not seem prudent to rely in the 1990s on a set of leading indicators that hadn't led anywhere a decade earlier' (2007, p. 199). But what then are his conclusions: that the reasons for the decline are largely a 'mystery', that 'large portions of the two-nation crime drop do not have discrete policy or economic causes'. Indeed, 'at least half of Canada's crime decline cannot be explained by old or new theories of crime causation. But if this holds for 60 per cent of Canada's decline, then it suggests that about 40 per cent of the US crime drop may also defy standard explanation'. And his conclusion: 'cyclical forces beyond the current ability of social science must get credit for a large share of Canada's decline' and ' become attractive candidates' for elements of the US decline (p. 133). One wonders what on earth these mysterious cyclical forces are, for whatever they are one would, of course, want to know what caused the cycle in the first place. More 'positively' Zimring maintains that the decline occurred without major changes in either the structure or culture of society. Indeed in New York City, where the change was most marked: 'The physical, social, and economic character of the city did not change much at all but, the crime rate did' (p. 208). 'But is this true?' one perceptive reviewer, Doris Provine (2008) asks, citing the enormous surge of immigration into New York that occurred over this time, with immigrants arriving from all corners of the world, constituting the hyperpluralism I discussed in the last chapter, which has transformed so many of the world's great cities. Indeed, recently the sociologist Robert Sampson (2008) has caused great concern among the widespread proponents of the immigration-equals-crime thesis by arguing the very opposite. He points to the well-known fact that first-generation immigrants tend to have lower crime rates than the indigenous population. The squawks of indignation from the right of the political spectrum about such a heretical suggestion alone makes the article worthy of celebration – just google in crime and immigration and smell the fumes. His initial desire, in a positivistic fashion, is simply to introduce a new variable for consideration and his data from Chicago, plus his examples from the surprisingly low crime rates of the border towns of San Diego and El Paso, support it. Yet he is praiseworthily cautious: 'correlation doesn't equal causation', and perhaps the possible rise in crime of the subsequent second and third generation of immigrants is something he doesn't want to contemplate. And there are obviously other processes in operation – the decline in crime of the indigenous African-American population is one. But his positivist *Zeitgeist* precludes him from trying to produce an explanation which pivots on meaning and perhaps begins to unite these various movements. Then, at the very end of his essay, he surprisingly takes a cultural turn. But, first of all note that this is one where culture is an added factor; culture is not something which responds to and shapes material change, it is separate, an addition to the equation. He speculates that perhaps what is occurring is a dilution of mainstream American values with its high valorization of violence. I hate to speculate how this is received in the South, although I have a degree of sympathy, given his suggestion that these values stem from the cultural transmission of the values of the Scottish-Irish, descendants of Celtic herdsmen who emigrated to the southern parts of what was to become the United States. This certainly does not sit well with my own personal feelings of ethnic heritage! For once again his notion of culture is something of an essence which is transmitted between the generations, not something which constantly adapts to changing circumstances. Lastly, in the very last paragraph Sampson, with laudable imagination, changes track somewhat; what may be happening, he suggests, is that the very diversity of immigration may lead to the greater visibility of competing non-violent mores.

So hyperpluralism may be a clue. And let us add to this a decade of continued structural change: the decimation of the manufacturing sector and the rise of a new service economy, the rapid expansion of the financial sector, so that the United States is beginning to look like Monaco as the AFL-CIO President, Richard Trumka put it recently (October 2009). Further, a proliferation of servants, almost invisible and *never* called servants, have emerged, who support the middle-class dual-career families with help in their homes, food in the restaurants, childcare, grandparent care, service in the hotels for business and pleasure. And of course there has been a vast expansion of security jobs from the manning of shops, hotels, clubs, to the criminal justice system with its elaborate varieties and 'families' of police. There has been an out-sourcing of manufacture and an in-sourcing of immigrant labour, two circuits in the process of globalization so powerfully outlined by Saskia Sassen (2002). Add to this the increased feminization of the public sphere with women's greater participation in urban life from pub to club to restaurant, which *just has* to have some effect on civility in the public sphere. And, culturally the change in the drug fashions of youth and, the further expansion of higher education, with its concomitant effects on youth culture. Thus class, gender, age and ethnicity, patterns of immigration and diversity, have all changed, and culture with them. Whatever the impact of such a mêlée of transformations, could anyone *really* seriously suggest, as Zimring does that there has been no change?

Overall, it is difficult to disagree with the tenor of John Hagedorn's assessment of the earlier book in this genre, Blumstein and Wallman's *The Crime Drop in America*: we need to look at the crime drop in the context of globalization, we need to listen to the voices on the street. For, as he puts it, such 'scientific' work betrays the 'one sidedness of positive science ... Such an analysis is limited in its ability to understand the human condition in the age of globalization ... through its display of good quantitative criminology [it] has the unintended effect of demonstrating that criminology needs some new theoretical blood' (2001, p. 496).

The Severely Restricted Concept Box

There is, therefore, as throughout this book, a critique on two levels. Firstly that, even if a positivist methodology is accepted, the range of variables available in the conventional toolbox is remarkably limited. It is a poor set of instruments selected from the possible range of demographics. Income, for example, is not only *very* likely to be misreported but is not as good an indicator of economic well-being as wealth – which is much more unequally distributed. Rates of unemployment do not measure economic inactivity but changes in the number of people actively seeking a job and unable to find one – a figure which can actually decline with depressed economic conditions; as people perceive that as there are no jobs to be had there is no point in seeking them. The measures of ethnicity are a scandal. To judge ethnicity, as in the United States, by a mixture of melanin level in the skin (black/white), continent (Asian), and, oddest of all, 'Hispanic' veers on the edge of the preposterous. The use of 'black' in terms of one 'drop' of African ancestry would have delighted a white supremacist from the apartheid days in South Africa. As the saying goes, a white woman can have a black baby, but a black woman cannot have a white one (unless of course, as is frequently the case, she is looking after it!). Thus American descendants of slaves, people from a large number of cultures in the Caribbean, African businessmen from anywhere south of the Sahara are all bundled together in the most chaotic categories imaginable. So many cultures reduced to one posited gene base. 'Asian' – from the world's largest continent becomes Chinese in the United States and Indian in the UK. 'Hispanic' includes a middle-class Argentinean, a poor indigenous Peruvian and a Catalan from Barcelona. And if any of these categories had even a modicum of approximation of reality in the past, they are utterly demolished by the hyperpluralism of today. What significance do they really have other than satisfying the prejudices of the right or creating fictitious power blocs for the left? Yet they are the very stuff of opinion polls, policy demographics and political analysis. The recent US 2010 Census does not even seem to have taken on board that 'race' is a biological nonsense; it is the false object of racism not the subject of ethnicity. Yet in a fashion which would make a national socialist bureaucrat rub hands in disbelief, the census deems to list Hmong, Laotian, Thai, Pakistani, Cambodian, Fijian and Tongan together with the usual 'black', Hawaiian, Korean as separate 'races'. It adds with caution 'for this census Hispanic origins are not races' (US Census 2010). And where is everyone else: white Brazilian, Israeli, Russian, Australian, French, German, British etc? They are, of course, in the most ragbag category of all: 'white'.

Let me add, as an aside, that the validity of the census as a sampling frame, and it will be used widely, is severely compromised by not only such categorizations but by low response rates, not to mention the asking of name and telephone number which surely must be a deterrent for undocumented immigrants.

Once again even if sociology were a natural science, the tools available are severely defective – they are a product in most cases of a certain academic laziness and the ease of accessing such data coupled with not so much a conceptual ignorance (nothing I have said here would come as a surprise) as an ability to skate on thin ice.

Moreover, if we go one step further and accept the cultural nature of the social world, the defects become even more pressing. What is actually relevant about 'income' is class position despite the fact that it has become *de rigueur* among some sociologists to avoid the word class and use socio-economic status. Class is a social relationship not a numerical point on an income scale. The change in class position from a factory worker, one of many, arrayed in opposition to management, to a service worker in a small or diffuse organization honed to respond to a series of particular clients, is remarkably different. The income may well be the same but the subjective experience a world apart. And, as I have noted, it may well be that the shift in class relationship from manufacturing to service may be a clue to the widespread changes in civility which have been encountered in the recent period.

All of the major structural 'variables': class, age, ethnicity and gender are social relationships. They are not the same as a standardized '15–20', or 'over 60', the two sexes male and female, the presence or relative absence of melanin in the skin, the inhabitant of a Continent or the posited descendant of someone from the Iberian Peninsular.

Such a loss of subjectivity extends to some of the key explanatory concepts. Take for instance relative deprivation. Here again subjectivity is difficult to measure and there is a great temptation to understand relative deprivation as a simple difference in income levels between two groups rather than the subjective comparison of just and fair rewards. To compare these is a much more difficult task. Yet it is culturally constructed differences which actually motivate people, engendering feelings of discontent or satisfaction, envy or anger, and which are of great importance in understanding human behaviour and emotion.

Part of the problem is, I suspect, because the work is not theory-led but also, as so often in such research, it is easier just to reach into the old toolbox and use the most simple things that spring to hand. Thus, when Sampson suggests immigration, it comes as something of a surprise while Zimring simply admits to being unable to see any significant change occurring during this tumultuous decade. Secondly, if one maintains that cultural change is capable of profoundly changing the weightings of variables (if that is what one wants to call these cultural products) then prediction from past cultural situations is always liable to uncertainty.

Put these two mistakes together and one has a recipe for disaster. Ironically, it results in the sociologist/criminologist being unable to assess both the material changes that occur across nations (e.g., hyperpluralism, the rise of the service industry, the feminization of the public arena) and the cultural context which leads to the particular interpretations and reactions to these changes. That is, both the similarities and differences between nations are missed. It is to the latter conjuncture, the way that fairly similar changes are interpreted differently that I will now turn.

New York Miracle

Let me for the moment touch upon the way in which social agencies construct narratives about such a decline, seeking to capitalize and intervene in these processes. One of the key institutions in these cases is the police, and to illustrate this I will focus in upon one of the greatest urban legends of our time, the New York 'miracle' under the watch of Mayor Giuliani.

In the last decade of the twentieth century the New York crime rate fell continuously. Indeed, the homicide rate dropped from 25.6 per 100,000 in 1990 to 8.4 in 1999, and continues to do so today. This was hailed as a miracle. As the story goes, Mayor Giuliani and his indomitable police chief, William Bratton, introduced a form of aggressive and targeted policing, backed by computer mapping of high-crime areas (zero-tolerance and COMSTAT) which drastically reversed the crime reputation of this great city. The result is history, or at least urban myth: Giuliani was lionized; his biographer, Fred Siegel in his somewhat unctuous *The Prince of the City: Giuliani, New York and the Genius of American Life* (2005), talks of this being an incontestable achievement. Indeed this was part of the reason he was so widely encouraged to put his hat in the ring for the 2008 presidential election. Bratton gained worldwide acclaim, and police delegates from all over the globe visited the NYPD in order to learn how they too could achieve miracles.

Let us clear up this urban myth once and for all: a major problem of this analysis is a problem of ethnocentrism for which New York is famous. Crime rates since the mid 1990s have been going down in many cities across the United States irrespective of what policing method is used – problem-solving, traditional policing, or indeed zero-tolerance. But more damning than this is that the crime rate has been going down in several major cities of the First World. It is not just a New York thing; it

is not even an American phenomenon. But what concerns me at this juncture is what actually happened in New York City, and how this relates to
the phenomenon of defining deviance down.

With this in mind, let us return to the work of the New York urban
anthropologist Ric Curtis. For his ethnographic research (1998) clearly
points to changes in the youth culture – the 'little brother effect', a coun-
ter-socialization, part of a general subcultural change independent of any
policy intervention, which we have noted earlier. But he goes further than
this for the response of police officers he interviewed about the downturn
was nothing short of desperate. The police need criminals and arrests,
just as academics need students and graduates. And just as when student
enrolment declines, entrance qualifications begin to lower, then as arrest
rates decline there is an instinctive tendency to define deviancy up. That is
to go down spectrum, to go for more minor crime and incivilities in order
to keep the arrest rate up. Even if this was unplanned and unintentional,
as Curtis puts it, 'the police were simply left with the lesser crimes' (1998,
p. 1275).

Curtis argues that the philosophy of zero-tolerance was a *post-hoc*
rationalization of already existing practices. Indeed, when I examined
the NYPD arrest statistics, his contention was fully borne out, index
crimes fell from 1990 onwards (that is prior to the introduction of zero-
tolerance in 1994). From 1989 to 1993 felony arrests dropped by 21.5
per cent, dropping year by year, while misdemeanour arrests steadily
increased, first of all compensating for the drop in felony arrests and
then soared ahead so that the ratio of misdemeanours to felonies, which
started out in 1989/91 at 0.8 to 1.0, became by 2000 over 2 to 1 (many
of which are cannabis related). Furthermore, the rise in misdemeanour
arrests started in 1993 – the year before the supposed introduction of
zero-tolerance.

Conversely, of course, during years prior to this, in a situation of
rising and plentiful crime, the police tended to define deviancy down, to
use Daniel Patrick Moynihan's phrase (1993). Such a contention parallels
the analysis of Donald Dickson (1968), who critiqued Howard Becker's
classic study of the emergence of the *1937 Marihuana Tax Act*. Becker
famously argued that the Act came into place because Commissioner
Anslinger, the Head of the Federal Bureau of Narcotics (FBN), acted as
a moral entrepreneur, issuing scary reports about marihuana in order
to generate public alarm and facilitate the passing of the Act. In fact,
Dickson argues, the scare stories came largely after the passage of the
Act and the real reason for Anslinger's strident advocacy of the new
legislation was the declining budgetary appropriation of the FBN. The
bureaucratic response was to argue for legislation to bring marihuana
under Federal control and thus substantially increase the number of

potential criminals under the Bureau's jurisdiction. As a result in 1938, the first full year of its operation, one of every four federal drug and narcotic convictions was for marihuana violations. Interesting here are the parallels: the FBN incorporated a lesser drug under its control, defining deviancy up from its perspective – rather like the NYPD (even down to the fact that marihuana is a major source of misdemeanours) and that both the Tax Act and the zero-tolerance campaign had remarkable international repercussions and influence.

The New York story is, of course, history: Commissioner Bratton arrived in 1994, introduced a zero-tolerance campaign, and claimed the decline in crime rate. Bratton and Mayor Giuliani fell out over who owned the policy and the Commissioner was subsequently fired. In fact, by the above analysis, the fall in the crime rate was largely a cultural product. Zero-tolerance was introduced because of the falling arrest rate. *Thus zero-tolerance arose as the result of the drop in crime, rather than the fall in crime being a result of zero-tolerance.* Bratton's magic was to reverse the causality of the process, to step in and make claim to the miracle, and as a result the police were, as Curtis remarks, congratulated rather than the youth themselves.

In this chapter we have encountered two levels of ethnocentrism: firstly, the amusing one, the focus on New York to the exclusion of the rest of the United States, the subject of the famous *New Yorker* cartoon, where America and the world shrinks beyond the Hudson, the second an American focus, which ignores the rest of the world. But, as we have seen, the crime rate has been going down in very many major American cities as well as New York, and in other developed countries as well as the United States. Furthermore, the phenomenon of defining deviance up was not only confined to the United States, for a growing intolerance of crime and disorder was present in many other countries, most notably in Britain where, as we shall see, the campaign against anti-social behaviour was taken to new levels and where, unlike in the United States, the decline in the crime rate was largely ignored by politicians and the mass media.

But note that those critics of policing as the key to the downturn in crime also tend to offer ethnocentric explanations: they explain in terms of changes in *American* youth culture, the decline in the *American* crack epidemic, a civilization of American culture. However much it is important to take cognizance of these local factors, we must heed not to neglect the general. But let us remind ourselves that the decline in crime is a common occurrence in the First World and the increase in intolerance of deviant behaviour and punitiveness to crime more and more widespread. As I have argued, the causes of these changes are changes in the wider economy and social structure of late modernity. My contention is that defining deviancy up is an international phenomenon and that this growing intolerance of deviancy is, as Edward Luttwak (1995; see Young 2007) has suggested is the product of fundamental insecurities generated in late modern capitalism.

Furthermore, it is important to understand that the moral entrepreneurial activities of the Mayor of New York and the NYPD were successful because they occurred in a climate of public opinion which was conducive to zero-tolerance policies. That is, although the NYPD in the early part of the 1990s were almost automatically arresting more individuals committing misdemeanours in order to compensate for the decline in felonies, such a clandestine 'bureaucratic' response (in Dickson's terms) was subsequently acknowledged, repackaged, and rebranded in a moral entrepreneurial fashion (in Becker's terms). Yet none of this latter expansion would have worked if it had not received widespread public approval. Of course its supposed efficacy was a major selling point, but decline in crime in San Diego, with the emphasis on neighbourhood (non-aggressive) policing did not receive anything like the enthusiasm and congratulation as that in New York. Further, the widespread dissemination of zero-tolerance crackdowns reflected global anxieties in the First World as did its well-nigh universal celebration as a best practice policy around the globe.

The UK Experience

Let us look now at the evidence from the UK. First of all, note the patterns are not the same as in the US, certainly not as close as in Canada – but why should they be? Of course the habit of using the US as the template and measuring all comparisons against it shows a rather complacent ethnocentricity as seen by Zimring's analysis, which judges Canada by the level at which its crime rate deviates from predictions based on US data. But, once again, think of the general and the local, and in terms of the difference that a specific culture makes both in terms of the rate of crime and the response to it. Secondly, note that the UK has the most neo-liberal policies in Western Europe, both in terms of political philosophies and popular culture (although one must be very careful not to exaggerate this) and free movement of capital and labour, hence its high level of multiculturalism and hyperpluralism. Lastly, note that despite the blatant parallel of the decline in crime in England and Wales, the common language and shared criminological tradition it was not an obvious comparison point for US criminology.

According to the figures from the British Crime Survey (BCS), conducted in the twelve months ending June 2008, the number of crimes against adults living in private households in England and Wales fell by 10 per cent compared with the preceding 12 months. Such a fall was echoed in the figures of crimes known to the police which showed a 9 per cent reduction in the period. Most significantly, the BCS indicates that there has been a consistent fall in crime year by year since 1995 with one year of stability in 2004/5 and that the present level of crime is the lowest recorded since the survey began in 1981 (Kershaw et al., 2008). Similarly crimes known to the police fell from 1992 until 1998/99 after which new counting rules were introduced and comparison became difficult (see Simmons et al., 2003). Even the homicide statistics are at present (2008/9) the lowest for twenty years, although for European countries, where homicide is much rarer than in the United States, any singular event such as a mass or serial murder throws the figures out of trajectory.

Thus, crime in England and Wales rose seemingly inexorably from the 1960s, reaching a peak in the mid 1990s – 1995 according to the BCS, and 1992 as far as police figures are concerned. Overall there was a reduction of crime in England and Wales of 48 per cent (including a similar 48 per cent reduction in violent crime) between 1995 and 2007/8. Furthermore, this reduction has occurred in every category of crime from vandalism through theft to violence. Let us put this in the context of my critique of the haphazard and, in my reckoning, reckless use of quantitative data, which I have outlined in previous chapters. The *precision* of any of these figures is, of course, palpably suspect, they ignore hidden figures and changes in public sensitivity to crime. Yet they occur across a lengthy period of time, a wide range of crimes and are in part corroborated from both survey and police data. What is most important, they indicate a dramatic reversal of an upward trend which stretched back decades and was seemingly inexorable. There is simply no adequate explanation of why such reversal should have occurred in terms of the statistical apparatus of either the survey organizations or the police. So let's forget about the 48 per cent reduction, as above; let us be more precise and say that it was about a half!

Some might have called this a miracle, yet no one in Britain has so far to my knowledge used this epithet – unlike on the other side of the Atlantic where, as we have seen, a roughly similar decline was trumpeted. As it is, the response of the public, the mass media, politicians and significant sections of the criminal justice practitioners in Britain has been a somewhat surprising state of denial. We have explored this process elsewhere (Mooney, 2003; Young, 2003a) but let us note at this point that the evidence from the BCS shows both a general unawareness of the crime drop and a heightened concern with anti-social behaviour. Thus, in

2004/5, two-thirds of people interviewed in England and Wales believed that the level of crime had risen 'a lot' or 'a little' over the last two years while only one in twenty believed that the crime rate was falling (Babb et al., 2006, p. 132). Further, a recent *Quarterly Update* indicates significant rises in fear of burglary and violent crime and both overall and increases in six out of seven indicators in concern about anti-social behaviour (Kara and Upson, 2006).

The Labour government coming into office after the landslide victory of 1997 encountered, throughout its first term and into its second, extremely propitious crime figures. The fall in crime was not, however, celebrated. Instead, the new administration embarked upon an ambitious programme of legislation centring on the control of anti-social behaviour. Commencing with the *Crime and Disorder Act 1998* where Anti-Social Behaviour Orders (ASBOs) were introduced, developed in the White Paper *Respect and Responsibility – Taking a Stand Against Anti-Social Behaviour* (Home Office, 2003) and realized in *The Anti-Social Behaviour Act*, which came into effect that year, the concept of anti-social behaviour became constructed, elaborated and focused upon. A whole range of behaviours were identified under the rubric of anti-social behaviour: begging, public drunkenness, letting off fireworks, neighbourhood noise, hoax calls, urinating in public, etc. What was special about this new territory for control was:

- *Defining Deviancy Up:* As mentioned earlier, Daniel Patrick Moynihan (1993), in his famous article 'Defining Deviancy Down', argued that the response to the rising tide of crime and disorder was simply to define less disorder as deviant. This is the reverse of this – in a situation of declining crime, deviance is defined up: tolerance becomes, in short, less lenient;
- *Blurring the Boundaries:* the boundaries of criminal behaviour and the anti-social become blurred, incivilities become criminalized (see Mooney, 2003);
- *Subjectivity of Definition:* From the start it is recognized that 'the subjective nature of the concept makes it difficult to identify a single definition of behaviour' (Home Office, 2004, p. 3). Anti-social behaviour is that which causes offence, or alarm, or distress, or harassment. 'As such what may be considered anti-social behaviour to one person can be seen as acceptable behaviour to another' (Home Office, 2004, p. 3). One cannot help thinking that this is a rediscovery of the sociology of deviance *circa* 1960. 'Deviance is not a property *inherent* in any particular behaviour, it is a property *conferred upon* that behaviour by the people who come into direct or indirect contact with it' as Kai Erikson famously put it (1966, p. 6). As such it sets itself up for

contest and disagreement, let alone questions of how such a multiplex and shifting thing could be measured;

- *Flexibility of Use:* ASBOs are a flexible tool of social control which can and have been used against widely different offenders in different parts of the country. Thus Elizabeth Burney, in *Making People Behave* (2005), points to their use against prostitutes in Manchester, drug dealers in Kings Cross, and fly posting in the London Borough of Camden; it can focus on clothing (e.g. balaclavas and hoodies), gang membership and criminal behaviour itself. Indeed, in the latter instance, it can allow police action where there is insufficient evidence to satisfy a court of law. 'It is apparent,' she writes:

> that the orders have become all purpose instruments to any type of crime or disorder, far beyond the neighbourhood problems originally envisaged. Within high-crime neighbourhoods, it is primarily outright criminal behaviour rather than mere nuisance, that is targeted, and police welcome the power that it gives them to use hearsay evidence in place of formal witness statements, nailing what one police officer described as their 'targets' and yet bypassing the criminal justice system altogether. (2005, pp. 101–2)

- *Predisposition not Action:* The anti-social individual once identified can, under an ASBO, be banned from future proclivities to commit an act. S/he can be excluded from areas, denied access to individuals, and refused permission to carry certain objects, and tools. Unlike liberal democratic notions of criminal justice, future activities are criminalized *as well as* actual acts. As Peter Squires and Dawn Stephen put it:

> As a society we have acknowledged a putative 'justice gap' but sought to fill it with enforcement practices based upon a dubious precautionary principle in which 'due process' and the 'rule of law' (hitherto regarded as constituent elements of Justice) become sidelined by political and administrative priorities. And the likely outcome is not justice at all, but the reinforcement of social exclusion and greater social injustice. (2005, p. 208)

Faced with a declining crime rate, the Labour government discovered, so to speak, a new territory of concern and a beguiled public found a new crime wave replacing the old. And to add irony to this, a fair proportion of anti-social behaviour was transmuted into actual crime, so that up to December 2003, 42 per cent of all ASBOs were breached and of these breaches 55 per cent resulted in custodial sentences (Liberty, 2006).

The concept of anti-social behaviour is a fascinating phenomenon, the construction of a problem which, because of the extraordinarily subjective nature of its base and the extreme flexibility of each category, could have the potential to generate an almost endless number of infringe-ments. And on top of this add the obsession with measurement (how many?) and targets (have we met them?). *It is a formula for a permanent moral anxiety*, it is a prescription for targets which will never be met. It is fairly easy, for example, to understand where burglaries begin and end and to provide reasonably good figures of their number and their increase or reduction. It is another thing to talk about eliminating rowdy behav-iour (how rowdy is rowdy?) or litter (how clean is clean?) and who is the judge? One has only to read the Home Office Development and Practice Report *Defining and Measuring Anti-Social Behaviour* (2004) to encoun-ter the ineffable, the vacuous, the intangible. The statistics bulge with the perceiver, they grow with the intensity of pursuit; they are a target which endlessly retreats.

In *The Vertigo of Late Modernity* (2007), I noted that at the annual Labour Party conference in 2005 the then Home Secretary Charles Clarke confidently assured the party faithful that anti-social behaviour would be eliminated in Britain by 2010. Such a Canute-like munificence was greeted with a degree of scepticism. So now we have arrived past 2010 and hopefully expect a Britain where apartment blocks are still and silent at night, the last ghetto blaster has been consigned to the bins, the teenagers have forsaken tinned lager imbibed in bus shelters and congre-gate peacefully in the local designated youth clubs, teenage girls go out with their beaus at night dreaming of homework and *distant*, dual-career families, young desperados stroll the parks with their neutered pit bulls in a city whose walls are spotless and lacking graffiti and there is not a single hoodie in sight!. All of this is, of course, a complete and utter fantasy, a Stepford land of New Labour thinking.

Convergence and Contrasts

The inability of social science to predict the future is legendary – from the fall of Communism to the movement in house prices. It goes without saying that the crime drop was a thing of astonishment to the criminolo-gist (present author included). It defied the status quo and it unravelled theories. Let us look at a prominent example of this. In 1996 David Garland published an extremely influential article 'The Limits of the Sovereign State', which pointed to the widespread acceptance of the 'normality' of high crime rates and that this placed the notion of gov-ernmental sovereignty and ability to provide public security in jeopardy. There arose out of this, both in the UK and the US, penal policies, 'adaptations to failure', which included the development of inter-agency cooperation, a shift in the responsibility for crime away from the state to non-state agencies and individuals, and most importantly 'the major system adoption' defining deviancy down. With regard to the latter, 'Its concern to let minor offences and offenders fall below the threshold of official notice – allows them to slip "a net" that is in danger of bursting at the seams' (Garland, 1996, p. 457). Thus the net-widening scenario famously envisaged by critical criminologists such as Stan Cohen (1985), where the net of the criminal justice system extended to include more and minor offences, was seen by Garland to reverse itself: the system was seen by necessity to be more and more tolerant of deviance. Indeed in a later book, *The Culture of Control*, Garland views Mayor Giuliani's zero-tolerance policies as 'a very public exception to this' (2001, p. 119).

But as we have seen, both sides of the Atlantic saw exactly the opposite of this: the net widened and deviancy was defined up, not down. In England and Wales a new crime wave was created in the minor key of anti-social behaviour, whereas New York City famously touted zero-tolerance. Either side of the pond walking down the street with a can of lager became a cause for suspicion. Yet there are obvious differences: the labyrinth of anti-social behaviour and the guileless optimism of targets and performance indicators are distinctively a British thing. Try explaining what is happening in terms of crime control to an American colleague and you will quickly register incredulity and disbelief. On neither side has the 'sovereign state' given up on the crime problem; indeed who would want to do so at a time of dropping crime? Yet there are crucial differences. Crime control, a central issue of policy, a major shift which marked out New Labour from Old Labour has been put on the back-burner of American politics, witness the last presidential election. In the 2010 British election it was still there, together with immigration, way out front. It was a central plank of the Labour platform, the two other major parties competing fiercely about how many new cops they would put on the street. For the Americans, especially the politicians of New York City there has been a spirit of triumphalism. The decline of crime was seen as a personal victory by both Mayor Giuliani and Commissioner Bratton (hence their falling out); it is a major selling point for the tourist industry; it has revitalized property prices and fuelled gentrification, it is a success story eagerly carried forward by Mayor Bloomberg. Criminologists who dare suggest that the NYPD was not responsible are lampooned by the popular media, who have bought the fact of decline (true) and the NYPD's role in it. (false) (see Karmen, 2000). In Britain, on the contrary, the decline is concealed by the newly discovered mountain of anti-social behaviour and moral panics abound about everything from public drunkenness to celebrity drugtaking.

In the United States the control of anti-social behaviour has been viewed as a secondary problem to that of crime control. Indeed the influential 'Broken Windows' theory revolves around the notion that the vigilant control of anti-social behaviour can normatively reinvigorate an area, and lead to drops in serious crime. That is, the control of anti-social behaviour is the handle on the control of crime. In Britain, in contrast, anti-social behaviour has been seen as more of a problem in itself, indeed it has almost become *the* problem and rather autonomous from crime itself.

The Embedded Nature of Culture

Both the origins of crime and the responses to it are shaped by the cultures from which they emerge. In the latter part of this chapter, I have taken two countries, the US and the UK, which have had similar (although scarcely identical) backgrounds in the last fifteen years. They have both had high levels of immigration, many of their great cities have become the epitomes of hyperpluralism, there has been a shift from manufacturing to service industries and there has been a degree of feminization of the public sphere. They have both experienced prolonged drops in the crime rates, although the patterning of change is not the same. The response to this situation once again shares similarities, the defining of deviance up occurred in both countries, but the accent on anti-social behaviour differs at times markedly and the degree of celebration of the decline is almost reversed. Although prison rates have gone up steeply in both countries, the US prison complex is quite exceptional in the developed world, with over 2.3 million people in prison and one in 34 of the population being under some sort of control by the criminal justice system at any one time. The spatial focus of the US criminal justice system on specific areas, a process aggravated by high levels of class and ethnic segregation, has led to the intense disruption and criminalization of specific areas of the city. Indeed, certain blocs have been identified as receiving over one million dollars of criminal justice intervention yearly, a process which gives rise to an increase in homicides in the poorest areas of the city in the context of an overall decline (Currie, 1997; Clear, 2007). In the UK, the campaign against anti-social behaviour which regularly prohibits two or more teenagers from gathering in the evening, or entering particular parts of a town, has an alienating effect and leads to criminal convictions because of the breaking of ASBOs. This is not the place to analyse in detail the deportment of crime control measures in the two countries; sufficient to say that in both cases the cultural settings result in situations of overall decline, although coupled with differing patterns of crime and because of what Dario Melossi (2001) refers to as the cultural embeddedness of penality, different social reactions to crime.

The inability to explain the rapid rise in crime in many developed countries in the latter period of the twentieth century and the decline that followed it are the two most blatant examples of the failure of the positivist model. I have indicated that this was due to faults on a technical level of the instruments used to predict changes in the level of crime and, more profoundly, defects on a cultural level. The cultural problems revolve around the unwillingness to countenance the cultural construction of crime and cultural change coupled with a resolute ethnocentrism. Canada was just about brought into the picture, Britain largely ignored, and who conceivably could discuss the crime drop in advanced industrial societies without taking consideration of the enormous 70 per cent decline in crime in Japan over the last fifty years? (Johnson, 2008).

I will turn now to examine ethnographic methods, both classic and contemporary, which place culture at the very centre of their analysis.

7
Mayhem, Magic and Margaret Mead: Towards a Critical Ethnography

Stare. It is the way to educate your eye and more. Stare, pry, listen, eaves-drop. Die knowing something. You are not here long.

(Walker Evans)

Late modernity brings with it a loosening of the ties between social structure and behaviour, between material predicament and the subcultural solutions which human beings create in order to facilitate and give meaning to their lives. That is, the rigid, fixed structures of Fordism, the fixity of work, family, community and place, with all their sense of embeddedness and 'naturalness', become more matters of chance or choice; they are no longer obvious and are, at any rate, uncertain and disrupted. The narratives are constantly in a process of being rewritten, at each turning of our lives we rewrite and recreate a thread of continuity with more and more frequency and with, in turn, greater fragility and variable success. And words, social concepts, which have always – as Durkheim pointed out – blurred one into another, become all the more blurred and liquid in late modernity.

Marriage, for example, becomes less and less distinguishable from co-habitation, its average length reduces remarkably; 40 per cent of marriages lead to divorce in the UK, one in two in the US; the idea of short-term marriage contracts gains wide support and currency; it expands controversially to include same-sex couples, and varies widely in its meaning between different ethnic groups and in different parts of the class structure.

Our most intimate experience and identities become transformed and contested. Ken Plummer, in his brilliant *Telling Sexual Stories* (1995), narrates how his own revelation of his sexual identity in the 1960s was phrased in the positivistic narrative of homosexuality as encapsulated in the infamous Penguin edition of *Homosexuality* (1968) by the Cambridge criminologist, Donald West, which he hurled across the room at his parents, exclaiming in tears 'that's about me'. Five years later the Gay Liberation Movement emerged and homosexuality became 'gay'. For the first time in human history, a whole lifestyle and community had evolved around homo-eroticism. Fancying one's own sex had, of course, occurred throughout history, but now it became a cultural entity, a lifestyle of great political and social significance. People uncovered their gay identity, they came out of the closet, they discovered and celebrated their new selves.

Likewise, Plummer examines changing notions of rape. What was once a subject of deep disgrace, and concealment among women, an experience immersed in self-blame and stigmatization, becomes transformed under the lens of the women's movement into a blatant example of patriarchal power; support institutions grow around it, it is discovered in marriage, during courtship, at work – it is extended to male rape. What is hidden becomes public, it expands, it is redefined, it is recontextualized. Thus the narratives surrounding 'coming out' or 'being raped' become transformed, but Ken Plummer goes further than this; he notes how in late modernity such narratives not only change but they are more fragmented, they are contested and they *co-exist*. That is, there are several possible/plausible narratives available at any one time. And, of course, in a media-saturated society one can note that these narratives are freely available in the public sphere in factional accounts such as the news or chat show, and most importantly in fictionalized sources whether on the radio, in TV drama, or the novel, whether in soap opera, movie or Booker prize-winning novel. Our world changes, we grasp around to understand our feelings, to find an orientation point or a narrative with at least a modicum of comfort. We are, so to speak, spoilt for choice. Yet none of the choices available has the weight of absolute certainty as in the past. Narratives, if you want, lose their singularity, their cohesion and their gravitas. And let me go a little further than this. The narratives are not only contested, but they are not coherent, well formed: they are contradictory and inconsistent not only between themselves but *within* themselves. There is always an element of mayhem in late modernity.

As we have seen, none of this is good news for numbers, but what does it mean in terms of method in general? We have seen the flaws of the quantitative method: its problem of *representativeness,* the existence of *masquerading and deceit,* the problem of *translation*: the way in which the actors translate your questions and the way in which you translate their answers and the *denial of relationship* with the people being studied. In an instant, ethnography holds up the promise of resolving all of these problems: its directness and immediacy seeks to give voice to the voiceless and to probe deceit; the cultural immersion of the researcher sets up a human relationship with the researched, the very object of research, the narrative of the subject and not of the observer. But, to counterpoise against quantitative methods, ethnography as a cure-all is clearly insufficient. Alas, all of these problems of quantitative research reproduce themselves in the qualitative, albeit in more subtle and insidious ways. Much ethnographic work is as stultified as its statistical counterpart. Researchers come back from the field with interesting vignettes of urban life which have as much validity as a posed photograph at a formal wedding. Only too often ethnography depicts too much consistency, too much constancy, too little contradiction, and too high definition of account. It replaces the reification of numbers with the reification of representation. It wants, in short, to tell a good story and in this it can be both self-deceiving as well as a vehicle of deception. We have to be constantly aware, then, of the underlying narrative about the subjects which the ethnographer is communicating to the outside world. What is the author's meta-narrative as well as what are the narratives of the subjects which have been recorded. That is, the narrative of the text and the narrative of the subject. This should be one of the initial questions which one asks of any study, particularly perhaps one which has gained popularity and appeal. For there is little doubt that these images of the other can reveal much about us, while in this process, concealing much about them. A critical methodology must be sensitive to:

- Incoherence
- Unresolved contradiction
- Hesitancy, tentativeness
- Concealment, problems of deceit, the masquerade
- Quick shifts in attitude
- Heterogeneity of opinion
- Strong feelings but just as much inconsequential feelings
- Reflexivity
- Social interaction and relationship in the research process
- Deeply felt and 'borrowed' attitudes (from the public media)
- Contra-socialization

The Meta-narrative of the Lens

In order to evaluate critically the problems of method with regard to ethnography, we need to establish first of all a few conceptual tools. The most useful of these are the notion of interior and exterior histories of a discipline, the concept of narrative and meta-narrative, the idea of a lens, an optic within the wider perspective of othering, of creating 'others' in a dualism against our own selves and culture. Ian Hacking (1981), the social philosopher, distinguishes two parts of the intellectual history of a discipline – its interior history and its exterior history (with regards to the history of criminology, see Young, 1988). The interior history is the particular debates within the academy, and the subjects and explanatory problems as they are seen from within the discipline. The exterior history is the socio-political context in which the discipline exists – the material predicament and ideological currents of the time. Such a formulation is in sharp contrast to the commonly held assumption that an academic discipline proceeds simply in terms of debates within its interior – of the exchange of ideas and evidence from competing scholars, each insulated within their ivory towers from the swirl of common preconception and opinion. Such a notion of insulated and 'objective' development characterizes the natural sciences, although even here there are widespread and inevitable external influences and it is the ideal that positivist social sciences would, of course, prefer for sociology and psychology. But, as we have seen in Chapter 4, such a notion of a gulf between the observer and the observed, of an 'objective' hiatus between the sociologist and his or her subjects, is false. Rather, there are relationships of class, gender, race, and age which exist between the sociologist and the observed world, while socio-political concerns of the moment are of great and pressing influence. Indeed, the exterior world drives the interior; the fortress academy, where the sociologist scurries out to collect data and returns to an insulated, pristine sanctuary, is an illusion.

Let us now look at the distinction between narrative and meta-narrative. The narrative is the subject's story; it is text which the ethnographic narrator gives voice to. The meta-narrative is the interpretative structure, the discourse within which the narrator interprets their story. It is a story told by an ethnographer to an audience and is truly shaped by both – its measure, its flair, and above all its reception are structured by such an exterior history as it is shaped by the personal interior history of the ethnographer. Such a meta-narrative, as I will elaborate later in chapter 9, can be usefully seen by the metaphor of a lens. It is a lens which focuses on a group of people (for example, the crack dealers of the East Barrio in Philippe Bourgois' *In Search of Respect* (2000)), at the expense, some would say, of the majority of people who live there, and in this suffers from the problem of representativeness. Further, it is, as I have stressed, a lens which will tend to bring out certain qualities of those observed: whether their fecklessness, or their misery, or their sense of fun or resistance. The lens can, moreover, give a greater coherence to the subject than actually occurs. Thus frequently the meta-narrative of the author can have a greater coherence than the narrative of the people observed and it is this meta-narrative rather than the narrative which drives the story. Finally, such lenses can be seen as part of the process of othering – whether from the right, the liberal centre, or the left, whether a demonization, an othering of deficit or of emulation and respect. All of this I will examine later, but let us return now to the crisis in ethnography.

Ethnography and Incoherence

Clifford Geertz famously writes, in *The Interpretation of Cultures*, that 'The culture of a people is an ensemble of texts, themselves ensembles, which the anthropologist strains to read over the shoulders of those to whom they properly belong' (1973, p. 452). This presents the ethnographer, as Dwight Conquergood puts it, as 'a displaced, somewhat awkward reader of texts' (1991, p. 188). Against this he quotes the critical work of Michael Jackson, who writes in *Paths Towards a Clearing*:

> The idea that 'there is nothing outside the text' may be congenial to someone whose life is confined to academe, but it sounds absurd in the village worlds where anthropologists carry out their work, where people negotiate meaning in face-to-face interactions . . . In other words, textualism tends to ignore the flux of human relationships, the way meanings are created intersubjectively . . . (1989, p. 184)

Conquergood talks of the rise of the performance paradigm in anthropology. What are the consequences, he asks, of thinking of culture as verb rather than as noun? He cites the works of both Jackson and Victor Turner's remarkable *The Anthropology of Performance* (1986). He writes:

> In a rhetorical masterstroke, Turner subversively redefined the fundamental terms of discussion in ethnography by defining humankind as *homo performans*, humanity as performer, a culture-inventing, social-performing, self-making and self-transforming creature. [He] was drawn to the conceptual lens of performance because it focussed on humankind alive, the creative, playful, provisional, imaginative, articulate expressions of ordinary people grounded in the challenge of making a life in this village, that valley, and inspired by the struggle for meaning. (1991, p. 187)

All of this connects, of course, to Goffman's dramaturgical perspective on social life (see Scheff, 2006). Such a perspective, true as it is to the human predicament, is all the more evident in late modernity. That is, there is nowadays a plurality of scripts on offer which are interpreted, reinterpreted, rewritten, bricolaged and often subverted and satirized in the actual business of human interaction. Thus there is no substantive text which unites the human being; rather there is a plurality of texts varying in coherence which are constantly devised and reinterpreted in the agency of human performance.

The creativity of the human actor is most apparent in the phenomenon of contra-socialization. Sociologists, perhaps inevitably, have tended to view socialization as a transmission which is more or less successfully achieved across the generations and between people, depending on the strength of family, community and peer group. All of this postulates passive social actors, all of this ignores human creativity, reflexivity and the constant generation of new responses to social predicaments. Thus, this gives rise to Ric Curtis' 'little brother effect', which we talked about in the last chapter. The little brother looks at his elder siblings and decides that he wants no part of the drug overdoses, of the out-of-your-face behaviour, of the killings and the violence – he does not want his life fucked up, thank you very much.

The Metaphor of the Photograph

Let me attempt to summarize so far, using the metaphor of the photograph – for so often we think of good ethnography as somehow akin to 'good' photography, or at least what is conventionally considered as well carried out photographs: clear, distinct, with a precise message. I really do not think this is what social reality is like and even more so in late modernity. Rather, if reality were a photograph, it would be blurred, some parts of the print would stand out, others would be extremely faint, there would be empty spaces here and there, the people and objects in the photograph would conceal their faces or purposes, or else present themselves falsely, there would be much indecision of expression – the photograph would be like a bad photograph, a between take – the ones you throw away. Yet again some photographs would be tightly regimented and presented like a wedding photograph, suggesting togetherness forever. There would be contradiction and disagreement – you would need several photographs of the same event from different angles. And of course they would move over time – like those wonderful photographs in the Harry Potter movies they would move – and they sometimes would shift rapidly in mood, demeanour and attitude.

Up till now I have, to continue the metaphor of ethnography as photography, concentrated upon the photograph; I wish now to turn more to the photographer and to his or her relationship with the photographed and, in turn, the relationship between the photograph and its audience in the outside world.

Hiatus and Relationship

The stance of hiatus and of othering, seen so clearly in quantitative work is scarcely mitigated by ethnography. Much of the best modern ethnography looks at the urban poor – in this it is in direct descent from Booth and Mayhew and, like these Victorians viewing the street Arabs, there is a gulf between the ethnographer and their subjects which mirrors that of quantitative researchers. In the most sensitive modern work, say Mitchell Duneier's *Sidewalk* (2001) or Elijah Anderson's *Code of the Street* (1999), there are interesting accounts of the personal relationships between the researcher and the researched, but none of this is put in any structural context. This is in marked contrast to the historical development of the ethnographic method in anthropology. Here the impact of decolonization across the globe brought home to researchers the degree to which classical anthropology echoed the colonial gaze. Listen to Claude Lévi-Strauss thunder about the colonial underpinning of anthropology:

> Anthropology is not a dispassionate science like astronomy, which springs from the contemplation of things at a distance. It is the outcome of a historical process which has made the larger part of mankind subservient to the other, and during which millions of innocent human beings have had their resources plundered and their institutions and beliefs destroyed whilst they themselves were ruthlessly killed, thrown into bondage, and contaminated by diseases they were unable to resist. Anthropology is daughter to this era of violence: its capacity to assess more objectively the facts pertaining to the human condition reflects, on the epistemological level, a state of affairs in which 1 part of mankind treated the other as an object. (1966, p. 126)

And Victor Tyler points to how 'Cartesian dualism has insisted on separating subject from object, us from them. It has, indeed, made voyeurs of Western man, exaggerating sight by macro- and micro-instrumentation, the better to learn the structures of the world with an 'eye' to its exploitation' (1982, p. 100). As Renato Rosaldo so pithily comments, this 'connects the "eye" of ethnography with the "I" of imperialism' (1993, p. 41). It is thus to critical anthropology that we must turn if we are to learn how to confront the problem of the late modern binary: of the postulated hiatus between cultures, between people, between concepts, between the observer and the observed.

The bustling, creative and discordant literature of critical anthropology revolves around two closely related concepts: the notion of how relationships of power structure perceptions and the permeability and porousness of the late modern/post-colonial world. The gaze of power carries with it, in Edward Said's poignant depiction, an 'orientalism' – a perception of other cultures as irrational, unreliable, often violent and sexually labile. And to this one might add that 'their' culture is seen as determined, a product of material circumstances that might perhaps be manipulated and made 'better'. But this projection of the Other carries with it a notion of 'us', the professional middle-class Anglo-Americans, our Self. Here, as Rosaldo has pointed out, 'our' culture is presented as something invisible:

> Social analysts commonly speak . . . as if 'we' had psychology and 'they' have culture . . . The temptation to dress our own 'local knowledge' of either the folk or professional variety in garb at once 'universal' and 'culturally invisible' to itself seems to be overwhelming . . . In practice, the emphasis on difference results in a peculiar ratio: as the 'other' becomes culturally visible the 'self' becomes correspondingly less so . . . analysts rarely allow the ratio of class and culture to include power. Thus they conceal the ratio's darker side: the more power one has, the less culture one enjoys, and the more culture one has, the less power one wields. (1993, p. 202)

Thus our 'self' comes to be conceived of as invisible, tacit, voluntaristic – in short the subject – whereas their culture becomes more visible, recalcitrant, determined – in short the object. The situation of power, of relationship, of class, becomes concealed in the notion of the objective, the observed, that which is detached from the subject. It is as true of modern urban ethnography as it is of the classic ethnography of indigenous peoples, indeed now, as Loic Wacquant points out, 'the black poor . . . stand at the epicenter of America's "urban orientalism"' (2002b, p. 1470). Such structures of perception ignore or distort the class position of the observed and render invisible the class position of the observer; that is, the turning of those who are an essential part of the economic circuit into the detached and the exotic. As such, urban ethnography, however sensitively conducted, leads to a focus on the peripheral: Mitchell Duneier on the sidewalk vendors of Greenwich Village, Philippe Bourgois on the crack dealers of East Harlem, Katherine Newman on the Burger King operatives of Harlem – almost as if these were typical of the populations despite the fact, in the case of fast-food workers for example, that these are only a small minority of the black labour force. Yet it is this relationship of power, this urban orientalism, which determines the lens through which we choose to observe the social world, upon whom it focuses and the images which such an optic provides. Indeed, it is our relationship with the poor which structures what we ask, what they say, and what we choose to hear.

Few within urban sociology seem to acknowledge and focus upon the relationships of subservience that exist within society. Rather this is left to feminists, such as Barbara Ehrenreich who, in *Nickel and Dimed* (2001), enters the world of humiliation where employees are routinely checked for drug use, pre-tip pay is a maximum of $2.13 an hour and unions are severely frowned upon. And, of course, she does this by a research technique which precious few academics would embrace – to take the jobs herself: an ethnography of total immersion. It is feminist scholars who have pointed out that part of the reason for this occlusion is that much of this work is that of poor women and that it is domestic labour. Witness the title of Ehrenreich and Hochschild's book: *Global Woman: Nannies, Maids, and Sex Workers in the New Economy* (2002). Here again the relationships of power are concealed, their work is not defined as 'real' work and not least of all is the irony that in part the emancipation of Western middle-class women is dependent on the domestic work of immigrants from the Third World and the periphery of the First.

It is not only the relationship of power that is mystified, but the relationship between the culture of the observed and of the observers. That is, as we have seen in quantitative analysis, there is posited an isolation, a discrete hiatus and difference between the two. In the case of classic ethnography this is epitomized by the anthropologist who travels to a distant land, studies the culture there with its strange norms and alien practices, and brings back to the home university a portrait of the people there and an exploration of their values and behaviour. Yet the very fact of colonization negated the notion of hermetically separate societies and the post-colonial situation of today's culturally globalized world further undermines this. This is all the more so for social groups within a society, whether indigenous or immigrant.

The Ethnographer's Audience

Ethnographers like photographers have audiences, their meta-narratives echo the major social philosophies of the times whether neo-liberalism, social democracy, or simply old-fashioned liberalism. These ideas slip into the marrow of the text sometimes unnoticed, very often taken for granted, a few times explicit, designed to proselytize and convert. The audiences expect these interpretative paradigms; they most often choose the studies which confirm their preconceptions, at times their stereotypes and their prejudices. Their reading tells them something about the outside world but also something of themselves; at best the ethnographer can hope to change the audience, to open their eyes; at other times the attraction of the reading is simply the confirmation and accentuation of their beliefs, deeply held fears and prejudices

Ethnography and the end of Innocence

John Van Maanen (1995) talks of the 'end of innocence', of ethnography, of 'a time – some might say a dream time', when ethnography was seen as a simple depiction of the lives of strangers, without great methodological pains or effort more like, as he puts it, 'a rather pleasant, peaceful, and instinctive form of travel writing' (1995, p. 1). George Marcus and Michael Fischer (1999) point to two texts which more than anything are emblematic of the crisis in ethnography: Edward Said's *Orientalism* (1979) and Derek Freeman's *Margaret Mead and Samoa* (1983). If the first signalled the ever-present possibility of othering, the second pointed to the problem of deceit, and both together can be seen as a potential system of deception where deceit moulds the contours of the other and othering encourages self-deception and deceit.

Said's famous book pointed to the way that Orientalism, the view from the West, allows us to portray the 'East' as an 'other', a scene of irrationality, chaos, sexuality, and violence, a viewpoint which allows us to present ourselves as the virtual mirror opposite and, further, permits social and political intervention on behalf of 'civilization' and humanitarianism. Marcus and Fischer portray Said's critique, although directed largely at targets other than ethnography, as the first major threat to its methods and claims to knowledge. Of course it came on the heels of a widespread awareness among anthropologists of the colonial gaze, of the fashion in which anthropology had followed colonization. So that, in the post-war era of decolonization, anthropologists became very much more aware of their colonial gaze and the relativism of interpretation (see Geertz, 1973) than, say, were ethnographers working in urban traditions such as that of the Chicago School. More recently, Loic Wacquant (1997) detects the emergence of a 'new urban Orientalism' in the depictions of the underclass and the ghetto. And most perceptively are Dwight Conquergood's comments in his paper 'On Reppin' and Rhetoric', pre-

sented at the University of Iowa, Philosophy and the Rhetoric of Inquiry
Seminar in 1992: here he sees the images of gangs in the inner city as
precisely a transplanting of Orientalism from the East to the inner city as
part of post-colonialist rhetoric. Thus, he writes:

> In the public sphere, the label 'gang' is a thickly lacquered representational
> screen onto which powerful and contradictory images are projected.
> The term 'gang' powerfully cathects and conjures middle-class fears and
> anxieties about social disorder, disintegration, and chaos, that are made
> palpable in these demonized figures of inscrutable, unproductive, preda-
> tory, pathological, alien Others lurking in urban shadows and margins,
> outside the moral community of decent people. 'Gang' has become a fan-
> tasy-fetish of primitivism that is co-extensive with other colonialist tropes
> deployed to erect barriers between Self and Other. In our post-colonial
> world the alien Other has migrated from the margins of empire and is now,
> in an ironic twist of history, colonizing our cities. The figure of the gang
> member in multicultural late twentieth-century urban America is an ethnic
> male member of the migrant and un- and underemployed classes. Like the
> representations of 'natives' in the colonies, representations of 'gangs' in the
> cities are deployed to contain and control the 'dangerous classes,' urban
> primitives. . . .
>
> In the contemporary theatre of primitivism, gang members are the
> post-colonial 'natives' of the urban jungle. The inner city and suburbs are
> polarized sites within a new economically articulated geography of power
> and domination that remaps the colonialist axis between capital and
> colony. The 'inner city', like Joseph Conrad's Congo, is spatially imagined
> as a journey into the dark interior, the penetration of a cavity, an orifice,
> an absence, a moral descent into an urban 'heart of darkness'. As an origi-
> nary site of gangs, representations of the inner city draw on and conjoin
> two major patterns of primitivist discourse: the violent primitive, and the
> diseased primitive . . .
>
> This conflation of xenophobic Third World stereotypes with gangs
> is a complex form of urban orientalism (Said) that conjured orientalist
> phantasms of gang terrorists that threaten the Enlightenment foundations
> of middle-class civility, indeed, western civilization. It is no accident that
> this new form of urban orientalism arises at a time when US cities are
> populated increasingly by non-Western immigrants and refugees from the
> hemispheres of the south and the east. Like its older colonialist form, this
> post-colonial orientalism functions as a discursive apparatus for control-
> ling and containing difference, managing the problem of diversity. (1991,
> pp. 4, 5, 7).

The gaze of the ethnographer moves from the colonies to the capital,
from the periphery to the centre, and yet, with irony, migrates from
the Third World at the global margins to the Third World populations
within the inner cities of the First World itself. The heart of darkness,

once to be found in the nether regions of the world, reconstitutes itself within the inner cities of the hinterland.

The criticisms of Said's *Orientalism* are well known: his brushstrokes are much too broad, he does not differentiate sufficiently the various responses of othering, nor attempt to locate these in particular groups or parts of the social structure. His project is political rather than sociological. And he does not give us an alternative position from where to base a critique (see Young, R., 1990). He tells us, in a marvellous passage, that

> above all, critical thought does not submit to state power or to commands to join in the ranks marching against one or another approved enemy. Rather than the manufactured clash of civilizations, we need to concentrate on the slow working together of cultures that overlap, borrow from each other, and live together in a far more interesting way than any abridged or inauthentic mode of understanding can allow. (Said, 1993 p. xxix).

As a statement of late modern reality, as an awareness of the difficulties of assessing similarity and difference in the present period, this assertion of position is excellent but Said does not present us with any notion of what a critical perspective would look like. I want, in the next chapter, to examine the phenomenon of othering in ethnography, bringing to Said's work the contribution of the social constructionist perspective, particularly within the sociology of deviance. But let me for the moment turn to the second volume which Marcus and Fischer identify as challenging the validity of ethnographic method, the famous or perhaps infamous book by Derek Freeman entitled *Margaret Mead and Samoa: The Making and Unmaking of an Anthropological Myth* (1983).

Mead's study of the Samoans is a salutary story which has been told many times, but still bears retelling. In 1928 Margaret Mead published *Coming of Age in Samoa: A Psychological Study of Primitive Youth for Western Civilisation*. Mead's research project was to critique the work of psychologists such as Stanley Hall, who postulated universal stages of human development which were biologically determined and independent of culture. In particular, that adolescence was inevitably a stage of storm and stress – a product of 'raging hormones' as we would have it today. Mead's hypothesis, to the contrary, was that culture shaped adolescence differently in Samoa from in the United States. Her findings – which became well known throughout the world – were that indeed this was true, and that, in Samoa, adolescence was relatively trouble free when compared with the United States. She pinpointed the reason for this in the sexual permissiveness of Samoan society – the lack of the repressions and taboos experienced by American teenagers. Further, that overall this indicated the plasticity of human behaviour and the importance of cultural determinants. Mead's influence has been considerable. She was, as the anthropologist Nancy Scheper-Hughes put it:

> in a sense, the mother of my generation. She and Benjamin Spock [who was Mead's only child's paediatrician] influenced the way we were reared and dared our parents to experiment with such 'radical' actions as tolerance, open communication and 'permissiveness'. (1984, p. 92)

It was against such an icon that Derek Freeman set his critique. An anthropologist who initially shared Mead's preconceptions, he found in his visits to Samoa, where he established close and intimate links, evidence which completely undermined her position. Where she found sexual freedom he found restrictions and the cult of virginity, where she found placidity he found teenage aggression, where she found a stress-free adolescence, he found turbulence, defiance and delinquency.

Derek Freeman suggested that Mead had been driven by her desire to substantiate her belief in the primacy of cultural over biological determinism and had been hoaxed by her mischievous and misleading informants, particularly two teenage girls: Fa'apua'a and Fofoa. Freeman's book set off one of the most famous controversies in the social sciences, one which continues unabated today. For here we have the doyenne, or perhaps diva would be more appropriate, of American cultural anthropology being systematically and tenaciously slandered. Indeed, Freeman's second book is even more direct in its accusation, witness its title: *The Fateful Hoaxing of Margaret Mead* (1999). At each stage of the argument, he ratchets his critique up. Margaret Mead was hoaxed, she deceived herself, she fooled the world at large – indeed, for what it is worth, he kindled a controversy which is listed among the top ten in Hellman's *Great Feuds in Science* (1998).

Let us note, first of all, the direct parallels with the controversy over the social research of Edward Laumann and his team, which I have discussed earlier. Ethnography seemingly is vulnerable to exactly the same flaws as survey research, indeed it might be suggested that the intimacy and hands-on nature of ethnography makes the possibility not only of deception, but self-deceit, all the more feasible. Let us recollect from Chapter 3 that there were three orders of problem in collecting information from other people: firstly that of representativeness – are the respondents representative of the population; secondly, that of masquerading: concealment, or simple deception – the respondents, for some reason or other, do not respond, or if they do, don't tell us the truth; thirdly, more subtly, that of translation: not only the misconstruing of categories, but where words have different meanings to different people and human action is differentially understood and categorized. All of these three problems emerge in the critique of Mead, but I will focus on concealment and deceit first of all, as this is explicitly the major thrust of Freeman's critique.

Although the image of Margaret Mead being misled by mischievous, somewhat embarrassed girls, has managed to stick in the public's imagination, the general consensus of informed anthropological opinion is largely supportive of Mead's findings. Yet sometimes one might have wished she had protection from her supporters. Thus James Coté portrays Mead as having basically got the facts right in spite of 'the scientific limitations' of her study, her limited resources and the restricted methodologies of the times. Thus, he writes:

> The perfect scientific study to examine Mead's problem would have been to use validated and standardized quantitative or clinical assessments measuring the prevalence and severity of storm and stress symptomology among representative samples of American and Samoan adolescents (both male and female) controlling for factors like the relative age of onset of puberty and nutrition. Mead did not have the means to undertake such a study, and it has not been done to date. (2000, p. 532)

Ethnography, here, is seen as an almost pre-scientific substitute for a quantitative study using 'validated and standardized' measures, whatever that might mean! One can only imagine what the measurement of the other variable – pre-marital sexual activity – would look like in this scheme. But we do not have far to look, because another one of Mead's other supporters provides us with the answer. Paul Shankman (1996) notes the problem (which I will return to later) of Mead comparing objectively the 'sexual activity' of Samoan and American girls, given that her argument hangs on the greater sexual freedom – or 'activity' as it is now formulated – of the former. He describes the American data as being 'more reliable' and cites the well-known research of Sandra Hofferth and her associates who work in the field of health science and demography (see Hofferth et al., 1987; Santelli et al., 2000). These studies are dependent on such data sources as the US National Surveys of Young Women, The National Survey of Family Growth, the Youth Risk Behavior Survey, etc. Here, pre-marital sexual intercourse is measured by interviews conducted at home or school, often with parental permission, and typically with non-response rates in the 20–30 per cent range. If the results of general sexual surveys outlined in the last chapter are gravely flawed, it can just be imagined how flimsy are these surveys of young people. Such arguments seek epistemological security in strange and unreliable places. It is not qualitative studies that have to be given substance by quantitative measures, but quantitative research which has to be shored up where possible and discarded where necessary by qualitative work.

A more sophisticated assessment of Mead's work in Samoa emerges from a series of acute observations on her work by fellow anthropologists. For the virulence of the exchange, the sound and fury of Freeman, obscures a much more striking problem for ethnographic research. The key question is not so much the absolute truth of Freeman's assertion that Mead was hoaxed, it is the awareness that the predispositions and preconceptions of the researcher can very easily shape the research. That is, the problem of translation rather than deception. And in this respect we have a further fascinating parallel between the pitfalls of the quantitative sex researchers and the ethnography of Margaret Mead. You will recall that the levels of sexual intercourse related not only to deceit because of modesty or boasting, but because of differences in definition of what actually constituted sexual intercourse. This was underscored by the discussion of levels of violence and of rape where, as was noted, the rates are dependent on the definitions held both by the interviewee and the interviewer. Nicole Grant, in an excellent article entitled 'From Margaret Mead's Field Notes: What Counted as "Sex" in Samoa?' (1995) engages precisely with this question. She starts by evoking Gayle Rubin's pithy remark 'Sex is sex, but what counts as sex is . . . culturally determined and obtained' (1975, p. 165).

A major part of Freeman's claim against Mead was that sexual freedom was extremely unlikely in Samoa given the low rate of pre-marital pregnancy which both he, and indeed Mead herself, had noted. But, as Grant points out, sexual freedom and a low incidence of pregnancy are not incompatible: 'The key to understanding why the young women of Samoa were sexually active and were not getting pregnant when Mead was there in 1926 is found in the consideration of what *counted as sex* in Samoa at that time' (1995, p. 679). She points to the fact that the Samoans separated out sexual play and procreative sex, the first was oral and manual, the second, of course, involved intercourse – the former was called 'play' by Samoans and was not frowned upon, indeed was encouraged, the second, which had the consequences of pregnancy, was considered deviant outside of marriage. Mead was, therefore, correct in her observations with regard to the sexual permissiveness of Samoan society, but:

When Margaret Mead published her study, readers interpreted her findings according to the dominant cultural construction of sexuality familiar to them. In Western industrialized nations, and in other areas of the world already under the influence of capitalism and Christian ideology, what counted as sex was primarily intercourse; engaging in sex before marriage or with more than one partner was considered deviant. It was assumed at that time that sex was a derivative of nature and not of culture, and that sexual practices were universal in form. Sex in Samoa as it was described to Mead was widely interpreted as promiscuous. But sex in Samoa was different from sex in Western cultures. Because sex and intercourse are considered synonymous in Western cultures, both are serious matters with serious social consequences. In traditional Samoa the most common word for sex is the word that means 'play'. It was intercourse, not sex, that had serious social consequences. Intercourse as associated primarily with reproduction, not with sex. Promiscuity in Samoa had nothing to do with sex. To be promiscuous meant to engage in intercourse when it was prohibited and thus to reproduce indiscriminately. Sexual play that did not result in a protracted monogamous sexual relationship involving intercourse was a normal part of the complex sex-gender system. That system functioned to protect the status of men, the autonomy of women, the integrity of the kinship structure, and the emotional and economic well-being of the entire community by assuring procreative control without sacrificing sexual pleasure. (Grant, 1995, p. 681)

Grant indicates how this binary of sex changed under the impact of missionaries and more importantly American sailors from the US Naval Base in American Samoa, whose sexual mores in their liaisons with the native girls helped move Samoan values towards those of Western 'civilization'! Thus, rather neatly, she explains Freeman's different findings almost twenty years later, including the retraction of the key 'witnesses', as reflecting a Samoan world of changed sexual mores. Indeed, by the time Freeman had re-interviewed Margaret Mead's informants (particularly Fa'apua'a and Fofoa), their retraction reflects the change in *their* attitude to the past. As Grant puts it:

As Western ideals were adopted, the Samoan ruling class lost the possibility for pride in the traditional Samoan ability to transcend the dictates of nature by culturally shaping sexuality so that pleasure and play were effectively dissociated from reproductive consequences. It is at this juncture that Freeman was able to publish his critique of Mead with little challenge to his premise that sexual freedom was precluded by the absence of reproductive consequences. What counted as sex among his colleagues – in Samoa and in most of the world – was by that time so different from what counted as sex in Samoa in 1926 that apparently no one guessed at his mistake. (1995, p. 682)

Here, then, we have an example of faulty translation – not so much on Mead's part but on the part presumably of the general audience and of Freeman himself, who mistakenly elides the dualism between 'play' and sexual intercourse and perhaps also intriguingly the informants themselves, now much older, looking back from a Samoa whose ethics had now changed.

But we must not let Margaret Mead off the hook so lightly! I want to turn now to more sceptical anthropologists who point to mistakes in translation on her part, although of a more subtle kind than the mere mistakes to which Freeman alludes. Nancy Scheper-Hughes begins what is a most perceptive piece on the Mead-Freeman controversy with the short poem of Wallace Stevens:

> Description is revelation. It is neither
> The thing Described, nor false facsimile
> It is an artificial thing that exists. In its own seeming, plainly visible
> Yet not too closely the double of our lives
> Intenser than any actual life could be
> *(Description Without Place*, Wallace Stevens)

This poem captures the inevitable accentuation and interpretation an ethnographer must make in the act of translation. Further, Scheper-Hughes talks very interestingly of Samoan society, like any society, being complex and contradictory:

> We know that when we talk about Samoan culture or Irish culture we are talking about an interpretation that is a result of a complex series of inter-actions between the anthropologist and his or her informants. Cultural understanding is essentially produced, not merely recovered. Ethnography is a very special kind of intellectual autobiography, a deeply personal record through which a whole view of the human condition, an entire sensibility, is elaborated. We no longer try to approach the world (as the natural scientist would) as a fixed array of objects, but rather as a reality that cannot be fully separated from our perceptions of it. It shifts over time and in response to our gaze. It interacts with us. (1984, p. 91)

Here we have quite correctly the dismissal of the positivist gaze that casts the object of study as separate from the ethnography. And here we have not only the possibility of multiple interpretations from different per-spectives but, in turn, a culture with multiple – and often contradictory – currents. To this extent, Mead captured:

> [a] Samoan truth . . . but *not* the Samoan truth. Derek Freeman, it appears, had access to another Samoan truth – again, not *the* truth. And this differ-ence in turn can be explained by differences between Mead and Freeman and their respective informants. Mead was a young woman, who inter-viewed Samoan girls exhilarated by the first blush of sexual experience. Freeman began studying the Samoans as a mature, later as an old man. His Samoan informants were high ranking chiefs. Freeman could never have asked Samoan girls of thirteen and fourteen the kinds of questions that Mead had asked without being run off the island as a 'dirty old man'.

Samoan pre-marital sex is relaxed among adolescent boys and girls – but it is decidedly not cross-generational . . . Freeman's informants on Samoan sexuality were, like himself, mature men who were the chief guardians of the 'public' morality. Freeman had access to what Erving Goffman called the 'front stage' performance on sexual behavior. Mead, however, had access to the 'back stage' performance . . . (1984, p. 90)

Freeman studies a different section of Samoa, from a different perspective, while also visiting a different Island ('British', as compared to 'American' Samoa) at a different time (from fourteen to forty years later). In a sense he was of the wrong gender, the wrong age, talking to members of the wrong class, studying the wrong island, at the wrong time!

Yet this formulation, as formalistic and as satisfying as it is, slips us back into the notion of universal truth. As far as gender, age and class is concerned, Scheper-Hughes is quite right that much ethnography has been conducted with a male gaze and further that Mead's youthfulness – she was twenty-four at the time – and willingness to talk outside of the Samoan hierarchy was a great gain. Yet she is also correct that various perspectives tap into various parts of the total reality and are truths in themselves. Let us recall how cultural criminology stresses that it is important to look at the underlife of the city, yet the formal rules of official society are not illusions, they exist as palpable influences and obstacles in the everyday lives of people. In this instance, the belief that pre-marital sexual intercourse should not occur had become elided with the belief that it did not occur. Yet the belief of the Samoan elders, however misguided, undoubtedly would have an effect on the lives of the young girls, even perhaps on their level of doubt and guilt. Other writers, notably Bradd Shore (1982) have written of the contradictions, paradoxes and 'mysteries' of Samoan culture, indeed that many such contradictions are never in fact resolved. Indeed it is difficult, maybe impossible, to think of any culture where its contradictions and incoherence are resolved. Thus against a notion of a monolithic cultural universe we have contradiction, incoherence and fragmentation. We can take this a step further by examining the comments of George Marcus and Michael Fischer on the debate. Their central concern is the dualism which Mead sets up. This is, they point out, on one side (the Samoan) in danger of caricature, and on the other (the American) based on complete conjecture. The aim of creating a critique of the supposedly repressive nature of American culture shaped a dualism which was 'static, unambiguous, over generalized and one-sided.' (1999, p. 159)

Let me attempt to summarize so far. Mead's approach to the Samoans was undoubtedly that of a romantic othering, she was out to find an almost utopian other in terms of sexuality and aggression in order to

contrast with and castigate the *Sturm und Drang* of American constructions of adolescence. We have seen how such othering was conducive to
mistranslation and it was this rather than deception which produced a
story which fitted so well the meta-narrative of how a permissive world
would give rise to benign behaviour. It is not simply that Margaret Mead
was misled by these mischievous and somewhat embarrassed girls. It
is that the meta-narrative – the story she had for the world and which
fuelled numerous lecture tours – was one which the world wished to
hear. For both versions of modernity – that of the West and that of the
Soviets – held a deep-set belief in the plasticity of human nature, in the
way in which, given the correct social institutions, aberrant behaviour,
from delinquency to sexual aberrations, could be eliminated in the wake
of progress.

But all of this is not to deny that Mead found some pretty exciting
stuff in Samoa which was remarkably at odds with the prevailing sexual
mores of American society. The separation of sexuality from procreation
permitted the possibility of sexual pleasure much less fraught with fear
and guilt than that of the United States at that time. Ironically, it was
only a lot later under the impact of the sexual revolution in the 1960s,
aided and abetted by the new technologies of contraception, of which
the likes of Kinsey and Mead were the ideological precursors, that this
most remarkable separation of procreation and pleasure came about in
the First World. So Nancy Scheper-Hughes is very right, Margaret Mead
was the mother of her generation.

But Mead got it in part wrong. Her social translation was faulty,
she conflated Samoan sexual play and penetrative sex (associated with
procreation) together because she was using the template of the Western
World where both were seen as a unity. Were the girl respondents mischievous or misleading? Perhaps to a limited extent Margaret Mead may
have been the right age and gender, but she was also an American. She
was a daunting visitor from the First World, the girls may have aided
and abetted Mead's translation a little, but this is scarcely more than
a blemish on the research. It is far from the calumny cast upon her by
Derek Freeman. Just think of the alternative. Mead could, like the missionaries, have seen Samoan culture as the other of primitivism: the
sexuality of the uncivilized. The missionaries arrived in Samoa with their
views fixed, nailed to the certainties of the revealed scriptures. If their
perspective had prevailed abroad, there would have been no need for a
Freeman and his 'revelations'.

But in Samoa itself Western views did begin to intrude: the unlikely
combination of the missionaries and visiting American scholars did
manage to propagate their values as well as themselves. Sex was for
procreation or else, until the recent period, was a world of fear, of guilt;

sex was of its nature penetrative. So it was when we came to the time of Freeman's follow-up interviews with Mead's respondents. Here in reality we have a mixture of contradiction, guilt, looking back on one's youth and then, in the interview situation, the opportunity to set up a narrative, a rewriting of the past concomitant with their age and respectability. If there was deception, then, it was probably here – not so much Freeman being hoaxed as, on the one side, the inevitable human creation of consistent narrative in the face of the expert (reminding one of Rissarro's interview with Sennett and Cobb outlined in Chapter 4) and Freeman's own commitment to the meta-narrative of evolutionary development, positivism and certainty.

8

Subcultures as Magic: Problems of Urban Ethnography

Respectable people have access to a limited body of information upon Cornerville. They may learn that it is one of the most congested areas in the United States. It is one of the chief points of interest in any tour organized to show upper-class people the bad housing conditions in which lower-class people live. Through sight-seeing or statistics one may discover that bathtubs are rare, that children overrun the narrow and neglected streets, that the juvenile delinquency rate is high, that crime is prevalent among adults, and that a large proportion of the population was on home relief or W. P. A. during the depression.

In this view, Cornerville people appear as social work clients, as defendants in criminal cases, or as undifferentiated members of 'the masses.' There is one thing wrong with such a picture: no human beings are in it. Those who are concerned with Cornerville seek through a general survey to answer questions that require the most intimate knowledge of local life. The only way to gain such knowledge is to live in Cornerville and participate in the activities of the people.

(Whyte, 1955, pp. xv–xvi)

The sheer surprise of a living culture is a slap to reverie. Real, bustling, startling cultures move. They exist. They are something in the world. They suddenly leave behind – empty, exposed, ugly – ideas of poverty, deprivation, existence and culture. Real events can save us much philosophy.

(Willis, 1978, p. 1)

I want now to shift attention from the ethnography of classical anthropology to urban ethnography, and in doing so to examine more fully the concept of othering. The ethnographer as urban anthropologist travels like the colonial anthropologist before him to distant and difficult parts.

He or she goes to a socially distant area of the city – whether it is the Washington DC of Elliott Liebow, or the Philadelphia ghetto of Carl Nightingale or the East Barrio of Manhattan of Philippe Bourgois. It is a place which is not usually visited, and more frequently avoided, for it is a place which frightens and vexes the middle-class public.

Ethnography: Three Forms of Othering

Simone de Beauvoir in *The Second Sex* writes of men and women as follows:

> The terms *masculine* and *feminine* are used symmetrically only as a matter of form, as on legal papers. In actuality the relation of the two sexes is not quite like that of two electrical poles, for man represents both the positive and the neutral, as is indicated by the common use of *man* to designate human beings in general; whereas woman represents only the negative, defined by limiting criteria, without reciprocity. (1953, p. 15)

Man is autonomous from woman, woman is defined by man; man is a neutral vantage point that does not have to be explained, woman is an enigma; man is sensible, sanguine, the font of reason, woman is frivolous, infantile, irresponsible; man is the tacit 'We', woman is the Other. 'The category of the other', de Beauvoir sugests 'is as primordial as consciousness itself' (1953, p. 14) and of all the numerous binaries of self and other, masculine and feminine is one of the most fundamental.

The notion of othering was further developed in the sociology of deviance and social constructionist literature in the 1970s to describe the way in which the threat of other social realities is defused by depicting them as a deviation from the 'normal' so that they are seen not as conveying alternative values but lacking the qualities of normality. The role of the 'expert', whether social commentator, social scientist or psychiatrist is, in this analysis, to shore up conventional – usually white middle-class – values, by presenting these as absolute (e.g. deferred gratification, the monogamous family, the steady job) and any deviation from this as a product of some deficit whether moral or material. Such a critique was most elegantly devised in Peter Berger and Thomas Luckmann's *The Social Construction of Reality* (1967), with its emphasis on the existential fear of the other, the ontological insecurity which difference engenders, and within the field of the sociology of deviant behaviour by writers such as Erich Goode (1994/1973), and Paul Rock (1973). It was these ideas which informed my own ethnographic work on illicit drug use in Notting

Hill, West London, carried out in the late 1960s and published as *The Drugtakers* (Young, 1971b). In particular I was interested in how such strategies shaped the image of the deviant other – the drug fiend/addict – and how in the face of moral panics such othering was self-fulfilling. We have already encountered Edward Said's concept of 'Orientalism' (1978), an analysis on a geo-political level which parallels the discussions in the literature of existentialism and the sociology of deviance and was developed quite independently.

The Ethnographic Other

> To what extent do anthropologists unwittingly abet the distorting tendencies of the popular media, where Third World peoples are typecast as political refugees and famine victims, defined in terms of the *absence* of freedom, as *lacking* in economic rationality, *wanting* in resources, illiterate, impoverished, undernourished? Seen as historically peripheral, they become for us negations of ourselves and needful of what we have. Specters of the not-self or objects of our compassion, it makes little difference. Their voices go unheard, their customs derided, their experiences masked, so that 'humanity' itself seems to belong only to the powerful and rich. (Jackson, 1989, p. x)

Othering is a perennial problem of ethnography. The process of othering varies with the political persuasions and perspectives of the social commentators. The type of othering that Conquergood describes is from the right and is akin to demonization. He graphically illustrates this by quoting from Lewis Yablonsky's classic *The Violent Gang* (1962) in which he refers to the 'defective personality and limited social ability' of these 'gang boys' which 'makes lying, assault, thieving, and unprovoked violence – especially violence – the major activity or dream of his life' (1962, pp. 3–4). Conquergood calls this 'the genre of cathartic textual violence thinly veiled as scholarly research . . . [where] Yablonsky sets out to dehumanize, demonize, and discursively destroy gangs' (1962, p. 22). But, of course, exactly the opposite type of othering can occur – one that romanticizes and exoticizes the subject – I will touch on this shortly, when I refer to Phil Cohen's self-critique of his work in London's East End. But, for the moment – and with the work of Elliott Liebow more in mind – I want to discuss a more common, yet least discussed, form of othering: that of liberal social scientists and political commentators.

It is an othering, but it is not one of the exotic or the alien – it has neither the resonance of the romantic projections of radicals nor the dystopian ruminations of conservatives. Rather, it is an othering of deficit

– they are different from us because they lack our qualities and our circumstances, not because they possess different qualities *per se*. they are not like us because of a deficit – and – this is a major theme – they would be *just like us* if this deficit were remedied. Liberal othering, in short, is a creature of deficit where social intervention is justified in order to make 'them' (the poor, the drug 'abusers', the deviant) like us – to share our civilization, comfort and orderly values. It is characterized, as Michael Jackson suggests in the introduction to this section, by a perspective which is close to images of popular media. In this it shares a further similarity to the quantitative methodology of positivism. Namely, that it gains credibility both scientifically and as a forceful narrative by echoing major currents in popular images of those who live on the margins outside of the First World and on the margins within it.

To do so I will start by examining Elliott Liebow's study of street corner men, *Tally's Corner* (2003/1967). I do so because it is famous and influential, the book has sold more than one million copies, many people's views of poor black men have been shaped by it, many more than those who have actually read it, further it is to an extent in the clear lineage of the Chicago school, albeit conducted in Washington DC, and a worthy representative of the American ethnographic tradition. To critique this single work is, of course, somewhat invidious, but I do so because its very clarity of purpose and exceptional literacy facilitates the task in hand, and I do so because it in many ways reflects the limits of conventional ethnography while displaying unusual insight. It is in some ways a typical example and in other ways exemplary. In doing this I will make linkages and comparisons with Liebow's British contemporary, Phil Cohen, Philippe Bourgois' celebrated *In Search of Respect* (1995, 2000) and, for a critical contrast, the work of Dave Brotherton and Luis Barrios (2004), the extraordinary radical iconoclast, Dwight Conquergood (1991, 1992, 1993), as well as the critical anthropology of George Marcus and Michael Fischer (1999), which I have already touched upon.

The Magic of Subcultures: Rationality and Deception at Tally's Corner

Elliott Liebow's classic study, *Tally's Corner*, first published in 1967 is one of the most durable and influential of ethnographic studies. It focuses upon a group of black street corner men living in Washington DC, within walking distance of the White House, and its major consideration is whether, as is often supposed, their behaviour (erratic work habits, unstable marital practices, drinking, drug use, short-term goals and irascible behaviour) is a product of the so-called culture of poverty. Liebow's conclusion is that, far from such behaviour being a product of some aberrant cultural trait, there is a genuine – almost utilitarian – logic to it all. Thus, when the pick-up truck glides past the corner looking for men willing to do a day's work, no one on Tally's Corner steps forward because the jobs do not pay enough to feed them, because ill health precludes heavy manual work, because there is no job security – because the jobs are dirty, uninteresting and underpaid. And, given this objectively erratic work predicament, chances of a stable marriage are remote: he has no hope whatever of supporting a family, to buy food for the table, to provide the regular rent for an apartment. Far from rejecting the values of the wider society, he is rejected by the society itself. And here Liebow articulates precisely the point that I have attempted to elaborate throughout this book: the lack of clear cultural and social demarcations, the permeability of the social order:

> This inside world does not appear as a self-contained, self-generating, self-sustaining system or even subsystem with clear boundaries marking it off from the larger world around it. It is in continuous, intimate contact with the larger society – indeed, is an integral part of it – and is no more impervious to the values, sentiments and beliefs of the larger society than it is to the blue welfare checks or to the agents of the larger society, such as the policeman, the police informer, the case worker, the landlord, the dope pusher, the Tupperware demonstrator, the numbers backer or the anthropologist. (2003, p. 136)

Thus, in an analysis greatly reminiscent of Merton, Liebow argues that the men on the street corner absorb the wider values of the workplace and the family and because of this experience their lives as failures. They are not a site of an alternative culture, which would insulate them from such definitions of success, but hold fast to the values of the wider world. Thus the job market speaks to them directly of their failure:

> A crucial factor in the streetcorner man's lack of job commitment is the overall value he places on the job. *For his part, the streetcorner man puts no lower value on the job than does the larger society around him.* He knows the social value of the job by the amount of money the employer is willing to pay him for doing it. In a real sense, every pay day, he counts in dollars and cents the value placed on the job by society at large. He is no more (and frequently less) ready to quit and look for another job than his employer is ready to fire him and look for another man. Neither the streetcorner man who performs these jobs nor the society which requires him to perform them assesses the job as one 'worth doing and worth doing well.' Both employee and employer are contemptuous of the job. The employee

shows his contempt by his reluctance to accept it or keep it, the employer by paying less than is required to support a family.' (2003, p. 36)

His series of broken marriages and liaisons, far from being part of a culture of serial monogamy, as is often postulated about the black family, are, in fact, a series of failures. For, 'armed with models who have failed, convinced of his own worthlessness, illiterate and unskilled, he enters marriage and the job market with the smell of failure all around him' (2003, p. 137). But on the corner this failure is transformed: the man's flaws become magically his virtues. Liebow posits his famous theory of 'manly flaws'. That is drinking, the need for independence, and sex are the core of masculinity. Marriages break down because of the masculinity of the man or as Sea Cat, one of the men, wonderfully put it:

> Men are just dogs! We shouldn't call ourselves human, we're just dogs, dogs, dogs! They call me dog, 'cause that's what I am, but so is everybody else – hopping from woman to woman, just like a dog. (2003, p. 78)

The street corner resounds with bravado, it is a place of comfort, of reassurance – of comradeship, *but* it is also a place of self-deception. Here Liebow's ethnography takes a critical twist, because he does not agree with the men he has made friends with, he does not merely reflect or transcribe their values and accounts, he radically questions their narrative. For to tackle the humiliation of the world:

> Increasingly he turns to the streetcorner where a shadow system of values constructed out of public fictions serves to accommodate just such men as he, permitting them to be men once again provided they do not look too closely at one another's credentials . . .
>
> From this perspective, the streetcorner man does not appear as a carrier of an independent cultural tradition. His behavior appears not so much a way of realizing the distinctive goals and values of his own subculture . . . but rather as his way to achieve the goals and values of the larger society, of failing to do this and of concealing his failure from himself as best he can.
>
> If, in the course of concealing his failure, or of concealing his fear of even trying, he pretends – through the device of public fictions – that he did not want those things in the first place and claims that he has all along been responding to a different set of rules and prizes, we do not do him or ourselves any good by accepting this claim at face value. (2003, pp. 138, 144–5)

Let us first make note of Liebow's analytical strategy. It is to argue that the men congregated in the street at Tally's Corner are not carriers of deviant values, rather they have precisely the same values as us, but act differently because of the limited and mediocre job opportunities open to them. Further their activities, although erratic and feckless, are, in fact, perfectly understandable. For, once their circumstances are understood, their behaviour is rendered rational. It is thus neither a product of a deviant culture or of individual pathology: both in values and in their instrumental rationality *these men are like us*: it is their poor material circumstances that make them act differently. It is easy to see why such an analysis appeals to a liberal audience: it reverses the culture of poverty thesis and it quite emphatically does *not* blame the victim (see, for example, Massing, 1995). But there are considerable grounds for suspicion as to its veracity, or at the very least, the weight of emphasis of its narrative. Let me now introduce a few criticisms:

The Evidence of Othering

The evidence of othering in *Tally's Corner* comes somewhat paradoxically from the *exaggerating of differences and the ignoring of similarities*. First of all, Liebow confuses the nature of difference in late modern society. This causes Liebow to exaggerate the difference between the streetcorner men and the middle-class, white, world to which he belongs. But, as I have argued in *The Vertigo of Late Modernity* (2007), there is considerable overlap in values; there is a convergence between the centre and the margins and between the margins and the centre. Secondly, he suggests in a classic liberal othering that they are just like us only less so. In a strange way, he exaggerates their similarity. Thirdly, he posits them existing in a vacuum outside of conventional society – the class relationships between street corner and the ethnographer between 'their' world and 'ours' is obviated. So from the first glance the binary logic of the research presents itself: the author speaks for *us*, he tells us about *them*. We are monogamous, they are serial marital failures, we are in steady employment, they are mostly out of it, we are moderate, they drink heavily/take drugs, we plan, they are impulsive, we have clarity of purpose, they deceive themselves. All of this is manifestly exaggerated. It does not for a moment grasp the convergence of values in late modernity and the key shifts in value orientation.

Let us start with the notion of rationality. The conventional world is implicitly conceived of as a haven of rational calculations, people who would step out of the sociology of James Coleman (1990) or the criminology of Marcus Felson (2002). I do not believe either 'normal' or 'deviant' behaviour to be constructed like some financial guidance plan. People fall in love and marry, they do not usually calculate income maximization. They become attached to localities, they do not move at whim. People laugh, cry, thrill, are bored, angry, disconsolate – they are moved by passions, they are more or less rational in the context of their passions. And, as Marshall Sahlin points out in his magisterial *Culture and Practical Reason* (1976): our most basic as well as our most intimate desires are social constructs – they are not fixed, pre-givens in which a logic akin to profit maximization can be applied. Rationality, of course, exists, but both in terms of goals and means it is always socially situated and normatively constructed (see Mouzelis, 1995). The neo-liberal language of rational calculation and interest maximization is the language of the urban planner, the financial advisor, the accountant and the corporate lawyer. It is the overt world of bourgeois society – it is not the ever-present underworld, the Soft City of Raban, the experiential city of de Certeau, the second life of Bakhtin.

But let us look at the specifics of behaviour: the characterization of the conventional world as involving deferred gratification, steady employment, monogamous marriage. None of these attributes are, in fact, characteristic of the modern world. It was incorrect when Liebow wrote in 1967, but of course it is even more untrue today. For the values of immediacy, short-term hedonism and expressivity once allocated to the ghettos of the underclass have now moved centre stage. Nor could we say that regularity of employment is characteristic of a late modern society, whether in the suburbs, in the industrial belt, or indeed in the ghettos. And as for serial monogamy being a special cultural attribute of 'lower-class Negro' culture, as Liebow would have it – this increasingly looks like a middle-class norm, not to mention a core theme of the lives of celebrities.

Nor is this to suggest that there is no difference between the poor and those better off. For, as I have argued, differences in the late modern world are narrower; indeed what we mean as difference is often confused. Outside of extraordinary groups such as the Amish, Hassidic Jews, born-again Islamists, difference is a much more nuanced affair – a fact that many multiculturalists frequently confuse (see Young, 1999). Even the very indigenous groups which set up the most oppositional of cultures and do so as a reaction to the decadence of Western culture, use Western values as a springboard and inadvertently retain and incorporate many of the values of the West.

In late modernity the massive forces of the mass media, education, consumerism, have made it extremely difficult for isolated subcultures to survive except with extremely rigorous measures of separation. These cultures, such as the Amish or the Hassidic Jews, are few and far between; for in general, within a nation, different groups are engulfed by the wider culture. The case of the Philadelphia ghetto documented by Carl Nightingale, (1993) is a case in point, as is Philippe Bourgois'

(1995) description of second-generation Puerto Rican immigrants in East Harlem. But to say that their cultures are penetrated, immersed, engulfed by the wider society and act out its major tropes is not to assume that they are identical – it is not to posit a blancmange of identity merely distinguished by cuisine or superficial lifestyle. On the contrary, the trajectories of national background or localism have great purchase and are of great importance, and the accommodations, the adaptations, the resistances and the responses to such a marginalization of reward and identity are profound and of great significance. Diversity does not end with globalization, it is generated by it albeit in a different form to the initial diversity of comparatively separate cultural groups.

Thus, when we turn to the men of Tally's Corner, one would object to the extent to which Liebow assumes similarity – in that he argues that their responses to their immiserized conditions, which would seem irrational, are, in fact, a simple rational reaction to their predicament. He vividly describes their humiliation, and quite correctly roots this in their perceptions of failure by the standards of the conventional world. But, their rejection of work, for example, seems to be too half-hearted, it becomes a rationalistic rather cool calculation that the work is not worth it. There is no notion of 'shit work', of any rebellion or defiance against humiliation. There is no *intensity* in this process. It reads like a liberal apologizing for the lifestyle of the poor.

Strangely, when we turn to the final chapter of his book, we no longer have African-Americans as people paralysed with self-deception but rather insistent on political change. For the book was written in the shadow of the Watts uprising where such deception was dispelled. And, even stranger, when we look at Liebow's Field Notes in the appendix of the book, no longer do we have a rather apathetic, joyless bunch but the emphasis is on fun and creativity . . .

Being Poor and Having Fun

Those who have wished to emphasize the sober constitutional ancestry of the working-class movement have sometimes minimized its more robust and rowdy features. All that we can do is to bear the warning in mind. We need more studies of the social attitudes of criminals, of soldiers, and sailors, of tavern life; and we should look at the evidence, not with a moralizing eye ('Christ's poor were not always pretty'), but with an eye for Brechtian values – the fatalism, the irony in the face of Establishment homilies, the tenacity of self-preservation. And we must also remember the 'underground' of the ballad-singer and the fair-ground . . . for in these ways the 'inarticulate' conserved certain loyalties – despite the inhibiting pressures of magistrates, mill-owners and Methodists. (Thompson, 1968, pp. 63–4)

Thus the eminent historian, Edward Thompson, admonishes liberal historians for their mistaken, if understandable, focus on a narrative of politics and struggle to the exclusion of all else. Earlier in this chapter I pointed to the way in which accounts of the world vary with the lens one brings to it. Sociologists and criminologists, I have suggested, are frequently preoccupied with the mundane and the miserable: in this case, despite the undoubted immizeration of the poor, much of the flavour, of the delight of life is missing from Liebow's account. Or at least this is true until one comes to the appendix and reads these two delightful observations in his field notes at the end of the book:

> Robert read the book slowly and with feeling, pausing only occasionally to take a swig of gin and chase it quickly with some beer. Lonny listened quietly and watched with blinking eyes as Robert changed his voice for each of the characters, assuming a falsetto for Snow White. But my own interest started to wander, probably because I had already read the book and seen the movie.
>
> Suddenly Robert raised his voice and startled me back into attention. I looked at Lonny – placid, eye-blinking Lonny – and at Ronald – a handkerchief around his head and a gold earring stuck in his left ear making him look like a storybook pirate – and wondered what the hell I was doing there with these two guys, drinking gin and beer and listening to *Snow White and the Seven Dwarfs*.
>
> I thought back to the events leading up to this situation. From this perspective, everything looked normal and reasonable. I retrieved my can of beer, sat back and listened to the rest of the story. Robert gave it a damn fine reading. [Field Note, April 1962] (1968, p. 151)

It is in these fragments of field notes that a sense of good times comes through which is, in general, obviated in the text. No more is this so as in the next sequence:

> It was very hot, it was very noisy, it was very smelly, and it was all very exciting. It was impossible to remain simply an observer in a place like this, even for someone as phlegmatic as I. It was only a few minutes after Jackie Wilson started singing that I discovered that the noise wasn't nearly loud enough, the heat wasn't nearly hot enough, and the odor from more than a thousand closely packed people was not really strong enough at all. Like everyone else, I wanted more of everything. (1968, p. 165)

This is Elliott Liebow on Saturday night going to a dance at the Capitol Arena where more than one thousand people were jammed together and he was the only white male. Apologetically, he notes, he can't keep to the beat, in fact, he cannot recognize some of the instruments. Surely they are not *just* like us?

Let me place this in a contrast, read any account of youth culture in a book on cultural studies or the sociology of popular music. Say Mike Brake's *The Sociology of Youth Culture* (1980), or Simon Frith's *Sound Effects* (1983), or Dick Hebdige's *Hiding in the Light* (1988), and compare it with a standard text on juvenile delinquency. In the first selection of studies, there is the emphasis on creativity, passion, innovation, rebellion, in the second a tome on misery and determinism. But they are talking about the same people! Indeed it is working-class youth, black and white, who have been the font of popular music and cultural creativity.

Ethnography and Choice

A critical ethnography must be aware of human choice, it must not assume, like some functionalist anthropology, that human culture springs obviously from material predicament. All the best ethnography, from William Foote Whyte's *Street Corner Society* to Paul Willis' *Learning to Labour*, is concerned with choice, indeed the particular focus of these works is social mobility. Why in Whyte's research some men stayed on the corner and why others went to college, or in Willis' book some were 'lads' and others 'ear'oles'? Liebow's street corner men in comparison are caught, trapped in the amber of the corner. They are like some characters out of a Samuel Beckett play outside of history, a solitary light focuses upon the corner of the street. In critical ethnography people must be seen as capable of movement: they are there because of a trajectory, because of praxis in the world. *Even people who stay still, whose role seems to be fixed, reified, habitual, do so with effort.*

Ethnography catches people at a point in time and at that juncture there will be various choices and adaptations while in the future all may change. Once again, the assumption that socialization into a predicament or a culture will lead to a static response is one determinism too far. The ethnographic photograph can fade and change. We have seen this earlier where Ric Curtis documents the 'little brother effect' and noted the remarkable way in which such subcultural transformations undermined the edifice of positivist explanation. Katherine Newman dwells on how the same family can produce such divergent pathways in life and regales against the simplistic assumptions we have about socialization. She talks of the message about the work ethic:

These messages, whether delivered by parents or by the culture as a whole, do not always get through, of course; they influence some children and bypass others in the very same family. Family trees among the working poor display a curious pattern of working siblings and jailed ones, of men and women who have made it to maturity alongside brothers who have died young. Tiffany has worked since she was fourteen, but her older brother has been a drug dealer in and out of jail since his own teen years. She barely completed high school, but has half siblings who finished college and now work as housing cops, as well as sisters who braid hair for a living and collect AFDC on the side.

To my knowledge, we have no compelling explanations of why the same family produces such divergent pathways in life. Undoubtedly we have made simplistic assumptions about family environments over time. The family into which Jamal was born was one with a working mother who had a good job in the Post Office. That 'same' family ten years later was one headed up by a mother addicted to crack. Is that the 'same' environment? Will the changes leave their mark not only on Jamal but on his little brother, who has never known a stable, working mother firsthand? (1999, p. 210)

Such an observation is a useful corrective to those who produce ethnographies where all the actors would seem to follow the same social line, yet here again the lack of 'compelling explanations' is because sociological positivism is taken as a backdrop to the analysis, a humanistic sociology would scarcely have problems with diversity of choice.

The Universality of Deception

> . . . concealment and ego-protection are the essence of social intercourse. (Hughes, 1958, p. 43)

Let us deal now with the problem of deception. Liebow's contention is that the men at Tally's Corner deceive themselves – they magically turn their failure into a virtue chiefly by the notion of 'manly flaws'. They do this by evoking the animal nature of their masculinity – 'the dog' in them. Here, once again, one implicitly gets the impression of a binary with clarity and overt purpose on 'our' side and deception on 'theirs'. My problem is that self-deception, far from being a prerogative of a few men on Tally's Corner, is not uncommon in society at large, nor among the male of the species for that matter. Once again Liebow's tendency to grant over-rationality to 'us' tends to evoke social actors who are far too neo-liberal and rationalistic in contrast to the traditional ghetto 'deviants' who are caricatured as creatures of determinism and deception.

Let me for a moment look specifically at the idea of 'manly flaws'. I am intrigued by the concept of manly flaws, I am in no doubt that such an excuse exists on Tally's Corner, but surely it is simple exoticism to believe that it only exists among poor men congregating on street corners. Middle-class friends emerging from a terrain of broken marriages, relationships and vows – will happily/unhappily evoke the world of temptation and opportunity which is concomitant with social successes. Indeed social and sexual success would seem to be seen as going hand in hand, although, of course, there is little reference to dog-like natures. Yet the only contact with street corners that my male friends have is en route to buy the *Guardian* or *The New York Times*. Indeed, the interesting thing is that whereas manly flaws are seen as an explanation of failure by the men at Tally's Corner, they are also seen as an indication of success higher up the structure.

Katherine Newman, in *Falling From Grace* (1999), which focuses on the neglected phenomenon of downward mobility, points to the way in which there is a peculiar vacuum in public discourse about this subject. It does not, of course, fit the imperatives of the American Dream and when it occurs the 'fall from grace' among members of the hitherto successful middle class is difficult for them to comprehend. Personal blame is, possible, but there is, she notes, an upper-middle-class version of 'manly flaws'. For some downwardly mobile executives, instead of blaming the capitalist market economy for their downsizing interpret their failure as an indicator of their manliness:

> Some downwardly mobile executives developed a managerial theory of manly flaws. They believe they were too aggressive, too rational, too smart, too experienced, or too committed to principle. These personal qualities threatened their superiors, gave momentum to their enemies, and led to their dismissals. Aggressiveness, rationality, and principled commitment (as opposed to political expediency) are praiseworthy attributes in American business. Executives are supposed to be tough and forthright; they are not supposed to bend with the wind. Hence to be fired for being too forthright is, according to the theory of manly flaws, a backhanded compliment. These unemployed managers frequently contrast themselves with those who managed to hold on to their jobs through political conniving and sycophantic behavior. They scorn the yes men and deride ex-colleagues who refused to make unpopular decisions.
>
> The weak may retain their jobs, but at the cost of their integrity and self-respect, a price some displaced managers claim was too high for them to pay. (1999, p. 72)

But this criticism is pretty minor stuff. Let us look at society as a whole and the role of self-deception within it. As I have argued throughout this book, late modern societies are characterized by exceptional levels of contradiction between the ideals of meritocracy and expressive identity and the actual opportunities available to most people. The inheritance of wealth and property, the limited access to decent education, whether at primary school level or at university, the actual very limited social mobility in the race road of life all daily present us with evidence which violate the dream. This is particularly true in the United States, where the dream is a central legitimation and where the very ambivalence of the word Dream – is it an ideal, is it just a dream? – has particular resonance. One solution is a realism – a feeling that nothing will ever change and you might as well restrict yourself to the small part of the race track which has been allocated to you and soldier on in a world which will never change. But very common is a false consciousness – a belief that the possibility of means is always there, you wait your chance or, of course, self-blame: limited wealth is your own fault, a product of your own lack of ability or effort. We all live in a world of illusion – not least is the pretence that class is not a potent factor in all our lives.

Liberal Othering: The Most Rational of all Possible Worlds

Let me sum up my assessment of the meta-narrative of Tally's Corner. Liberal othering is immensely seductive and has an easily deceptive power. Our world is taken for granted as obvious; its superiority is tempered by our sense of largesse, for we offer an analysis and suggest policies which would provide for the betterment of our objects of study. They could become just like us. In doing so we assume that if they were better off morally and materially, they would produce exactly the same cultural solutions as we have. Thus middle-class culture, as it is at present, is the embodiment of reason; that whoever had our material blessings would inevitably come to our moral conclusions. Note the implication that we have little to learn from the subcultures we study, in terms of values and lifestyles, for example, having fun, taking it easy, the place of children, of old people, attitudes to status and to consumption, the ordering of life's priorities. In *The Vertigo of Late Modernity* I outlined how precisely such an othering occurs in the social exclusion literature. For example, I analysed the negative assessment (indeed pathologization) of teenage pregnancy. Here the implicit narrative seems to say that if only these working-class girls had our material advantages, they would *automatically* and *logically* embrace dual career families and postpone their childbearing to later in their life. The norms of middle-class women *at this moment in time* have become accepted as normal and *ipso facto* rational.

That they were evolved in order to deal with the problems of the the dual earning family, the promotion dangers for professional women of leaving their job for a time early in their career and that they carry with them inevitable biological drawbacks is somehow ignored. That the decision is only a fairly recent one for middle-class women, that it is a subject of doubt and uncertainty and that it might change in the future, particularly if employers are forced to recognize the demands for flexible employment, is swept under the banner of obvious rationality. Suffice it to say the two strands of rationality: means and ends, are not abstractions but are normatively constituted. That is, what are desirable ends and what are desirable means (exciting or pleasurable, challenging or comfortable, old or new, etc.) – what is desirably effective – is a matter of human choice and construction. The notion of an instrumental rationality pursuing the social equivalent of profit maximization is only one of many models, just as it is in reality the most mundane and surely the most miserable. There is much I feel we could learn from the denizens of Tally's Corner, whether it is in terms of avoiding work, learning to sit back and look at the world, pursuing the pleasures of everyday life or engaging in the virtues of a good drink and pleasing music. But to do this would involve what Marcus and Fischer call defamiliarization (of which more shortly), of returning to our own social world and learning from our subjects.

I have talked of the universality of deception, but let us examine also the liberative quality of dreams – not the dreams propagated by the central institutions of the system, but the subcultures which people evolve to give identity, expressiveness, and warmth to their lives. First of all let us note what a difference a lens makes.

Three Perspectives on the Poor

Let us examine at this juncture another ethnographer whose work in the East End of London was almost contemporaneous with that of Elliott Liebow, although his politics were somewhat further to the left. Phil Cohen, in the early 1970s, was studying a skinhead gang in London, 'the Collinwood', and in the process created one of the most imaginative theorizations of social change which was to greatly influence the subcultural and ethnographic work of the Centre for Contemporary Cultural Studies at the University of Birmingham. Cohen, writing years later, very candidly reflects on his preconceptions at that time:

That first position of childish omniscience, from which I had looked down upon a culture about which I knew nothing, mirrored all too accurately the standpoint of an uncritical ethnography, which projects onto the tabula rasa of some 'unknown continent' the figures of its own inner phantasms of The Other Scene. From slum novel to community studies, from urban sociology to subculturalism, working-class life has been portrayed as an exotic underworld, holding out the promise or the threat of overturning 'bourgeois domestic order'. This literature both creates and draws upon a vicarious concern about how life is lived on the 'other side of the tracks'. It is a voyeurism which cares about its objects only because they have first been rendered fascinatingly different by some kind of 'inside story' and then been humanized by the application of a superior reason which demonstrates that 'underneath' they are 'just like us'. From such a vantage point there is much that is shocking but few surprises, since what is discovered is always already what is suspected to be the case. Looking back it seems as if my early work was pitched in and against the twin impositions of the 'view from below' and the 'view from above'; even as it oscillates uneasily between the two, it is struggling, and usually failing, to find a third position from which to address what is bracketed out by both: the lived interiorities of gender, class and 'race'. (1997, pp. 9–10).

The poor are like a canvas and the other projected upon them varies with the preconceptions of the researcher. For socialists, such as Cohen, the subculture holds promise of revolt, it is the cockpit of resistance; for liberals, it is a site of misery and worklessness; for conservatives it is the eyesore of fecklessness and indiscipline. One lens sees the romantic and the exotic, one the miserable who need to be rescued, one the feckless who need to be coaxed and corralled into work. In fact, it is not that such subcultures do not harbour resistance, that they are often places of misery, or that their denizens are sometimes feckless. All of these things; but meta-narratives, in the process of othering, tend to plump for one lens rather than another, and the consistency and appeal of a story well told overrides reality. I am not suggesting here a relativism – you see what you see simply as a function of the lens – nor even an empiricism, although certainly these features of resistance, determined misery and fecklessness are more or less present in different subcultures of poverty. Rather, of course, that this is a matter of theoretical perspective, it is a question of fundamentals: for what you see is a function of one's conception of human nature and social order. David Brotherton and Luis Barrios, in their book on gangs, *The Almighty Latin King and Queen Nation* (2004), have considerably widened our perspectives on critical ethnography. In this they contrast the conventional criminological approaches to the gang which stresses the pathological, the reactive, the creature of disorganization and anomie, to that which views it as resistant, evocative, quasi-political, a nascent social movement. Of course, their study focuses upon the Latin Kings, a group which has developed considerably as a social movement over the last fifteen years. But the point is this: if you start from the theoretical perspective of a creative notion of human nature and an unequal and denigrating social order, you will be not surprised to find elements of resistance *everywhere* within subordinate groups. This was the message that the Birmingham School forged in their transformation of subcultural theory as conveyed in the title of their famous book on youth culture: *Resistance Through Rituals* (Hall and Jefferson, 1975). Skinhead gangs, mods, teddy boys – all these subcultural formations in their aesthetics, their style, and in their social trajectory, all evidence resistance. This is the core message also of the study of prisons and total institutions from Gresham Sykes (1958) through to Erving Goffman (1968) and Cohen and Taylor (1972), that even in the most dire circumstances people form cultures which seek to protect their identity, their human dignity, and help manage the material predicament that they face.

So, if we return to the three perspectives on the poor – resistance, misery and fecklessness – we can *and must* bring them together. The resistance is to the determinacy and misery of their material existence and – often forgotten – the denigration and humiliation of their social position. It is sometimes overt, frequently stylized and symbolic; the feck-lessness can involve brutality and exploitation of each other, but is mixed up and elided with cultures of fun, warmth, comradeship – cultures which undermine, intrigue and fascinate the more sober moral regimens of the middle classes. Brotherton and Barrios cite the pioneering work of Dwight Conquergood:

> The homeboys are keenly aware of class differences in communication style, and are critical of what they take to be the tepid, distant inter-personal mode of the middle class. . . . Against a dominant world that displaces, stifles, and erases identity, the homeboys create, through their communication practices, a hood: a subterranean space of life-sustaining warmth, intimacy and protection. (1993, p. 47)

Subcultures as Magic

So, just a little after the time that Liebow was writing *Tally's Corner*, at the other side of the Atlantic the subcultural tradition of United States sociology was being transformed. The rather wooden actors of American theory became people of style, aesthetics and panache, the emphasis moved from the frustrations of work to the excitement of leisure, the narrow instrumental rationality of monetary reward received or thwarted became augmented with the problems of boredom, tedium to be overcome. Music, dress, sexuality, expression – it became more an emphasis on the hum rather than the humdrum.

Phil Cohen, in his influential 1972 essay 'Subcultural Conflict and Working-Class Community', explores the reasons for the emergence of the spectacular youth cultures of Britain at the time, in particular the skinheads and the mods. He starts from the rapid changes occurring in the East End of London in the 1960s. The forces of post-war development, rehousing, gentrification, coupled with the drastic reconstruction of the local economy – the death of small craft industries and their replacement by larger concerns often outside of the locality. Thus:

> There was a gradual polarization in the structure of the labour force: on the one side, the highly specialized, skilled and well-paid jobs associated with the new technology and the high-growth sectors that employed them; on the other, the routine, dead-end, low-paid and unskilled jobs associated with the labour-intensive sectors, especially the service industries. As might be expected, it was the young men, just out of school, who got the worst of the deal. Lacking openings in their fathers' trades, and lacking the qualifications for the new industries, they were relegated to jobs as van boys, office boys, packers, warehousemen and so on, and to long spells out of work. More and more people, young and old, had to travel out of the community to their jobs, and some eventually moved out to live elsewhere, where suitable work was to be found. The local economy as a whole contracted, became less diverse. Girls, on the whole, negotiated the transition to the new serviced-based economy more easily. They travelled 'up west' to work in shops and offices much more easily than their brothers, who were afraid to leave the protection of their local 'manors'. (1997, pp. 53–4)

The effects on the traditional working-class extended family and the community were considerable. The high-rise blocks dispersed the families into nuclear units, the decline of the craft trades and apprenticeships often located within the family broke down local employment and structures of respect, the changes in the economy began to polarize the community into the upwardly mobile and the downwardly mobile. Cohen's analysis suggests that the response among youth was an attempt to compensate for these changes; in a famous phrase he suggests that subcultures create 'a magical solution' to the problems of community decay, of the loss of traditional jobs and the props of masculinity, even of inequality and the predicament of the working class.

It is difficult to know what to make of this magic: is it a cultural gain, this strange masculinity of shaved heads and Doc Marten's boots? Indeed, for both Cohen and Liebow, their magic does not go far enough. It is a magic underlain with illusion, the men on Tally's Corner fool themselves about their own failure, the skinheads of the Collingwood gang create an imaginary solution to the loss of working-class community and tradi-tional masculine roles – they are not fighting for a real transformation, they are lost to the politics of progress. For Cohen there is a romanticism clouded with a sense that all we have is a sort of cultural substitution for the real thing, for Liebow a sympathetic commiseration for group failure.

We all make magic; culture itself, as Bauman points out in *Wasted Lives* (2004), is the supreme magic, it's what gets us through the night, it endows us with a sense of eternity, blinkers the notion of death, it is the balm that calms our existential terrors. Subcultures can magically transform things: they can turn stigma into pride, humiliation into resist-ance, adversity into success, the street corner becomes a warm place of comradeship, the language glows with innovation and versatility. Recall Dwight Conquergood's evocation of the homeboys' street gang, and contrast it with the liberal pictures of immiserization or the conserva-tives' attempts at denigration. For Conquergood the homeboys create identity in a situation where their ontology is threatened and heavily stig-matized, they create warmth of relationship and comradeship in a world which is divisive and atomized. But sometimes this magic goes wrong: it creates cultural solutions which entrap or fail, or it involves a bad faith, a sense of social falsehood which impoverishes the self as it threatens others. Thus, hippies believed they were in a world beyond scarcity until they looked down and found themselves like Mickey Mouse characters over the cliff without anywhere to go but fall; Paul Willis, in *Learning to Labour* (1997), famously describes how the culture of resistance of the lads traps them finally in working-class jobs, and Philippe Bourgois (1995) graphically depicts how the search for respect in East Harlem results in a culture which is isolated and disrespected.

Magic can be evasion, magic can be delusion but magic can also be liberation and sometimes it can embody the deepest forces of reaction. As for liberation sometimes this can evolve an explicitly political agenda other times one which is embedded in symbolism and aesthetic signs of revolt. But it would be wrong to see rebellion as necessitating some forward looking political goal. Such a position characterized by some of the work of the Centre for Contemporary Cultural Studies and many socialist historians is insightful in its analysis yet limited in its notion of resistance. Let us look for a moment at the work of Michel Maffesoli.

Power, Puissance, Resistance

Michel Maffesoli, in *The Time of the Tribes* (1996) makes the key distinction between the two French words for power: *pouvoir and puis-sance*. *Pouvoir* is power in the conventional sense, power from above, the institutions and paraphernalia of power. *Puissance* has no direct translation in English; in French it carries the notion of the vital force of the people, their inherent energy and dynamism. As Maffesoli uses it, it conveys a sense of irony, of laughter, perhaps of taking the piss, a resistance not in the sense of seizing power in an institutional fashion, it is not the power as in the Anglo-Saxon 'power *to* the people', but rather it is the power *of* the people, often expressed in dissociation, in acting cool, in indicating that you may be in their world but you are not of their world (see Pountain and Robins, 2000). It is a bracketing off from the official world and a concentration on the moment, the here and now.

It is *puissance* which maintains the sense of group and of solidarity, of endurance and survival. It is, Maffesoli maintains, a deeply held source of sociability, which to the social scientist is only too frequently a mystery. Thus Maffesoli writes:

> "Noi siamo la splendida realtà. This slightly clumsy phrase was discovered in a lost corner of southern Italy, and without any claim to pretence, it sums up what sociality is all about. It contains in miniature all of sociality's various elements: the relativism of life, the grandeur and tragedy of the everyday, the burden of the world around us which we bear as best we can; all of which are expressed in that 'we' which forms the glue holding everything together. We have dwelled so often on the dehumanization and the disenchantment with the modern world and the solitude it induces that we are no longer capable of seeing the networks of solidarity that exist within. (1996, p. 72)

Agreeing with this one commentator remarks: 'Perhaps contemporary theorists are more alienated from social existence than social existence is itself alienated.' (Peterson, 1997, p. 324). Thus the attractiveness of the notions of the isolated individual in contemporary capitalism, the family as being the last 'haven in a heartless world', the death of community and the rise of the rampant individualism is entailed.

It is important to stress that Maffesoli clearly recognizes the intensity of everyday life, the energy that is entailed holding things in stasis, coupled, at times, with the pleasure and at others the extreme boredom of the moment. He writes: 'I would like to insist on this point: there is a poetics of banality, a poetics harbouring a high degree of intensity. I would tend to view it as a wellspring of societal energy, a water table (so to speak) hidden from view but crucially important to collective survival' (2004, pp. 206–7).

Maffesoli characterizes this sociology of the present as Dionysian in its character over against the Promethean nature of modernist conceptions of politics, society and, indeed, subcultures. That is the warmth of collectivity, its here and nowness, rather than its *projective* qualities, 'where everyday life is lived for its own sake and not a function of any sort of finality' (1996, p. 32). Such an epicureanism of everyday life focuses on not where we are going nor where we have been but on what has been called 'the laboratory of the present'.

It is in this light that one must view the emergence of clubcultures (see Thornton, 1995), of raves held illegitimately in deserted warehouses or in clandestine country locations, of the myriad club venues from New York City to Ibiza. All of the youth cultural forms viewed so sceptically by an earlier generation of subcultural theorists as lacking political edge and direction but which are, in fact, part of a youthful colonization of the present, a temporary abolition of the mundane.

Magic as Reaction

Magic can be reactionary: the magic of blood, of the holy book, of tradition, of imaginary boundaries and made-up countries. Othering is itself a form of magic. The actors make up for themselves an inviolable essence, that exists between, after and beyond the individual; they bolster their magic with the evocation of the other – a contrast which serves to substantiate the ontological certainty of the self. The fixated masculinity of the skinhead, the rigid certainties of fundamentalism, the writing and rewriting of histories of irremediable evil pitched against unquestioned virtue, the conjoining of the forces of war both in the real world and in virtual realities, all smack of this. The aim of a critical ethnography is to break such casts and to demystify such rigidities. This task is made all the more difficult, as I have argued, because such processes of othering are a frequent part of the academic itinerary. But our job is to dispel the nightmares of essentialism; it is not to deny the dream.

Discovery and Self-Discovery

Marcus and Fischer are famous for their concept of *defamiliarization*. The task of a critical anthropology, they argue, is not merely that the researcher depicts the world of other cultures but that the anthropologist returns to their own cultures equipped to question their own taken-for-granted reality. That is, field research enables one to deconstruct one's own world, to become aware of how what one takes for granted to be solid, uncontested, things are in fact social constructions rooted in time and place. You will recall Berger and Luckmann's parallel notions in the sociology of knowledge, our social world presents itself as reification, a reassurance, other realities – whether different civilizations, subcultures, or even dreams – present themselves as *threats* to our secure symbolic universe. Furthermore, as we saw earlier, in an intensely pluralistic, and media-saturated late modernity such threats reach a new pitch of potential instabilities. Berger and Luckmann present two modes of 'universe maintenance': 'nihilation' and 'therapy'. In nihilation we turn alternative norms either into non-norms (or lack of norms), or we attempt to destroy rival symbolic universes. Of course, this is precisely the insight behind the notion of Othering. In therapy we attempt to persuade the denizens of other normative systems that their thoughts and feelings, are misconstrued, uneducated and irrational and that our own symbolic universe is the sole repository of reason, of common sense and naturalness. (See Thomas Scheff's 1968 article on 'Negotiating Reality'.)

Defamiliarization does not countenance this – it is the very opposite of othering. It is to learn from encounters with other societies or subcultures that one's notion of rationality, of desirable means and inevitable ends, are social constructs. It is not defining the certainty of oneself by the shortcomings of others, but precisely the uncovering of one's own uncertainties. It is not the recipe for relativism, merely the medicine to cure absolutism: a humanistic awareness that moral choices and mores are human constructs, not things of absolute truth and certainty. So, if you go out to do research, expect changes in your attitudes, your beliefs, yourself, and if you do not experience change, you are not engaging in critical research. Contrast this with conventional social scientific research. Here the job is to relay back the information with as little normative 'interference' as possible – you mustn't change (the very notion of objectivity demands a steadfast unchanging observer) and beware of changing the subject (for that would contaminate the research). Thus, as Marcus and Fischer point out, Margaret Mead was a paragon of defamiliarization. She changed and her views helped to change Western views on sexuality, childrearing and adolescence. Contrast this to the majority of modern urban ethnographies where the researcher dips into an exotic world, then dips out again producing a coffee table ethnography where the subcultures of our society are presented like pages from the *National Geographic* magazine.

But just as research should change the researcher, genuine research should inform and change the researched. This may be full on as when Luis Barrios offered his church in East Harlem to the Latin Kings as a meeting place and David Brotherton acted as their biographer and mentor. Or it may be less direct but influential for instance where domestic violence research shows that such assault is endemic in our society and the dissemination of findings allows victims to recategorize themselves as scarcely abnormal. To believe that it is possible to conduct any form of research which actually makes contact with people without having some effect on them is an error of the first order and a constant illusion of positivism. Even the most desultory interview, say the NORC study of the the unemployed in Chicago, which I described in chapter 4, underscores their humiliation and exclusion, while the very basis of participant observation is the interaction and change which is part of any human exchange. The point, as Pierre Bourdieu points out, is not to deny such change but to reflexively understand how and why this change is occurring. Thus he writes:

> If its objective of pure knowledge distinguishes the research relationship from most of the exchanges in everyday life, it remains, whatever one does, a *social relationship*. As such, it can have an effect on the results obtained
> . . .
> The positivist dream of an epistemological state of perfect innocence papers over the fact that the crucial difference is not between a science that effects a construction and one that does not, but between a science that does this without knowing it and one that, being aware of work of construction, strives to discover and master as completely as possible the nature of its inevitable acts of construction and the equally inevitable effects those acts produce. (1999, p. 608)

Transformative Research and Dangerous Knowledge

Nancy Fraser (1997) makes a pivotal distinction between affirmative and transformative social policies. Affirmative policies, however liberal or ameliorative, merely affirm the existing divisions within society, transformative policies break down division whether it is in terms of the class distribution of income or the rigidity of cultural differences (see the discussion in Young, 2007). I would like to end this chapter by suggesting a similar dichotomy between methods of social investigation. Affirmative research reaffirms the hiatus between the observer and the observed, makes a pretence of social distance and couches its descriptions in the language of othering. Transformative research traces the concealed links between observer and observed, makes visible the invisible, seeks to break down the barriers between the social scientist and their objects of study, its success is to defamiliarize the investigator and to facilitate change in the investigated. It seeks in short what David Sibley (1995) calls 'dangerous knowledge'. So should we.

9

Dangerous Knowledge and the Politics of The
Imagination

Imagination is one thing, criminology is another.

(Klockars, 1980, p. 93)

Now is the time to ascertain the limits of this imagination, to summarize the contentions of this book, recapitulate its main arguments and pull the threads together.

If the sociological imagination involves placing the individual in the context of structure and history, of creating a biographical timeline of narrative in a world of possibility and circumstance, imagination itself is not a detached characteristic of a fortunate individual. For the vicissitudes of history create periods when imagination runs fast forward and times when everything appears static and solid. And particular strata of individuals are caught up in the maelstrom while others are cocooned and protected from ambiguity and disturbance. One particular reaction to change, as I have described in *The Vertigo of Late Modernity*, is to withdraw into certainties to demand solid bearings in the vertiginous currents of the modern world. The academy itself is prone to such a temptation of retreat, of ivory towers and the contemplative life: the ivy clad quadrangles and the isolated country campuses. Sometimes the very intake of academics recruited into a discipline may shape the subject at times giving it a sensitivity to the marginal and the offbeat and others to the staid and the conformist. Indeed C. Wright Mills in an early, celebrated article published in 1943, talks of the 'the professional ideology of social pathologists' referring to the small town background of American sociologists entering the field of social problems at that time and how this shaped their perceptions of the world around them. Thus society was viewed as an organism, values as a consensus and deviance as a pathology. In contrast the perspectives on society of those who live in the great multicultural cities of late modernity bear the imprint of a far different world. These are cities made up, as Zygmunt Bauman reminds us, of diasporas, where a larger and larger proportion of the population are born in other countries, cities where there is a majority of minorities, cities of hyperpluralism with a magical cubism of perspectives, where everyone is simultaneously normal, deviant or incomprehensible from one vantage point or another. And, of course, sociology has greatly benefited from those individuals who are cosmopolitan in their outlook – very often those who are Jewish or ethnic minority or socially mobile in their origins; carrying with them a double or triple vision, they are social travellers, perpetual strangers, in Simmel's sense, caught between cultures, unable ever to see the world as natural and unambiguous.

It is a central paradox of this book that positivism has developed in precisely a world which is most inimical to its development. We live in a world of extreme pluralism which we encounter everyday in the street and on the screen. This pluralism is itself subject to constant change and the hybridism between cultures creates an incessant blurring of boundaries. Such a state of fragmentation bedevils any attempt to have the fixed agreement or constancy of definition that 'science' necessitates. Yet it is on such an ill-suited soil that positivism in the social sciences flourishes, develops and proliferates and where despite the evidence of human cultural creativity all around us, determinism is so avidly evoked. Nowhere is this more evident than in criminology and the sociology of deviance. Yet, as I have argued throughout this book, in late modern society both the causes and the effects of deviance are manifestly diverse as, of course, are the definitions of what constitutes deviance. For the vocabularies of motive available to explain, countenance and, indeed facilitate, deviance are myriad. We have a vast google of references ranging from soap operas, through to news stories, through personal contacts and observation to, excuse deviance, justify it, or indeed, deny that it is in fact deviant. We are, because of the changing exigencies of work, family and community constantly in the process of writing our personal narratives. We do not have fixed narratives that tell us definitively who we are, what is right and what is wrong and indeed what sort of a person we are, on the contrary, we are constantly open to retelling the story, reassessing our self. We are in the market place of identity and the market teems with ideas.

Proposing Dangerous Knowledge

> Many criminologists believe that crime has no universal definition. They
> see crime as subjective, whereas society and its justice system 'manufacture'
> crime by changing the definition. Their intellectual lawlessness makes a
> mess of our field by
> • Giving it no boundaries and keeping it vague
> • Requiring a different criminology for each legal system
> • Letting criminology students get an easy A, no matter what they write
> (Felson, 2002, p. 17)

Let us forget, for one moment, how easy it is to get an A in a syllabus
which is rote learnt and where imagination is shunned and the intellectual challenges which are an intrinsic part of scholarship, are described
as 'making a mess'. One can only conjecture what Mary Douglas author
of the seminal work on social categorization, *Purity and Danger* (1966)
would have made of all this talk of lawlessness, breaking boundaries,
antipathy to vagueness, over-liberal assessment, and . . . mess, all in one
short paragraph, punctuated by bullet points! But, the fact is *their* fear
is rational, for Marcus Felson – like Hans Eysenck before him – fully
recognizes that science necessitates objective, fixed, measurable, categories and that to describe crime, deviance or any other human behaviour
otherwise – however much it actually corresponds to reality – is a threat
to the scientific enterprise. Physics envy is, in short, a constant desire but
an impossible dream.

David Sibley, in his remarkable *Geographies of Exclusion*, talks not
only of spatial and social exclusion – the exclusion of dangerous classes
– but the exclusion of dangerous knowledge. He writes:

> The defence of social space has its counterpart in the defence of regions
> of knowledge. This means that what constitutes knowledge, that is those
> ideas which gain currency through books and periodicals, is conditioned
> by power relations which determine the boundaries of 'knowledge' and
> exclude dangerous or threatening ideas and authors. It follows that any
> prescriptions for a better integrated and more egalitarian society must also
> include proposals for change in the way academic knowledge is produced.
> (1995, p. xvi)

Both the traditional positivism of sociology or psychology, or the new
'crime science' of Marcus Felson and the rational choice/routine activities
theorists, have exceptional interest in maintaining rigid definitions and
demarcations between science and non-science, between crime and 'normality', between the expert and the criminal, between criminology and
more humanistic academic disciplines – and even between the individuals

studied themselves as isolated atoms incapable of collective activity. It is the nature of critical criminology that it questions all these distinctions and this is, of course, an anathema to the project of criminology as a natural science of crime. As such its 'intellectual lawlessness' is, of course, a threat to such a position. Just for a moment, think of the benefits of orthodoxy: the privileged access to research funds, the size of the burgeoning criminal justice system with all its patronage and prestige, the jealous guardianship of the truth, the respect accrued from the 'scientific' presentation of data or even, dare I mention it, the personal feelings of ontological security that such a stance enhances.

Early in this book I explored the various reasons why the paradox of positivism occurred; why, if you want, social and methodological fundamentalism occurs despite such a seemingly hostile environment of pluralism, individualism and existential openness. In this I have tried to describe how the social processes in which the parallel exclusions: social exclusion and epistemological exclusion, of the rejection and marginalization of threatening social norms and of the dangerous knowledge, which Sibley points to, have a common basis. This is both ontological and material: social blindness, caution, the inordinate growth of the criminal justice system and the search for funding, insecurity, vertigo, the pursuit of certainty, of physics envy and the nomothetic impulse for objectivity and a secure base. Underlying both exclusions is the process of othering, whether it is the middle class looking across the tracks or the social scientist surveying the poor. But let me add to this a historical dimension, for the fact is that such a process of blinkering and stifling of the sociological imagination occurred most stridently within one particular Western country: the United States. This is of significance because of the paramount position American criminology (and sociology) has within the social sciences and because, in terms of the narrative of this book, it is the precise context in which C. Wright Mills wrote *The Sociological Imagination*. For it is out of this particular history that one can begin to understand both the expansion and uneven development of criminology in the United States, the bursts of extraordinary creativity punctuated by periods of stagnation and narrow-mindedness.

Crushing the Imagination

Imagination can be blinkered by social situation and by those historical times where stasis or the end of history would seem to be the order of the day, it can be becalmed by financial inducements, socialized out of you by professional training, the formation of the 'cheerful robots' so scorned by C. Wright Mills. But it can also be crushed, by threats of loss of jobs, professional ostracism and worse. The pivotal events which shaped, one might say cowed the social sciences in America, in the early post-war period were McCarthyism and the strident interventions of the FBI, which lasted from the late 1940s until the late 1950s. We all know of the persecution of Hollywood and the blacklisting of directors, actors and playwrights who were suspected of having communist sympathies. What is lesser known is the extent and impact of this upon the academy. Mike Keen in his remarkable book *Stalking Sociologists* (2004) utilizing data available since the passing of the Freedom of Information Act, 1966, sheds light upon the extraordinary level of FBI surveillance that occurred and the drastic effects as reflected in the title of the first edition of his book: *Stalking the Sociological Imagination*. Keen investigates the FBI files of prominent sociologists from staunch patriots like Samuel Stouffer to progressives such as W. E. B. Du Bois. All have extensive files as, of course, did C. Wright Mills himself, whose investigation commenced in 1943 and continued until his death. Perhaps the most surprising of these revelations is the account of the investigation of Talcott Parsons as the suspected head of a communist cell at Harvard. Such accusations continued for two years and involved lengthy interrogations as to his loyalty to the United States. At times they took on a surreal quality when it was reported that Parsons' son, at that time still at high school, had got up at a party at his home and recited the Communist Manifesto by heart! It is difficult to imagine this disciple of conservatism, whose major political activity was recruiting ex-Nazis to collaborate as experts in anti-Soviet intelligence, as being at heart a secret Soviet agent. The parallel, of course, is on the other side of the cold war where social scientists of similar patriotic disposition were being accused of deep-seated and clandestine disloyalty to the Party and the Soviet Union. Similarly the files reveal that Robert Merton was suspected as being in the same cell as Parsons, sent on to Columbia to foment communism there!

But it would be wrong to believe that it was only the famous and the prominent who were seriously affected by the red scare. The purge scoured deeply into the academy. In 1955 Paul Lazarsfeld and Wagner Thielens of the Bureau of Applied Social Research at Columbia University carried out a survey of just under 2,500 American social scientists on the political pressures they experienced (Lazarsfeld and Thielens, 1958). The findings are remarkable: 60 per cent said that they had been interviewed by the FBI in the last twelve months and one-third of all had been interviewed more than three times in this period. The feelings of paranoia, of canniness, of watching your back with the administration, with other faculties and students were widespread. Further given the political sensitivity of such a survey the results are, as I have discussed earlier in this book, undoubtedly underestimated. The chilling effect of McCarthyism on American intellectual life was widely felt. It had three levels: firstly governmental centring around those who were blacklisted for refusing to give names to the various investigating committee, secondly academic, the response of the colleges to the scare which controversially included forcing faculty to sign loyalty oaths as to their patriotism and freedom from communist influence, and thirdly individual. It began in the late 1940s and by the middle of the 1950s, as Ellen Schrecker put it in her harrowing *No Ivory Tower* 'no academic who refused to cooperate with an investigating committee was able to find a regular teaching position at an academically respectable American college or university' (1986, p. 266). They left academia, they seriously tempered and scaled down their scholarship, syllabuses were rewritten, faculties were careful with their contacts and lectures to students. Some went to Europe: an enormous brain drain occurred either out of the profession or out of the country. The irony was that very many of them were *ex-communists*, they had left the Communist Party of the United States because of their disillusionment with Stalinism. What was being purged was a generation of intellectuals, some Marxists, some not, who still had faith in human progress and social justice, who embraced the notion of looking at the social world on a macro-scale and demanding radical social intervention to achieve change. But the universities, from the highest Ivy League to the least prominent liberal arts college, scarcely produced any barrier or protection to this unruly violation of academic freedom. Schrecker gives the pitiful example of Leon Kamin, the psychologist who, although having left the communist party, refused to name names of his past comrades to the adminisration at Harvard and subsequently felt obliged to prove himself as an 'objective' scholar. 'He worked with rats for years until his academic reputation was secure enough for him to tackle the work that definitively refuted racist theories about the genetic basis of human intelligence' (Schrecker, 1986, p. 424). He is, of course the same Kamin who we encountered in Chapter 2 in his collaboration with Richard Lewontin and Steven Rose in their critique of Herrnstein and Murray's *The Bell Curve,* in their celebrated book *Not in Our Genes.*

It was thus not merely the most prominent and in some ways the most protected who suffered from the red scare. As Keen puts it 'Perhaps the most important story that remains untold, if not untellable, is that of the uncountable numbers of relatively unknown and anonymous sociologists, at institutions small and large across the nation, who either did not survive, or quietly censored themselves out of fear of the consequences, stunting the growth and development and blunting the critical edge of the sociological imagination' (2004, p. 207). But he goes a little further than this because he points to the intellectual consequences of keeping your head down. He suggests that one protective mechanism is to detach from any theoretical and speculative research about the total society and to engage, just like Kamin, in 'hard', 'factual' research. Thus the emergence of quantitative research, abstracted empiricism, without any political attitude becomes very attractive. He points to parallels occurring in the USSR among young Soviet sociologists in the 1950s. Indeed, as Zygmunt Bauman sarcastically notes with regard to his native Poland, such scholars ardently imported the work and methodologies of American empiricists such as Lazarsfeld and Festinger while avoiding Mills on his visit to Warsaw as if he were 'a sort of Typhoid Mary' (Bauman and Tester, 2001, p. 27). Furthermore, looking back at the early Chicago School, the decision by Park and Burgess to create a scientific sociology and to break with Jane Addams and the radical women of Hull House occurred at the time of the first American red scare from 1917 to 1920 after the revolution in Russia.

In *The Sociological Imagination* the shift to abstracted empiricism is seen as a result of the bureaucratization of the social sciences and the financial incentives of corporate and state research. I have no doubt that this is true but must also point to more directly coercive factors, certainly in the United States. It is this trauma which is *in part* the reason for the sharp differences between American and British criminology and indeed, as has been widely remarked upon, between the sociologies of the two countries. Ironically it was precisely such pressures which C. Wright Mills directly experienced both from state authorities and within the academy and which he scornfully chided his contemporaries for so easily succumbing to.

The Two Criminologies: An Imagination Lost and An Imagination Gained

There are two criminologies: one grants meaning to crime and deviance, one that takes it away; one which uses an optic which envisages the wide spectrum of human experience: the crime and law-abiding, the deviant and the supposedly normal – the whole round of human life, the other a lens that can only focus on the negative, the predatory, the supposedly pathological; one which encompasses a world of creativity and is an agent of *verstehen*, one which is fixated on the scientific and the nomo- thetic; one whose vista is emotion: it is a criminology of excitement, anxiety, panic, repression and frequently boredom, another whose actors are miserable creatures of rational choice and determinacy, either a pas- sionless foreground or a mechanistic background; one that is the voice of those below and the investigator of the powerful, the other which echoes the white noise of the criminal justice system; one which seeks to reclaim criminology for sociology, the other which sets up a 'crime science' divorced from the great modernist tradition of Marx, Weber, Durkheim and Simmel. One is the criminology of the imagination; the other frowns on such exuberance and resolutely proclaims the mundane nature of the everyday world. One carefully patrols its borders, shutting out the philosophical, the overly theoretical as too reflective, and carefully excluding war, genocide, state crime, crimes against the environment and so on, as outside its 'scientific focus', while the other views such boundaries as there are to be crossed and there are to be learnt from, and constantly expands the lens of criminology.

The first begins in the nineteenth-century investigations of Booth, Mayhew and Engels, the attempt to explore the nooks and crannies of the great cities of London and Manchester, these 'Africa's' and 'unknown continents' of the metropolis; it re-emerges in the burgeoning Chicago of the first three decades of the twentieth century; contradictory and hesitant, its ethnography far outrunning its theory, yet bustling with a nascent inventiveness, it flourished greatly in the extraordinary burst of creativity of American deviancy theory of the mid 1950s and 1960s, which was elaborated and developed in the late 1960s and 1970s with the transatlantic crossing to Britain and the work of the National Deviancy Conference and the Birmingham School; it matured immensely with the influence of second wave feminism and the intense and creative debates with the abolitionism of Northern Europe and is represented by the cultural criminology of today. The second is an orthodoxy which started with the iconic figure of Lombroso at the end of the nineteenth century, which gained speed with Enrico Ferri's positivist revolution, meandered into multi-factor theory with the work of Cyril Burt and the Gluecks in the middle of the twentieth century and is manifest in the work today of such authors as Travis Hirschi, James Q. Wilson, Richard Herrnstein, Michael Gottfredson, Marcus Felson, David Farrington and a host of others too numerous to mention. It is the dominant criminology at the moment in the United States, despite the extraordinary intellectual heritage that preceded it in the Chicago School and the revolutionary New Deviancy Theory of the 1960s. It is much less of a presence in the United Kingdom, a fact which should give pause for thought as British criminology is second only to that of the United States in its infrastructure of postgraduate and undergraduate degrees, research institutes and specialist departments. One glance at *Criminology*, the pinnacle American journal in the field and another at the *British Journal of Criminology*, might make you think that there were two different disciplines. You might even ask yourself what percentage of the British journal's articles would get published if submitted to *Criminology* and what proportion of manuscripts from the American journal would be returned if proffered to the *BJC*. Indeed at a recent conference I asked, as a thought experiment, some prominent

American and British criminologists what numbers they would put on this transaction: the unanimous answer was nil, in both directions. It would certainly give rise to doubts as to positivist claims of scientificity and the triumphant progress towards a 'normal science'. The Japanese, American and German journals of astrophysics are surely more similar: they all sing from the same scientific hymnal, they all share the same paradigm and investigate the same problems and anomalies (see, of course, Kuhn, 1970).

Divergences and Underdevelopment

Such a yawning gap between American and European Criminologies has been noticed frequently in the literature. Ellen Cohn and David Farrington in their empirical study of the differences in citations of other journals in the most prestigious journals of each country, note that the *British Journal of Criminology* had only 1.5 per cent of the citations in *Criminology* and conversely *Criminology* had only 2.2 per cent of the citations in the British journal. Further that the rate of citations of *BJC* articles in *Criminology* increased with their 'quantitativeness'. As British positivists they conclude, wistfully, that 'if British criminologists wish to influence their American counterparts they should carry out high quality quantitative research using the most sophisticated and up-to-date statistical techniques' (Cohn and Farrington, 1990, p. 481). Ineke Haen Marshall (2001), in a wide-ranging article on the difference seeks social and philosophical reasons for the gap. She notes to begin with that the gap is not obvious to American criminologists themselves, for because of the tremendous output of the American criminological enterprise and its almost autarchic nature: 'not surprisingly, for most American scholars, criminology is *American* criminology' (2001, p. 16). At root she sees the difference being centred around the longstanding philosophical tradition of American pragmatism, where 'intellectual thought embodies the primary importance of the scientific method, a practical problem focus (rather than on abstract issues) and a need for the ideas (theories) with practical implications' (2001, p. 19). In essence it is: 'policy driven, and lacking theoretical lustre, diversity, and short of a critical edge' (2002, p. 22). Thus to the political pressures we have already documented we must add the tradition of American pragmatism.

But one must also note that not only are American and British criminologies species apart but the same is true for their sociologies. As David and John Gartrell (2002) point out in their study of the differences between articles in the American and British *Journals of Sociology* there is a sharp contrast between the quantitative orientation of the first and the much more humanistic and interpretative mode of the second. In line with Mills' notion of abstracted empiricism there is in American sociology not only an over-emphasis on the quantitative but a tendency to avoid any high level theorization. Indeed, the distinguished American sociologist Stanley Aronowitz argues in his recent book on C. Wright Mills, 'With some exceptions theorizing itself has migrated to Europe, Asia and Latin America. The United States does not have its Pierre Bourdieu, Edgar Morin, Norbert Elias, Jurgen Habermas or Anthony Giddens' (2010) and to this one might add Zygmunt Bauman and Niklas Luhmann. Europe, he concedes, does have its positivists for 'American positivism and empiricism have become a global phenomenon in those societies where intellectuals wish to free themselves from the burdens associated with theories, pointing to social transformation particularly historical materialism' (2010).

Zygmunt Bauman is particularly cutting on this. In his interview with Keith Tester he comments: 'It is extremely treacherous and utterly unwise to generalize about American sociology. America is a big country and it takes little effort to find ample exceptions to every rule. And yet I must admit that in 'mainstream' American sociology as represented by the *American Journal of Sociology* for instance, I do not feel at home. Some products I find downright boring, uninspired and uninspiring; others put technical sophistication above the significance of the issue' and he cautions that 'European sociologists should not copy the style and particularly not the fads and foibles, of their transatlantic namesakes' (Bauman and Tester, 2001, pp. 28–9). He has of course many exceptions one of which is the work of Richard Sennett, who ironically, as we have seen in Chapter 2, has a very similar view with regard to mainstream American sociology as does Bauman himself.

The Problem of Uneven Development

I would be much more sanguine about the differences between American and European social science than Bauman, although the situation in criminology is patently more dire than in sociology itself. But the winds of globalization blow in two ways: there has been a growth of positivism in Europe and a parallel development of critical thinking, some homegrown, some influenced from abroad, in the United States. But the contrast certainly remains. Elliott Currie (1998) described American criminology as having three strata: a large technocratic 'mainstream', which rarely sticks its neck out in the public arena, a small extremely influential right wing, very vocal, the likes of Charles Murray, James Q. Wilson and John Dilulio, and a comparatively small radical contingent with its own organizations and journals almost ghetto-like in its relationship to the wider academy and society as a whole which has 'too often gone along with the definition of itself as a fringe, or as a kind of sub-specialization within the larger field' (1998, p. 18). In Britain, in contrast, critical work dominates the majority of academic courses, the syllabuses from secondary-school sociology onwards rehearse the radical texts, the major distance learning institution, the Open University is critical in its orientation and the editor of the *British Journal of Criminology* can reflect in a recent article that she sees it rather unnecessary to use 'evangelical' titles like critical or cultural criminology as 'the centrality of meaning, representation and power has been a taken-for-granted assumption in academic criminology since the 1960s' (Carlen, 2010). What after all is the point of talking about critical criminology if all criminology worth its name is critical? Beneath this there is, of course, a burgeoning technocratic industry of government research and evaluation studies, although much of this is discreetly subverted to carry a critical perspective and, finally, there is no right wing criminology to speak of outside of the journalists in the tabloid newspapers.

Uneven development is like an assertion or a gaze which occurs both ways. It is like the famous vase and face of the phenomenologists: from one perspective it looks like a vase which can be measured or calibrated, from the other like a human face caught at one point in time which is expressive, changing, meaningful. Positivist criminology sees America as the New World with Old Europe lagging behind, critical criminology views positivism as unrealistic and out of touch with the reality of the human situation. What positivists see as methodological sophistication, critical criminology sees as ingenuous and naive. What one side sees as a lens of scientific objectivity, the other sees as an optic which distorts and obfuscates. I will turn to examine this lens shortly but, as I have argued throughout this book, there can be little doubt that what has occurred is the latter, the sort of scientism which Mills so strongly warned against. The particular manifestation of underdevelopment in the United States can be seen as a result of a conjunction of factors. Firstly, the bedrock philosophy of pragmatism which is so central to American exceptionalism; secondly, an extraordinary concert of coercive interventions by government agencies in the near past, throughout the cold war and beyond, which has generated a chilling effect on the discussion of macro-structural transformation; thirdly, the bloated development of the criminal justice system which through funding initiatives has, at best, encouraged research on the efficacy of very low-level administrative interventions, at worst, pursued a martial narrative of wars – against crime, against gangs, against drugs, against illegal immigrants, against terrorism, and so on. Lastly, a political climate which had been neo-liberal long before the term came into common usage, where transformative politics have been largely absent from its political institutions or ascribed to the other side in the cold war and where the end of history has so often been so prematurely announced.

The Loss of Legacy

None of this is to totally berate American criminology or sociology of deviance. At its best it has produced by far the most creative and imaginative work in this area. It is difficult to imagine the subject without the Chicago School, the seminal work of Merton on anomie theory, the innovations of Edwin Sutherland on white-collar crime, the subcultural theories of Albert Cohen and Richard Cloward, the symbolic interactionist studies of Howard Becker, Kai Erikson and Aaron Cicourel, the dramaturgical genius of Erving Goffman, the radical work of the Schwendingers, Tony Platt and Paul Takagi and others too many to mention. The ethnographic work from Thrasher to Willam Whyte puts Europe to shame. All of this, as we shall see, was the flame and inspiration which set off the British contribution to the field and prepared the groundwork for a critical criminology worldwide. Even today it has produced remarkable scholarship; it is after all the birthplace of cultural criminology with the inspired work of Jeff Ferrell and Mark Hamm (1998). And it continues to produce fine scholars such as Todd Clear with his empirically grounded yet theoretically informed *Policing Communities* (2007); Jonathan Simon's *Governing Through Crime* (2007); Elliott Curries' pivotal work from *Confronting Crime* (1985) to *Crime and Punishment in America* (1998); Jack Katz's *Seductions of Crime* (1998); and, albeit in critical anthropology, Philippe Bourgois' brilliant ethnography of East Harlem, *In Search of Respect* (1995), to name just a few; although it has to be said that a considerable proportion of the contemporary critical work is by emigrés; just think of Piers Beirne, James Messerschmit, Stuart Henry, David Brotherton, David Garland and Loic Wacquant.

What concerns us is the explanation of the precipitous decline in American theory, the fall from grace which preposterously elevated theorists such as Travis Hirschi, James Q. Wilson and Marcus Felson to the top of the citation list, with their minimalist theory consisting of a mixture of the mundane and the tautological, and which is associated with the decline in the centrality of theory in general. It is, in short, an investigation of a loss of riches.

Let us now have a closer look at establishment criminology.

The Lens of Establishment Criminology

If you want to understand orthodox criminology's vision of the world, the way in which the criminological gaze is structured and distorted, it is best to think of the discipline as an optic, as a lens through which the budding scientists peer down at their objects of study. Let us look at its attributes:

(1) The Focus on the Mundane and the Miserable.

The delinquent and the criminal are seen as creatures of misery or of mundanity: they are either propelled by determining circumstance (a 'bad' background whether genetic, family or environment) or they make the most lacklustre of decisions in the face of the most obvious of opportunities. The narrative is desperately thin, the human spirit notably absent. It is as if the lens is so subtlety constructed as to take the magic out of the world, to render their life worlds arid and energyless. It is as if a slide is slipped under the microscope, previously sterilized and sanitized, so as not to disturb or distress the gaze of the onlooker. It was not always like this; the early studies on juvenile delinquency, for example, often stressed the sheer fun of transgression. For the kids in the street – now and then – the mundane can become the magical, the housing estate up the road forbidden territory, the corner shop a constant source of temptation and disturbance, the police an endless source of excitement. Thus for Thrasher, writing about the gang in 1920s Chicago, the city is for the boys 'a place of mystery and mythical wonders'. He notes:

> The gangs dwell under the shadows of the slum. Yet, dreary and repellant as their external environment must seem to the casual observer, their life is to the initiated at once vivid and fascinating. They live in a world distinctly their own – far removed from the humdrum existence of the average citizen.
>
> It is in such regions as the gang inhabits that we find much of the romance and mystery of a great city. Here are comedy and tragedy. Here is melodrama which excels the recurrent thrillers at the downtown theaters. Here are unvarnished emotions . . . The gang, in short, is *life*, often rough and untamed, yet rich in elemental social processes significant to a student of society and human life. (1963/1927, p. 3)

A whole tradition of ethnography follows this; think of Ned Polsky's *Hustlers, Beats and Others* (1967); Howard Becker's *Outsiders* (1963); Erving Goffman's *Asylums* (1968). A whole tranche of critical ethnography echoes this today from Philippe Bourgois' *In Search of Respect* (1995) to Loic Wacquant's *Body and Soul* (2004) But for establishment criminology it is as if the light was turned out in the 1970s. For in the eyes of today's social scientists, mischief has become mundanity, magic maladjustment.

(2) The Focus on the Negative

As I have mentioned before, William Foote Whyte, in the foreword to *Street Corner Society* noted how to the outsider, the inhabitants of Cornerville were viewed as simply a collection of social worker's clients or defendants in criminal cases; their kids are juvenile delinquents and their parents on relief. Yet, in real life these Italian-Americans from the North End of Boston play baseball and cards, they have a rich social life, eat good food; they are joyful of life and loyal to each other. There is a rich leisure culture of bonhomie and support as well as a modicum of delinquency and political skullduggery. The study was set in the 1940s where there were no shortage of public and media concerns about the Mob and about the political sympathies of Italian-Americans yet Whyte does not fall into the trap of importing into his study the one-dimensional media narratives of prejudice. Instead he presents both corner boys and college boys in the round.

This is entirely the opposite of how orthodox criminology approaches the world. It as if they view human reality through a slide stained to block out the majority of life and to bring out only the vicious and the predatory. The act of transgression, the moment of offence, the most negative of all the actions and beliefs of an individual or a group become pivotal in the definition of their very essence or nature (see Lea, 2002). Nowhere is this more evident than in the gang literature. Thrasher's classic study of gangs has no explicit reference to delinquency, but present-day gang 'experts' have made it central. Thus, Malcolm Klein's (1971) widely used work explicitly includes delinquency as part of the definition. There is, of course, more than a hint of tautology here: for the gang is evoked to *explain* delinquency, at the same time as the gang is defined *by* delinquency. So presumably any social grouping of young people that is non-delinquent cannot be a gang! (See Brotherton, 2008.) Furthermore as Jack Katz and Curtis Jackson-Jacobs, in their wonderful essay 'The Criminologists' Gang' (2004) point out, what has to be proved if the concept 'the gang' has any causal validity, is that gang members have a higher level of criminal violence than a sample of non-gang youth from the same place and the same time. They point to the glaring flaws in data collection: the common use of police records and assessments and self-report studies based largely on adolescent school student populations, the shakiness of which we have already fully documented, as well as numerous alternative hypotheses as to the relationship between gangs and crime, most of which have never been considered (e.g. gangs may reduce everyday violence by providing a 'protective habitat'; gangs shape the form not the incidence of violence).

It is as if the conclusion that the gang is the cause and focus of juvenile violence is already decided and the discussion is all over. As a result of this the study of gangs occurs largely outside the study of youth culture in complete contrast to the legacy of Thrasher who saw gangs as a recurrent part of youth culture with movements in and out of violence eminently possible.

It is an illustration of the peculiar perspective of orthodox criminology if we compare the depictions of poor and marginalized youths held by different traditions in sociology. As we have seen, exactly the same young people who are viewed by the sociologists of youth and of popular culture as the font of creativity are seen by the criminologist as the locus of determinism and negativity. This perspective has built into it policy conclusions which tend towards the restrictive and the repressive. Let me give an example of this. A colleague of mine from a university in the west of Britain – let's call it Torchwood for reasons of confidentiality – became concerned that his students were spending too much time clubbing and too little time on criminological research. He therefore set his students the task of doing ethnographies of the local club scene: a seemingly adroit combination of business and pleasure. A week later one young woman came back and said that apart from having something of a hangover nothing had happened, she had nothing to report, her notebook was empty. He could not believe that *nothing* had happened in a week of clubbing! Being a good sociologist he asked what she had been looking for, what lens had she brought with her to this mini-ethnography. She recounted the mass media stories of binge drinking among British youth, of profligate and disgusting behaviour and how this was backed up by a series of research articles in the academic journals. And indeed the moral panic about binge drinking had spilled over into the academy, funding was at hand to research this very subject and the criminologists and sociologists had dutifully turned themselves into moral entrepreneurs, temperance warriors denouncing the perils of drink, condemning the brewers, the low price of alcohol and its easy access by the young. With this vision of debauchery in mind the student had seen nothing, for there was nothing to see. In fact all sorts of things had happened, some people had a great night out, the music was fantastic, the *craic* amazing, the culture of youth had colonized the night, some people had got off with each other and some had fallen in love. What more do you want . . .

If we start from the negative moment and then proceed to see this as what Everett Hughes called a *master status*, a clue to the very 'essence' of the individual or group we are observing, we preclude much of human action and potentiality. For it is, as Whyte suggests, a critical distortion to eliminate the majority of peoples' lives, to concentrate on the most negative and predatory moment yet hope to understand the person in the round. At the very least, it fails to see the possibilities inherent in a neighbourhood, the many kids who don't commit dramatic acts of violence and ignores the major part of people's everyday lives rather than what is frequently momentary and fleeting. There are significant policy implications of such systematic blindness. Because if the individual or the group is defined by their criminality and if the prognosis revolves around such a master status, then the clear implications are that the lead response should be from the criminal justice system. This it feeds into the increased tendency over the last two decades in so many liberal democracies to make the criminal justice system the major instrument of social intervention (Simon, 2007). That is responses to social problems which are educational or welfarist or medical – or even the simple denial that they are problems in the first place – are sidelined or co-opted into the ever expanding orbit of the criminal justice apparatus.

(3) The Narrow Focus of the Lens

> The Law, in its majestic equality forbids the rich as well as the poor to sleep under bridges, to beg in the streets, and to steal bread. (Anatole France. Le Lys Rouge, ch. 7)

The lens of orthodox criminology not only distorts, it leaves out. It has a narrow focus which leaves out much more than it sees. These omissions are of as great an interest as the inclusions. In particular it omits all those acts and activities which would suggest that there are wider structural forces involved in the generation of social harms. Let us take violence as an example; it omits the violence of war, of genocide, of injuries at work, of corporate malfeasance, of the state, of torture, it largely ignores the violence of imprisonment, of police brutality and until recently it ignored domestic violence. Indeed it ignores the vast majority of violence in our society. But what you might ask are we to make of a criminology of homicide that ignores most homicides? Let us take a dramatic example, genocide. Wayne Morrison in a remarkable essay 'Criminology, Genocide and Modernity' (2004) talks of criminology's 'silences' and refers to the manner by which this extraordinary locus of killings, rape and atrocity is absent from the canon. He refers to Gottfredson and Hirschi's *A General Theory of Crime* (1990) and writes 'The authors were clear that criminological theory must be faithful to the data on crime . . . [but] what constituted the data? It is no surprise that again there is no inclusion of the millions of murders, the hundreds of thousands raped, the vast amount of property confiscated, the houses occupied . . . Instead they find that the "the vast majority of criminal acts are trivial affairs that result in little loss and gain"' (1990, p. 16). From that basis they argue that criminality has much in common with accidents and other forms of "deviant" behaviours and is a function of low rates of "self control". This self, however, is an abstracted self. Nowhere do they face up to the European tradition that asserts that all "selves" ... need to be understood in terms of social, historical and economic processes; nor the narratives of taking control of the situation, or "another" and "yourself" that hold out to "individuals" a way of asserting they are anything but in "control"; nor is the normalcy of the (mainly) American statistics ever questioned' (2004, pp. 72–3). And, of course, it is in this European tradition that Mills placed himself. To this one should add, as I have argued in *The Vertigo of Late Modernity*, that the very idea of low self control has become a core value in advanced, consumer capitalism and is scarcely a sign of low socialization as these authorities presume (see, Young, 2007). It is by this process of widening out: historically, structurally, in terms of the type of crime, and beyond the shores of the United States, that that need for such socially grounded explanation becomes more apparent. Paradoxically what might be construed as the search for a universal explanation, the nomothetic impulse, leads us to the culturally and historically specific. As it is, this attempt to introduce genocide into the criminological canon was not a great immediate success. As Morrison ruefully describes in a footnote at the American Society of Criminology Conference in November 2000 there were 1,800 delegates, yet a round table discussion on the relevance of genocide to criminology drew only an audience of three (Morrison being one of them). He notes that the 2001 session had an audience of six from whom he 'would draw the response from a "positivist" analysis of a 100 percent increase in appeal!' (p. 85 n. 2).

(4) The Selective Vision

The figure below shows the process by which the criminologists' sample is 'scientifically' selected. Let us note that this is a curious process which sieves at every stage, narrowing down the focus and ending with a 'sample' which is remarkably similar in most countries of the world. It starts with a wide section of the population including the rich, the powerful, the corporate, the military, the older, the elite and it ends up with the poor, the ill educated, the minorities who fill the prisons, It is a process engineered by power at every stage. It is a strange science which has at its disposal such a sampling procedure. One can only wonder what ornithology or particle physics would look like if they adopted the 'scientific' methods of positivist criminology!

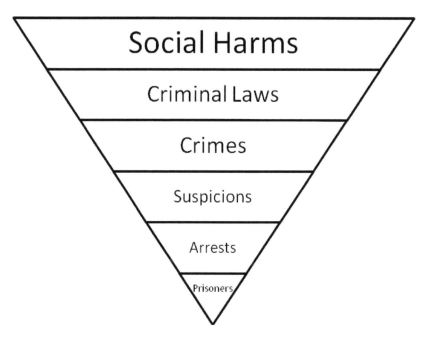

(5) The Superficial Focus and Cosmetic Criminology

The lens of establishment criminology only illuminates the surface of social problems; it does not penetrate beneath the surface, indeed, it does not conceive that there is anything of importance lying there. What we have, as I have pointed out earlier (1999), is a cosmetic criminology which would have us believe that crime and many other social problems are mere blemishes on the body politic which can be dealt with by superficial, administrative measures. The gross inequities of society, the daily indignities of prejudice and stigmatization are either blatantly ignored or cast into another realm unrelated to the problems that the lens reveals. (See Felson, 2002; Wilson,1975). Indeed the image of crime revealed by the lens involves an inversion of reality; rather than social problems being caused by the endemic and chronic contradictions of the system, the problems are seen to be caused by crime and leniencyetc. *Ergo* get rid of crime, drug use, violence, terrorism, etc and there would be no problems! Further these problems are viewed as having individual causes. They are lapses on the part of the individual due to faults of character and socialization or rational choices made because some mundane opportunity has presented itself. The thread connecting the individual to society is snapped and the analytical individualism so effectively criticized in the nineteenth century by Emile Durkheim has been almost magically resuscitated. In a jiffy this reverses Mills' axiom of turning personal issues into public problems; public problems become the result of a series of individualized personal issues. The problem of deleterious drug use thus becomes the problem of addiction, which is to be solved in a clinic; the problem of crime some sort of cognitive lapse which should be dealt with by therapy, the problem of anti-social behaviour to be sorted out by a myriad CCTV cameras or benches which it is impossible to sit in comfort for any length of time.

(6) Refraction: Sharp Lines and Reflected Images

The social world is full of many things which are amorphous, shape-changing, hybrids which blur at the edges and are contested both by onlookers and onlooked alike. As we have seen Durkheim fully realized this at the beginning of *Suicide* before he famously proceeded to ignore his own advice throughout the subsequent text.

Number of gangs and gang members

It was estimated that 30,818 gangs and 846,428 gang members were active in the United States in 1996.

Prior to the 1995 National Youth Gang Survey, the estimates of gangs ranged from 8,600 to 9,000 with 375,000 to 400,000 gang members (Curry, Ball, and Decker, 1996a; 1996b; 1996c; Klein, 1995). However, the samples used in previous surveys were limited in size and scope.

The sample of jurisdictions reporting gangs in the 1995 National Youth Gang Survey included counties and was much larger (2,007) than any used in previous studies of gang activity. Results of the survey indicated that approximately 23,000 gangs and 665,000 gang members were active in the United States in 1995 (Moore, 1997; National Youth Gang Center, 1997). These figures were based on actual reports or estimates by city and county law enforcement agencies. The data were not extrapolated to account for agencies not included in the survey, because the sample was not representative.

As noted in the introduction, the 1996 National Youth Gang Survey was designed to be representative of the Nation as a whole. Therefore, inferences can be made about gang problems in cities and counties not included in the survey. After extrapolations were conducted for the random samples and nonrespondents for large cities and suburban counties, it was estimated that 30,818 gangs and 846,428 gang members were active in the United States in 1996.

Source: 1996 National Youth Gang Survey, July 1999

The lens will have none of this: it distorts to uncover deviant entities which are more clearly delineated than they are in reality; it seeks
things with hard distinct edges and unambiguous essences. It wants
numbers, it wants to know how many of x are there? How large is y? It
doesn't want to be told it all depends on what you mean by x or y or,
even worse, it depends on who is doing the defining. The most fascinating, some might say amusing, example of this is the discussion as to
the number of gangs and gang members there is in a city or particular
locality. For having conjured up the gang as the magical cause of youth
violence it is obviously of great importance to discover their *exact*
numbers.

One wonders – 30,818 gangs? Why not 30,819 or indeed 30,820! And as
for 846,428 members, the mind boggles at the precision.

But more than this, the lens has a problem of refraction so that it
misleadingly reflects the delineated worlds of the investigator. It sees
structures, whether in the gang, in the Mafia, in Al-Qaeda, which are
simply not there. Thus they are perceived as too hierarchical, too delineated, with too fixed membership and too clearly defined roles and
organizational shapes. In other words, they mysteriously begin to look
like corporations or academic departments or the Metropolitan Police or
the NYPD or whatever . . .

(7) The Frozen Optic: The Coldness Each Side of the Lens

The lens is seen as an instrument to be used dispassionately; objectivity
itself demands that emotions are no part of the scientific process. The cli-
nician looks at the cancerous tissue without passion; the social scientist,
likewise, does not want his or her vision clouded by the effects of passing
emotion.

There has been in the last ten or so years a vast output of scholarship
which actively denies this (e.g. Katz, 2001). In a riveting article, 'Strong
Emotions at Work' (2009), three social scientists: a Canadian, working
in management studies, a Dutch anthropologist and an American sociologist dramatically bring together accounts of how emotional responses
helped them connect with their subjects and radically revise their theories. The Canadian, Gail Whiteman, was investigating the community
impact of mining and forestry in the Amazon interior and from the
perspective of stakeholder theory. The situation in Port Kaituma on
the Guyana–Venezuelan border was a million miles from the seeming
rational discourse of such theory. There was violence, drunken miners,
and a fearful community – particularly of Amerindian women. She
describes the gang rape of one her interviewees, seemingly a common

occurrence, the miners acted with impunity, the police paid off with a piece of gold and her own fear of being in the mining town, the pounding on the door at night, the sounds of drunkenness outside. It is like a scene out of Conrad's *Heart of Darkness*. Later when presenting her findings to an international conference she breaks down in tears. Her superiors frown at this lack of professionalism. Elsewhere she writes of this experience: 'What emerged from this challenge was surprising. I discovered that my intense and vulnerable response to these data was a powerful analytic signal. That, is when I begin to engage analytically with my "data" without stripping away my raw emotional interpretation of these interviews, stakeholder theory and related phrases (relations, consultation, management, etc) suddenly seemed strangely devoid of the flesh, blood, fear and humiliation of women and communities who were affected by the natural resources development that I was studying. I asked myself, 'What the hell can stakeholder theory say about "banking" [gang raping] a woman?' I thought: not much. However, this in itself tells us quite a lot about the limitations of stakeholder theory' (Whiteman et al., 2009).

The second story is of the anthropologist, Thaddeus Muller who sets off to see a football game between Feyenoord and Ajax, the classic rival teams from the cities of Rotterdam and Amsterdam, with the aim of investigating the concept of *communitas* – which he supposed paralleled the strong we-feeling associated with religious pilgrimages. He is suddenly plunged into a world of extraordinary excitement, finding himself in a crowd fighting with the police, in a stadium filled with 60,000 people, largely men, 'big tall men with tattoos', singing, embracing each other when a goal was scored. He felt 'totally excited. All my senses were aroused. I had an extremely heightened awareness of the surroundings and it was like I was in survival mode. But this need to survive gave me a very positive feeling. I felt no fear. It was great. My body was alive. It was tantalizing' (Whiteman et al., 2009, p. 52). But when he came to write up this experience for his thesis, he neglected all these emotions; he wrote it up 'rationally' omitting: 'wrong or strange emotions, e.g. the arousal experience of violence, and physical and emotional but non-sexual male intimacy' (p. 53). It did not seem appropriate but as he recollects this could well have been used to expand and enliven the concept of *communitas* away from its disembodied and rationalistic usage.

The last story is that of John Johnson, an American sociologist researching the death penalty. He turns up to witness the execution of Jesse James Giles on 13 January 1999 at the Death House in the main prison in Florence, Arizona. The witnesses consisted of victims and their relatives, media representatives, inmates and those representing the state, many from other state agencies, mostly women who had the day off for the task. The latter group included Johnson himself with the four groups of witnesses being segregated from each other. The execution by lethal injection proceeded without complications, in the quasi-medical setting. Nobody in his group was emotionally upset or at least expressed it; it seemed almost a rational, mundane procedure. It was in bureaucratic terms 'a good execution'. Afterwards he interviews some of them in the prison car park. Driving back he records his ethnographic observations into his recorder. But about half of a mile from home he almost loses control of the car and has to pull in to the side of the road. He breaks down and cries for about twenty minutes. He was not crying for Jesse Giles; he realized, he was crying for *himself*: because 'the bureaucratically rationalized ritual of a state execution is a very degrading one, for all parties concerned; we are rendered less moral and less human because of these actions taken in our names' (2009, p. 55). This made him recognize that the notion of being a detached by-stander, of being non-responsible in the face of state-execution is a myth and, in turn, fundamentally changed his symbolic interactionist account of capital punishment. And let us add to this, the tawdry, quasi-medical setting of the execution arises out of a desperate attempt to suppress emotion. It is far from *emotionless*: it is an attempt to turn killing into a medical procedure.

The message of this is quite clear. It is cold either side of the lens of establishment criminology and little human understanding will pass across it. For without emotional involvement it is very unlikely that you will pick up on what is going on; you will eliminate the expressive and fixate on the instrumental, the 'rational'. The situation of one human being looking at another and purposively suppressing emotion will only allow you to see behaviour and by that measure block out meaning.

(8) Peering Down the Class Structure

In 1968 at the annual meeting of the American Sociological Association in Boston, Martin Nicolaus gave a famous speech castigating 'Fat Cat Sociology'. 'The professional eyes of the sociologist', he said, 'were on the down people, and the professional palm of the sociologist is stretched toward the up people.' His portrayal is a calumny of course, to this packed audience of well-meaning liberals; there is a tinge of infantile leftism, a shade too much conspiracy; he grants sociology too much power, far too much influence. Yet the cartoon image remains in my mind's eye: a respectable looking gent, bespectacled and tweed suited, one hand high in the air, palms flat, waiting for the next grant, his head turned sideways, eyes peering down looking at the next social problem that official society has identified, his body twisted uneasily, he looks both preposterous and liable to fall.

As I outlined in *The Exclusive Society* and *The Vertigo of Late Modernity* this act of peering down is facilitated by the notion of a social hiatus between the researchers and the researched. The poor are seen as an underclass economically disconnected from society, they live in spatially segregated areas, they are morally deficient from us in their socialization and they are the source of all social problems. All of these axioms are incorrect: they are very much part of the new service economy, their labour subsidizes the living standards of the middle classes, they regularly traverse the city in their roles as shelf stackers, drivers, restaurant helps, nannies, gardeners, labourers, porters, cleaners, and so on; they live anyway in a highly mediated world where the lives of the better off are always in your face, they are well socialized into the values of the wider society, indeed their discontent is because of failures of the American – or First World Dream – rather than rejection of it. Violence is central to our culture, witness Hollywood, video games and our constant wars; it is certainly not the monopoly of the poor, nor, of course, is low self control and short-term hedonism in a consumer society and, as we have seen, to view the poor as the problem, rather than poverty being produced by a grossly unequal society, is a complete inversion of reality. Yet it is this sense of hiatus, part of what Barbara Ehrenreich (2001) calls the solipsis of the middle class, which generates an epistemological hiatus, a false sense of distance and objectivity. And, of course, all of this is reinforced by the habits of buying in data, questionnaires and the quantification of everything. Indeed, Dario Melossi, in *Controlling Crime, Controlling Society* (2008), points to the reverse scenario. He notes the appreciative stance of the early Chicago School as stemming from their own backgrounds as immigrants, deviants and outsiders. As he puts it: 'The connection between such a proximity and the particular methodology used by the Chicagoans, an ethnographic approach that involved the need for talking to, living with and getting to know the people they were writing about, seems self-evident enough' (2008, p. 105).

In a fine dig at the pretence of objectivity, Mike Presdee (2004) takes this notion of solipsis a little further. He argues that 'numerical life' has little if any relationship with 'actual life', that there is a chronic split between academic knowledge, the gaze from above, and everyday experience and the view from below revealed by ethnography and biography. He maintains that orthodox criminology is driven by the administrative concerns of the powerful which presents problems as obvious and uncontested, and sets the research agenda for the social scientist. Why he asks is it 'obvious to all . . . that we need research into the "evilness" of young people rather than the oppression of young people; the evils of drink and drugs rather than why we take substances that might even include enjoyment and the excitement of transgression'? (2004a). Such a power driven knowledge presents itself as part of a rational research agenda where the very presence of power is occluded. Mike Presdee then turns to the researchers themselves noticing their poverty of experience, their exclusion from the lived worlds of the people they research, thus neatly reversing the conventional nostrum: it is the social scientist who is very often marginalized from the social world rather than the objects of social science who are supposedly marginalized.

(9) Orthodox Criminology as Liberal Othering

In *Vertigo* I describe two forms of othering: conservative and liberal. Conservative othering is the act of demonization where negative images are projected on the other; they are evil, the very inversion of ourselves. It grants us virtue in contrast to the alien other. Liberal othering as we have seen, is less well recognized; it is where the deviant other is seen to lack our attributes, they would be *just like us* if only they had our level of self control, our family background and socialization, our steady employment and habits of work. There are two moments in this process *diminishing* (they are less than us) and *distancing* (we have no direct relationship with them). That is, it grants our professional middle-class world an implicit, unquestioned superiority and it definitely rules out the fact that it is our social relationship with the deviant which is part of the problem. The interesting tactic of orthodox criminology is that it takes up a critical pose by being fiercely dismissive of the conservative othering found in the stereotypes of the mass media and popular imagination but it does this – not by rejecting othering – but by adopting its liberal version.

(10) The Lens as a Block to the Imagination

This, then, is a lens which tends to individualize problems and to present them in a way where the human actor is observed as an isolated atom without social context. It involves a process of radical disconnection: the actor is bereft of culture, the collective and personal narrative created in a specific place and time and his or her social predicament is detached from the social structure. Furthermore, from this viewpoint power is simply a resource, not part of the structure that shapes the circumstances that people find themselves in, and values are the consensual stuff which holds the social universe together rather than the ideas which legitimate power or inspire resistance. And most *certainly* such power is not the force which selects and shapes the individuals who find themselves under scrutiny! It does not look at those behind the lens: an ethnography of the rich would be hard to find let alone of the academic world, these things are left to novelists; it does not really listen to those in front of it. It is a lens honed by power, guided by money, distorted by othering, haunted by the nomothetic impulse: the pursuit of science. Our job is to wipe the lens clean, widen its focus and detach it from its bearings.

For let us underline the fact that the modus vivendi of orthodox criminology is in all of its aspects, the very opposite of the sociological imagination proposed some fifty years ago by C. Wright Mills. For orthodoxy offers the disconnection from power, the loss both of structure and meaning, and acts bereft of the context of history. It is to restore these things that critical criminology must set as its central task.

Becoming Deviant: The Struggle for a Critical Criminology

David Matza in 1969 published *Becoming Deviant*, a book which looked back over these years of intense creativity in the 1950s and 1960s, and back beyond that to the Chicago School and the early days of the development of the sociology of deviance. It is a volume extraordinary in its perceptiveness and pivotal in its influence. He argues for a position of *naturalism* towards the phenomena of deviance, a methodology quite simply characterized by its commitment to being faithful to the phenomenon under scrutiny. Naturalism, on the face of it, might be seen as an approach which argued for the use of the natural scientific method in studying society. Indeed the assumption that positivism typically makes. But for Matza this is a grave mistake. For as we have seen, in the case of human behaviour, to be faithful to reality means that we must of necessity take notice of subjectivity. That is, that, although human beings like natural objects can act merely adaptively or reactively, they are never mere objects even when they act *as if* and believe themselves to be the creatures of forces beyond their control. Human culture, in particular, can be, as we have seen, the site of human creativity but also an unwitting resource of stability and consensus where codes of behaviour are looked upon as natural and not of human creation. For Matza the history of criminology and the sociology of deviance is one of an emerging naturalism. But it is a struggle against a positivist tendency deeply ingrained in the subject, and extensively financed and encouraged by the various agencies of social control. He contrasts two approaches to deviance, the *appreciative* and the *correctional*. The appreciative is the methodology of naturalism, of human culture and creativity. The correctional arises out of the technical needs of social control, with this in mind, it is drawn towards positivistic, natural scientific models of human behaviour. Basing itself on the hugely successful achievements of natural science, it seeks deterministic laws of causality which are universal in their explanatory power. Because of this, *nomothetic impulse*, the mindset which seeks either to eliminate culture as part of the understanding of human behaviour, or view it as fixed and static, becomes clear. For an ever-changing created culture will always undermine the possibilities of wide-scale generalization.

Culture is an anathema to positivism. For, whereas science demands agreement of definition, clear lines of delineation between concepts, the possibility of quantification, the universalism of laws and regularities, regardless of time and place, culture undermines all of this. For science, as we have seen, a zebra is a zebra, not a horse, H_2O and C_2H_5OH are separate, distinct molecules (only turned one into another on very *special* occasions). The zebras do not talk among themselves and decide to be horses, horses do not look like zebras through one person's telescope yet appear as horses through another's.

Note that the idea of an appreciative methodology does not rule out the need to control predatory and anti-social behaviour – it merely denies a positivistic approach which negates human creativity and culture. Thus the appreciative stance does not imply that of the romantic: it does not have to applaud behaviour, it certainly does not need to view all deviance as, of necessity, well organized, culturally sophisticated or morally commendable. It may shun the behaviour in question yet enter into an understanding of its norms and values; *verstehen* does not mean valorization. To be naturalistic towards deviance is to see both the defects and merits of a phenomenon: it is not to view deviant behaviour as being a construction made up of flaws or a paragon of virtue. That is, in short, neither to view deviance as a pathology nor to romanticize it. Rather it is to understand it and so determine if it is actually a problem which warrants social intervention and if so, of what sort and at what point in its development should intervention be applied, the criminal justice system being only one agency of many that may be appropriate (Young, 1992).

In contrast a positivist stance 'interferes' with our ability to engage with, 'to appreciate', the phenomenon under study. It has a series of implications: deviant behaviour becomes perceived as a 'pathology' to be eliminated. Such a biological metaphor, a shift from the social to the organic, is facilitated by our own nature as both organic and social beings: thus deviance comes to be seen as a fault in social homoeostasis – of the equilibrium of society seen as an organism; it is a determined condition, marginal to human behaviour, a nuisance problem, worthy only of a separate yet ancillary discipline. The sociology of deviance, or, even more stridently, criminology, is conceived of as outside of sociology proper, with its own canon of scholars and texts (Lombroso, Hirschi, Felson, etc.). In cultural terms, crime becomes understood as a lacking of culture, and culture itself not as a creative act, the most quintessential characteristic of human beings, but rather as a cement, a consensual unifier, which holds the social structure together, somehow detached from human choice and construction. (See Bauman, 1999: Ferrell et al., 2008.) Deviance, in these terms is a an absence of culture, a breakdown of the socialization process. Further, the stance of correctionalism gives rise to the possibility of losing the phenomenon.

> The purpose of ridding ourselves of the phenomenon manifests itself most clearly in an overwhelming contemporary concern with questions of causation, or 'etiology'. The phenomenon itself receives only cursory attention. The ultimate purpose of liquidation is reflected in this highly disproportionate division of attention between description and explanation ... traditional studies of deviant behavior have been highly vague and short winded about the phenomena they presume to explain. Why bother with detailed and subtle description? The task before us, in the correctional perspective, is to get at the root causes in order to remove them and their product. (Matza, 1969, p. 17)

Such a correctionalist stance explains the strange phenomenon which Jack Katz noted years later: that orthodox criminology has an extraordinary lack of interest in the subject it purports to study. There is thus an extremely:

> thin narrative between cause and effect. There are causes (unemployment, broken homes, etc) and there are crimes but inbetween up to *and including* the crime itself there is precious little detail or description. The story, the causal narrative of meaning which actually explains a crime, and intrigues and interests the rest of the world, is seemingly of little interest to the professional criminologist. (2002)

Elsewhere, Katz and Jackson-Jacobs note that 'it is a revealing paradox that gang life is at once a symbolic image sufficiently powerful to justify study after study, and at the same time never worth actually describing'. (2004, p. 101)

Becoming Deviant is the chronicle of the struggle for the emergence of an appreciative stance in American criminology and the sociology of deviance. Matza is intrigued by the way in which writers in the Chicago School of the 1930s attempted to wrestle with the correctionalist impulse, on one hand, which would seek to pathologize deviance and, on the other hand, the facts of social diversity which they encountered in their advocacy of open, engaged and appreciative methods of research. Their painstaking ethnography and fascination with diversity constantly undermined their tendency to depict diversity as simple social pathology. Herein lies a neat irony for as Jack Katz and Curtis Jackson-Jacobs (2004) point out, it was the Chicago School's initial attachment to the natural sciences which brought about this change. For their very immersion in the meticulous natural scientific approach to the documentation of data brought them nervously, hesitantly to the very brink of the realization that the social world with its inherent creativity and diversity was fundamentally unlike the natural world. The Chicago School is fascinating because its researchers were constantly poised between appreciation and correctionalism (see Hayward, 2001). It was to take the work of the New Deviancy Theorists, the Neo-Chicagoans to shake off the dead weight of correctionalism.

The New Deviancy Revolution

> Deviance is not a property inherent in certain forms of behavior; it is a property conferred upon those forms by the people who came into direct or indirect contact with it. (Erikson, 1966, p. 6)

> This is a large turn away from an older sociology which tended to rest on the idea that deviance leads to social control, I have come to believe the reverse idea . . . social control leads to deviance. (Lemert, 1967, p. v)

The decade 1955 to 1965 was a time of exceptional creativity in American sociology of deviance. The names alone: Becker, Cicourel, Cohen, Cloward, Erikson, Goffman, Gusfield, Matza, Scheff, Sykes, to mention just a few, jog the mind and convey the intellectual intensity of the period. It was a time when society shifted from what seemed like a post-war sea of prosperity and harmony to one where both the anger of those excluded from the 'great society' and the rebellion of many of those included reached a fever point. It was a period when, for a while, the sociology of deviance became a central focus of sociological debate and when, as Howard Becker reminds us in the introduction to *The Other Side* (1964), it regained its connection within the mainstream of sociological theory. For a long period, in the aftermath of the Chicago School, the sociology of deviance had succumbed to becoming a hand-maiden of administration, 'a practical pursuit, devoted to helping society deal with those it found troublesome' (1964, p. 1). Images of pathology had replaced those of *verstehen* and deviance was viewed as a lacking of culture (because of inadequate socialization) rather than as a culture to be understood and appreciated. For, as Stan Cohen was to note later in the introduction to *Images of Deviance* (1971), the traditional perspective towards deviance involved 'an annihilation of meaning' and a whole array of experts were mobilized to achieve this process of deculturation.

The two strands of the new deviancy theory, subcultural and labelling theory, roundly subverted this. Subcultures, whether these involved drug taking, violence, burglary or vandalism were seen, in the tradition of cultural anthropology, as human creations, attempts to tackle the problems of material and social existence (see Cohen, 1955), while labelling theory pointed to the ways in which those in authority attempt to take meaning away from deviant individuals or groups. Both strands are social constructionist in their orientation, stressing that deviance is a constructed category rather than some fixed essence and that *both* the subculture and the culture of control are necessary subjects of a fully social theory of deviance.

The new deviancy revolution involved the rejection of absolutist notions of value and the highlighting of the ironic and self-fulfilling nature of social control. We live in a pluralistic society with a magical cubism of perspectives, where one person's deviancy is another person's normality and where there are numerous audiences and evaluators. *Deviance is not inherent in an action but a quality bestowed upon it*: the ascription of deviance demands both actors and reactors. Furthermore, the definitions of those in power are proclaimed as absolutist standards of normality and are given top ranking in what Howard Becker (1967) termed 'the hierarchy of credibility'. These are imposed with varying degrees of success upon those in lower structural positions through a social control apparatus ranging from the mass media to the criminal justice system. In this rubric of control orthodox criminology, together with cognate disciplines especially psychiatry, has a key role in *explaining away* deviancy as a lack of values rather than alternative norms and realities (see Young, 1971b). In this the *label* criminal or deviant carries with it essentialist connotations of undersocialization, irrationality, mindlessness, impulsiveness etc., often caricatured in positivist terms.

The second axiom was that social control frequently has effects which are counterproductive and self-fulfilling. This insight runs through the critical tradition in criminology, it is at the heart of its intellectual enterprise from the discovery of the criminalizing effect of imprisonment to the repeated demonstration of the counterproductive effect of the war on drugs. In this the new deviancy theory moved beyond a liberalism that insists that images of crime and deviance are mistakes in knowledge, misperception or badly grounded stereotypes, to one that suggests that however true this may be at the initial phases of a criminal career or the onset of a deviant enterprise, over time such stigmatization can become self-fulfilling. For, in certain circumstances, people become like the label. The folk devils conjured up out of moral indignation and prejudice are actually constructed by the forces of social control. Fantasy is translated into reality. Something like the stereotype of the psychopath is created by the long brutalization of the prison: lockdowns, isolation, alternating with the ever present threat of inmate and warden violence. The amorphous grouping of the young people on the street become reconstructed into the hierarchical structure of the gang by the targeting of police patrols and the persuasive narratives of the mass media (see Cohen, 1971; Hallsworth, 2000).

Bringing Culture Back In

The impact of the new deviancy theories was, for a time, enormous; their influence seemingly irreversible. Their contribution was to bring culture into the study of crime and deviant behaviour, not in the sense of acknowledging the inevitable presence of culture in social life, an obvious platitude, but in stressing the creative characteristic of culture and hence the cultural and creative nature of human deviance *and* the systems which attempt to control it. For the majority of commentators in criminology, 'normal' law-abiding behaviour was conformity to the cultural; crime and deviance was a *lacking* of culture, while social control was simply the rather automatic and mechanistic enforcement of cultural norms. Crime was caused, therefore, by institutions unable to transmit culture or individuals unable to receive it: by social disorganization on a societal level or lack of socialization on a personal level: most frequently some combination of both. Such a positivist criminology, as I have argaued, seeks to explain, by a series of factors (most commonly, for example, community disorganization, unemployment, broken families, or even genetic predisposition and biochemical imbalance) why such a successful socialization into an unquestioned consensus of values had not come about. Crime is thus, in short, the failure of society to inculcate culture and, as such, the criminological gaze can be seen as an act of othering. It is the presumed 'well-socialized' scrutinizing the 'under-socialized', the social viewing the asocial, the socially evolved examining the atavistic, the world of meaning explaining variously 'meaningless' behaviour, 'mindless violence', 'the mob', the menacing and the malevolent – all the words that seek to describe and depict a lacking of culture. The role of subcultural theory, then, was to grant criminal and deviant behaviour meaning and culture while that of labelling theory was to explain the process by which othering occurred, how criminological theory, the mass media and the wider public tended to stereotype deviancy – to distort and take away meaning.

As we have seen, Zygmunt Bauman distinguishes two interpretations of culture. First there is the notion of culture as the cement of society, the normative support of the given structure and institutions of society; secondly culture as the font of creativity, of that which challenges reification and the monolithic and unquestioned notions of the social order and the acceptable. The new deviancy theorists whole-heartedly embraced the latter – culture as innovation and resistance, although, as we shall see, they took great pains to expose the cultural extemporizations of the powerful which attempted to maintain the opposite: the pretence of culture as somehow natural, a social given beyond human action. The two notions of culture are thus not empirical alternatives, they both exist in the real world and both these and their social productions are acts of creativity, the acts of innovation and resistance and also the bad faith which attempts to portray the social world as solid and somehow beyond human creation. A thorough understanding of deviance must embrace both how human action involves the creative generation of the cultural and how powerful agencies attempt to take meaning and culture away from the deviant. The first of these realms is the focus of subcultural theory and the second of labelling theory – the first is concerned primarily with the origins of deviant behaviour, with the deviant *act*, the second is concerned with the social *reaction* to deviance, with efforts at social culture and the effects of such interventions.

1968: A World Turned Upside Down

Such a reinvigoration of theory did not, of course, occur out of the blue: it was very much a product of the tumult of the time. It is more than forty years since 1968, a time when the *world seemed turned upside down*. The sanity of psychiatry, the honesty of the police, the veracity of the mass media, the respectability of the politician, the comfortable world of the middle classes, were all relentlessly questioned. The war in Vietnam, the emergence of dramatic expressive youth cultures, the challenge of new bohemianism and a strident second wave of feminism, all raised questions of the status quo, reversing the traditional questions of criminology and the sociology of deviance (see Ferrell et al., 2008). A whole stratum of middle-class youth came into collision with the police on demonstrations, on civil rights marches, and in the policing of their everyday lives (see Lilly et al., 2009). The new deviancy theory and the new criminology which came close after it, was organically linked to this. 'The troublesome', traditionally located with seeming obviousness in the realm of the deviant and the criminal, become relocated in a polar elsewhere. 'Trouble' *was* the police, the prisons, the judges, the mental hospitals, the journalists, the 'normal' man in the street. The focus of the problematic shifted, where meaning had been taken from the deviant, it was now returned appreciated, and whereas the powerful had somehow magically been seen as existing outside of the world of explanation, their activities and impact became the centre of attention. As Bill Chambliss,

1978, put it 'a change in the sociological weather' occurred which made everyone look again at what was once taken for granted; no longer was the view from the police car looking out but from the street looking in (see Dario Melossi, 2008).

It is important to stress how a younger generation of sociologists identified with the process of cultural change that pivoted around 1968. We were all moved by the times: the possibility of social change, the worlds of diversity that the new bohemia promised, the youthful colonization of leisure and the rejection of austerity and discipline in a world seemingly in fast forward, all of which made the choice of being on the side of progress well nigh inevitable.

The culmination of this intense period of creativity in the American sociology of deviance was Albert Cohen's 1965 article, 'The Sociology of the Deviant Act: Anomie Theory and Beyond'. In this he made an imaginative attempt to synthesize the two strands of deviancy theory: anomie and labelling, and set up the groundwork for the British endeavours to create a 'fully social theory of deviance' which were to follow in the early 1970s. Let me say at this stage that the passage across the Atlantic was not so much a translation as a transposition. The British radical criminologists just like the American sociologists, whose imagination inspired the new deviancy theory, were revolting against the tradition of positivism and correctionalism which had dominated criminology and the sociology of deviance in both countries in the 1950s and early 1960s. This was the reason why the American ideas were so attractive to them. Yet, as we shall see, the ideas were significantly transformed in the transition and, ironically, their impact was more influential and sustained.

The Transition to Late Modernity: The Emergence of British Deviancy Theory

It was an exciting period for criminology. Radical ideas were everywhere. The National Deviancy Conference in 1968 had really shaken things up. We didn't talk any more of criminology *per se* but of the sociology of deviance. We had made a cleaner break with the positivism and with siding with the agents of state control. We spoke of trying to create a society where the facts of human diversity would not be subject to the power to criminalize'. (Arnott, 1999, p. 280 – *A crime novel set in the 1960s; made into a BBC TV film in 2004, directed by Bille Eltringham*)

I have traced the development of subcultural and labelling theory, the flourishing of the new deviancy theory in the United States in the 1950s

and 1960s. At this juncture the baton passed to Britain. The two intellectual bases for this were, first of all, the National Deviancy Conference,
an organization of radical criminologists which was inaugurated at the
University of York in 1968 and, subsequently, the work on youth subcultures conducted at the Centre for Contemporary Cultural Studies of
the University of Birmingham, which would become world famous in
the area of cultural studies. The periodization of the shift in activity to
Britain represents a conjuncture; the later development in Europe of an
affluent consumer society, and the general transition of the advance of
industrial societies into late modernity.

Let us first briefly situate this work intellectually in the tumultuous
world of the late 1960s and early 1970s. Eric Hobsbawm, in *Age of
Extremes* (1994), describes what he calls the Golden Age of the post-war
period in the First World from the 1950s onwards. This was a world of
constant economic growth, rise in real incomes and full (male) employment where consumer spending increased year after year and affluence
and prosperity became taken for granted. Such economic progress was
coupled with a social stability in terms of job security, marriage, the
family and community and a sense of shared and relatively uncontested
values. The years that followed involved a widespread restructuring of
work, the rise of unemployment, uncertainty and insecurity, increased
marital breakdown, the decline in community and a wholesale contest
of values. The periodization of this transition into and out of the Golden
Age varies with the nation concerned. As Hobsbawm points out, the
United States, which had witnessed continued expansion through the war
period, sustained economic progress and prosperity which started much
earlier than the war-torn countries of Europe. Indeed, the United States
in the 1950s represented to the Europe of reconstruction, regimentation
and rationing, very much a shiny contrast: a material utopia of aspiration
and desire (see Hebdige, 1988). But if the onset of the Golden Age varied,
its demise was more of a unity: for from the late 1960s onwards social
commentators talk both of a cultural revolution and of fundamental economic restructuring which transformed the social order of the developed
world. The shift into late modernity had begun (see Young, 1999). It was
at this cusp of change that an extraordinary burst of creativity occurred
within sociology and within the sociology of deviance in particular, this
time on the other side of the Atlantic. The major site of this intellectual
tumult in Britain was the National Deviancy Conference (NDC) which
held its first meeting in 1968 and lasted for about ten years (see Cohen,
1981; Young, 1998). The NDC was, in the words of David Downes, the
site of an 'explosion' of work, the 'fall out' of which was to change the
terrain of criminology and the sociology of deviancy for many years to
come. One gauge of this explosion would be that in the first five-year

period from the inception of the NDC in 1968 to 1973, there were sixty-three speakers from Britain who produced between them just under one hundred books on crime, deviance and social control. The NDC was hectic, irreverent, transgressive and, above all, fun. It took no notice of disciplinary boundaries, it was as important an arena for the emerging field of cultural studies (Stuart Hall, Mike Featherstone, Paul Willis, Dick Hebdige, all gave papers), anti-psychiatry (Peter Sedgwick, Jeff Coulter) critical legal theory (Alan Hunt, Boaventura de Sousa Santos and Sol Picciotto), the sociology of sexualities (Ken Plummer, Mary McIntosh), as it was for the sociology of deviance (see the account in Cohen, 1988; Young, 1998). Perhaps, however, it was the pluralism and social constructionism of deviancy theory that gave it such a pivotal role. There was a frenetic quality to the NDC, there were fourteen conferences held between the end of 1968 and the end of 1973 and papers, articles and books seemed to emerge in an endless stream – exciting and excitable.

The basis of such work and the widespread interest it generated (there were ten national conferences in the four years 1969 to 1972) undoubtedly the first airing of what was to be known as 'post-modern' themes. As Stan Cohen put it, 'After the middle of the 1960s – well before Foucault made these subjects intellectually respectable and a long way from the Left Bank – our little corner of the human sciences was seized by a deconstructionist impulse' (1988, p. 101). Indeed the arrival of *Discipline and Punish* in English translation in 1977 was scarcely a revelation, many of the themes and concepts of Foucault were already well rehearsed, the door was wide open to deconstructionism.

For the conference was deconstructionist to a person, anti-essentialist in its stance, it evoked a myriad voices and viewpoints right to the edge of relativism; it dwelt on the social construction of gender, sexual proclivity, crime, suicide, drugs and mental state. It inverted hierarchies, it read total cultures from the demi-monde of mods, rockers, teddy boys, hippies, skinheads – it traced the bricolage of the old culture by which the new 'spectacular' youth cultures constituted themselves, it focused on their media representatives and the fashion in which media stereotypes shaped and at times became reality. And beneath all of this was an underlay of critique of both strands of State intervention: positivism and classicism. For the twin meta-narratives of progress: social engineering and the rule of law, were consistently subject to criticism. Positivism was perhaps the main enemy: its ontology was seen to take human creativity out of deviant action, its sociology erected a consensual edifice from which deviants were bereft of culture and meaning, its methodology elevated experts to the role of fake scientists discovering the 'laws' of social action and its policy, whether in the mental hospitals, the social work agencies or the drug clinics, was self-fulfilling and mystifying. But the rule of law also came under close scrutiny. The NDC was concerned with how the criminal justice system was selective and ineffective. That is how crime occurred endemically yet the justice system focused on the working class and on youth. Crimes of the powerful were ignored: middle-class deviancy tolerated. And the prison itself was brutalizing, scapegoating and ultimately counterproductive: two of the most blistering indictments of the prison system, *Psychological Survival* (Cohen and Taylor, 1972) and *Prisoners in Revolt* (Fitzgerald and Sim, 1977) springing out of this. But such irrationality in terms of social reaction to crime was not limited to the institutions of the State, but also to those of civil society. For the mass media were seen to select out deviant groups creating folk devils and engendering moral panics (see Cohen, 1972; Young, 1971b).

The major fulcrum was the sociology of crime and deviance. This is scarcely surprising in that the sociology of deviance (and by implication that of crime) has a privileged position within sociology: insofar as from its vantage point, power, stigmatization and the contest of norms are palpably visible. The subject revolves around the point where norms are broken and norms made. It was from here that the two imports from the American sociology of deviance which we talked about in the last section came. The first was labelling theory and the second the sociology of subcultures.

The deconstructionist impulse commenced, as we have seen, in the United States around the work of the labelling theorists: Edwin Lemert, Howard Becker, John Kitsuse, Kai Erikson, Edwin Schur and many others. It was revolutionary in its discourse (social control generates deviance rather than deviance necessitates social control), it was relativistic in its analysis (deviance is not an inherent property of an act but a quality bestowed upon an act), it inverted orthodoxies, lambasted positivism, defended and celebrated human diversity: it was tremendously *attractive* to the young and to the radical at this time of change.

At the same time as this radical deconstructionist literature was imported to British shores, the second more established but scarcely less radical strand became incorporated and transformed within the sociology of deviance. American subcultural theory, in particular the work on gangs and delinquency of Cloward and Ohlin (1961) and A. K. Cohen (1955), and the studies of prison subcultures by Gresham Sykes (1958) and Donald Clemner (1940). A major intellectual conduit of this importation of American theory were sociologists working at the London School of Economics commencing with Herman Mannheim's *Juvenile Delinquency in an English Middletown* (1948) and brought to fruition in Terence Morris' *The Criminal Area* (1957) and Terence and Pauline Morris' *Pentonville* (1963), and culminating in the extremely influential *The Delinquent Solution* by David Downes, published in 1966. It is out of this tradition that Stan Cohen's (1972) study of mods and rockers emerged as a PhD thesis, as did related studies, for example, my own work on drug taking (1971b) and that of Mike Brake (1980) on youth culture (see Hobbs, 2006).

It was in the debates and presentations which occurred within the NDC that a series of transformations occurred to these two American traditions – labelling and subcultural theory. First of all, the two were brought together in a synthesis. This was facilitated by the logic of their focus, namely that labelling theory focused on construction downwards (the *reaction* against deviance) and subcultural theory in construction upwards (the deviant *action*). Secondly, the rather wooden American subcultural theory was given a zest, an energy, a feeling of creativity: further the synthesis between the two traditions demanded likewise a sense of passion in the response to deviance. Thirdly transgression was given a much more positive valuation: it was a sign of resistance, an overcoming, a creative flourish: it was not predominantly a site of failure or simple adaptation. American sociology of deviance became in Britain a sociology of transgression.

These twin strands of North American criminology became transposed and woven together in British deviancy theory. Transposed in that they were shifted to a society which was more aware of relationships of class and transfixed, at that time, with the emergence of ebullient and dynamic youth cultures. Thus class and youth became the major social areas around which the work pivoted (gender was to come a little later and race/ethnicity to wait until the 1980s). Woven together, in that both strands, which in American criminology were separate and somewhat antagonistic, were brought together. In a way this was only logical because both were complementary. The great contribution of labelling theory was its unpacking of the dyadic nature of crime and deviance. Deviancy is not a quality inherent in an act it is a quality bestowed upon an act. To have deviance one needs action and reaction, behaviour and evaluation, rule making and rule breaking. Yet having said this, labelling theorists, as did the social constructionists who followed them, tended to bracket off action from reaction and concentrate on the latter and its impact. They were interested in social construction, human agency was never lost but became ephemeral embracing a rather ungrounded, existentialism. Subcultural theory, on the other hand, was interested in the actual generation of behaviour; its weakness was the creation of rules, the other half of the equation. Yet even though it was able to chart the determinants of actors, the actions themselves were wooden. In *Delinquent Boys* (Cohen, 1955) they rather petulantly inverted middle-class morality like spoilt automata reversing their programmes; in *Delinquency and Opportunity* (Cloward and Ohlin, 1961) they went through a series of pre-programmed options like bearings in a pinball machine (see below). The task of British theorization was to try to bring these three concepts together: to deal with action and reaction, to postulate human actors who were neither capriciously free-willed nor stolidly determined, to place actors both in a micro-setting and in the context of the wider society.

Finally and distinctively, both theories had limitations with regard to the macro-level of analysis. Labelling theory, in particular, was concerned very fruitfully with the immediate interaction between the actor and the labelling process, it was essentially a remarkably insightful micro-sociology but it had little theory of the total society outside of the clash or disparate interest groups and moral entrepreneurs. Subcultural theory was excellent in terms of its emphasis on the contradiction between structure and culture on a macro-level, but it had little sense of what were the dynamics of society as a whole and with the realities of power. As Laurie Taylor put it in a brilliant passage:

> It is as though individuals in society are playing a gigantic fruit machine, but the machine is rigged and only some players are consistently rewarded. The deprived ones then either resort to using foreign coins or magnets to increase their chances of winning (innovation) or play on mindlessly (ritualism) or propose a new game altogether (rebellion). But in this analysis nobody appears to ask who put the machine there in the first place and who takes the profits. Criticism of the game is confined to changing the pay-out sequences so that the deprived can get a better deal (increasing educational opportunities, poverty programmes). What at first sight looks like a major critique of society ends up taking the existing society for granted. The necessity of standing outside the present structural/cultural configurations is not just a job for those categorized in the rebellion mode of adaption – it is also the task of the sociologist. (1971, p. 148)

It was this task of synthesis which confronted the radical criminologists who grouped around the NDC and it was these tasks which shaped the structure and discourse of *The New Criminology*. But before we turn to the questions which such debates engendered, let us look briefly at one area of work in which the NDC was greatly involved, for it is these exploratory tasks which were the laboratory within which the framework of *The New Criminology* was developed. We have talked about transposing American theorization onto the current British preoccupations with class and youth. It was, in fact, the *combination* of class and youth which was a major focus of the NDC. Thus we have papers on football hooliganism and working-class youth (Taylor, 1968), on student, middle-class drug taking (Young, 1968), on hippies (Hall, 1970), Phil Cohen's path-breaking paper on working-class youth cultures in 1970, Paul Walton on political protest and the student movement in 1971, Paul Willis on motorbike subcultures in 1972. And this was followed over the years by papers on youth culture by John Clarke, Mike Brake, Geoff Pearson, Geoff Mungham, Dick Hebdige and Paul Corrigan.

What is clear from these various essays is that there is a very overt attempt to go beyond the wooden determined actors of American theorization, to place them in a specific class position rather than invoke the notion of a universal youth culture (see Hall et al., 1975) to place such cultures in particular local settings with a consciousness of space and change over time, and to stress the creativity of youth culture. For subcultures were seen as human creations, attempting to solve specific problems which were constantly rewritten at each nook and cranny of society rather than centrally orchestrated scripts mechanically enacted by actors deterministically allocated to their position in the social structure. There is a lineage certainly between Albert Cohen and Paul Willis and between Cloward and Ohlin and Phil Cohen, but there is also a wealth of difference.

In this work there is a clear influence of the English socialist historians, such as Edward Thompson, Eric Hobsbawm, Christopher Hill and Sheila Rowbotham (see Downes and Rock, 1988; Cohen, 1980). That is, among other things, of *'writing from below'*, of history written from 'the material experiences of the common people rather than from above in the committee chambers of high office' (Pearson, 1978, p. 119). Of revealing a world which, in the title of Sheila Rowbotham's book, was 'hidden from history' (1973). The socialist historians of this period undoubtedly had an extraordinary influence on this second wave of subcultural theory presented at the NDC and developed particularly around the work of the Centre for Contemporary Cultural Studies at the University of Birmingham under the directorship of Stuart Hall. Indeed the cultural turn of the historians was matched by the turn to culture of the deviancy theorists. Here we have subcultures of imagination and creativity rather than of flatness and determinism, resistance rather than of negativism and retreatism, of a world of leisure as well as school and work, of meaning rather than malfunction. And just as socialist and feminist historians read from the activities and aspirations of lowly people the dynamics and ethos of the total society as high culture in understanding the total society – perhaps more so. Here the work of the Marxist literary theorist, Raymond Williams (1958) who elevated popular culture to the some aesthetic status and significance as that of the elite, was particularly important. Thus Phil Cohen's (1972) 'mods' and 'skinheads' tell us about urban dislocation, working-class de-skilling, destruction of community; Stuart Hall and his colleagues' analysis of changing youth cultural forms relates to the wider processes of embourgeoisement, mass culture and affluence (1975), Paul Willis' 'lads' intransigence and bloody mindedness becomes transformed to Pyrrhic resistance to wage labour and subordination (1977).

But it is not only deviant action which is given meaning in such a holistic fashion, it is the reaction against deviance. Here the other strand of North American theorization, labelling theory, is reworked and transformed. For, in a parallel fashion, labelling theory became re-cast into moral panic theory. For if subcultural theory interprets the seeming irrationality of delinquency in a rational fashion, moral panic theory offers the possibility of interpreting the seemingly ill thought out, gut reactions of authority and the wider public to deviance in a similar manner. That is, just as on a superficial level delinquent vandalism is negativistic and unproductive, yet at the same time becomes meaningful and understandable in a wider social context, so moral panics about crime, although disproportionate, wrongly conceptualized and even counterproductive, become understandable and *'reasonable'* in the light of conflicts existing in the total society (Young, 2009).

Of course, once again, one of this is to say this does not mean that subcultural behaviour is inevitably tenable (see Matza, 1969) – it is frequently not; nor that moral panics are correct in their foundation – they are not by definition. Rather it is to stress that deviant action and the reaction against it is not mindless behaviour, rather it is meaningful behaviour which may or may not involve mistakes in rationality.

The New Criminology: For a Fully Social Theory of Deviance

It is out of this background that *The New Criminology* emerged. It was heavily influenced by C. Wright Mills, stressing individual actors placed in immediate predicaments set in a wider social structure and historical period combined with the notion of the dyad which insisted on the need to explain both the deviant action and the reaction against it, which emerged out of the new theories of deviance. Thus the core agenda of the book concerns itself with establishing both the formal and substantive requirements of a fully social theory of deviance and to examine the extent to which the criminological canon from the past to the present measures up to this task. In terms of scope it was concerned at the macro level that theories explain both the origins of the deviant act and the reaction against it, in terms of the wider links to the culture and structure of the total society, while at the immediate level it looked to their ability to place the act in particular social contexts. Furthermore, it stressed that the interaction between action and reaction over time should be placed in a processual and historical context. Thus it took on board the Millsian injunction to place individual action and concerns within the wider culture and structure and place this in a historical context but melded this to the twin demands of the new deviancy theory, namely to perform this *symmetrically*; that is for both actor and reactor: drug user and the police apprehending them, both criminal and judge, both deviancy and its representation in the mass media.

On a substantive level *The New Criminology* demanded that an adequate theory should first address the problem of human nature and social order and to take cognizance of the human predicament, which involves actors who are both determined and determining, that they make history but in circumstances not of their own choosing. Further, that in terms of social order it must recognize the class nature of society, of the extraordinary inequalities of wealth and power and the extensive pluralism of values, some of resistance, some of acquiescence in modern capitalist societies. On an individual level it evoked a sequential, processual model of human action which involved a dialectic between structure and consciousness, that is, related typical sets of motives to situated historical contexts. The attempt therefore was to create a politically informed economy of criminal action and of the reaction it excites, and a social psychology of these ongoing dynamics. To sum up: 'It was critical not only of the inadequate notions of human nature and social order but about the *partiality* of existing theory: we have constructed . . . the formal elements of a theory that would be adequate to move criminology out of its own imprisonment in artificially segregated specifics. We have attempted to bring the parts together in order to form the whole' (Taylor et al., 1973, p. 279).

Above all it placed crime and the response to it in the context of the total society. A few of the most perceptive critics within American criminology realized that this was their key weakness. Thus, Albert Cohen, reflecting on the state and prospects for criminology at the 1977 meeting of the American Sociological Association, pointed to how 'American criminology has been disproportionately concerned with the social psychology and microsociology of crime. It has been too little concerned with the macrosociological question . . .' (1978, p. 152). He described such criminology as being 'grossly undeveloped' a phrase resonating with our previous discussion. He noted, quite correctly that Merton's famous paper on social structure and anomie (1938) had the potential for allaying this but, in fact, only a few beginnings had been made on this basis and the same remains true until today. He went on to say that 'the chief exception to this is the Marxists'; not a position he himself endorsed but this was simply the fact of the matter.

The overall response to *The New Criminology* was mixed to say the least. Radicals such as Al Gouldner (who was kind enough to write an introduction) welcomed the revelation of the 'silences' with regard to so much criminological theory where the social and philosophical underpinnings were unspoken and concealed in a technical rhetoric. He placed the work in the line of Mills and the early Merton and stressed the need to place crime and deviance in the context of the wider society and 'to explore its *Lebenswelt* without becoming the technicians of the "Welfare" State and its zookeepers of deviance' (1973, p xiv). But from establishment criminology there was a mixture of annoyance and mystification. Clarence Jeffrey, 1978 President of the American Society of Criminology, commented with characteristic mixture of clarity and alacrity of the dangers of: 'The communist ideology of anti-positivism, anti-bourgeoisism, radical sociology/criminology' (1980, p. 119). Quite so! Absolutely! Nearly all of the members of the NDC and the Centre for Contemporary Cultural Studies were on the libertarian left: Marxists, Anarchists, Left Social Democrats. It was this predisposition to meta-narrative that enabled them to take New Deviancy Theory and place it in the structural context of a total society. For the majority of the rich American tradition, whether it was Goffman or Garfinkel with all their magical insights, was trapped at a micro level and it was only in subcultural theory that the total dynamics of capitalism were even hinted at. For not even in Merton's seminal article, 'Social Structure and Anomie' (1938), with its undoubted influence of Marx and the radical Durkheim, is the actual gearing behind the American Dream in all its seductiveness and institutionalized failure (a theory of legitimation crisis if there ever was one) spelt out or even implied, and, of course, Karl Marx does not even merit a footnote (Young, 2010).

As I have argued, this silence about the dynamics of the whole society, this loss of meta narrative, whether Marxist, anarchist or social democratic, and the concentration, however imaginatively, on the micro level, is understandable in terms of the differing social and political contexts of the United States and Britain – and is even more glaring in the contrast between America and Western Europe as a whole. As we have seen, American academics faced, during the twentieth century, two Red scares and, in the late 1960s, something of a third, seemingly incessant political surveillance and worked in the context of political philosophies emphasizing individualism and neo-liberal values. In contrast, Britain was a country with collectivist politics, an extant Labour tradition, and where, for example, membership of the Communist Party or an anarchist organization, would in the academy scarcely warrant a mention. Every now and then in the United States radical scholars would, so to speak, put their heads above the trenches only to face extremely hostile responses. Two particularly notorious cases were events in Berkeley and New York City. In 1976 the influential and popular Berkeley School of Criminology with a gifted minority of radical criminologists was infamously closed by direct political pressure. Somewhat earlier Richard Cloward had devised the Mobilization for Youth project which directly implemented Merton's ideas that delinquency was a product of lack of job opportunities. In 1964 the project was exposed by the *New York Daily News* as a 'commie' front. The city offices of the project were raided by FBI agents, files seized, and staff systematically called in to be interrogated (Brotherton, 2010). Yet, as Stephen Pfohl put it, 'What could be more American than trying to incorporate people into the opportunity structure as a whole?' One might reflect what could be more American than government intervention against any project which suggests transformative change. Needless to say no such responses occurred in Britain or in the rest of Europe, in the numerous countries where critical criminology took root.

Critical Criminology: The Ten Ironies

Let me pause for a moment and summarize the major features of critical criminology. These present themselves as a series of ten 'ironies' which serve to turn establishment criminology on its head.

Ontology	That crime has no ontological reality and that the 'same' behaviour can be constructed totally differently. Thus, for example, a serial killer could be either a psychopathic monster or a hero if dropping bombs daily in the Afghan War.
Dyadic Nature of Crime And Deviance	That crime and deviance includes rule makers and rule breakers; explanation necessitates, therefore, a double problem; why people make and enforce rules and why people break them. Furthermore, that the enforcement of rules shapes crime and deviance and the existence of rules invites transgression.
Socialization	That the core values of competitiveness, acquisitiveness, individualism and hedonism are close to the motivations for crime, so that the well-socialized person is more likely to offend than the undersocialized.
Contradiction	That the ideals and institutions which legitimate and hold the system together are the very ones which society thwarts and the frustrations generated deep dysfunctions in the system.
Function	That the system called forth deviance and disorder focuses on 'the criminal', 'the outsider', 'the other', creating a major mechanism of governance which

	reverses causality so that instead of an unequal and unmeritocratic system creating problems, it is the scapegoats themselves who are seen to be the major problems of society. Systemic dysfunctions are then transformed into the very material which helps hold the fabric of society together.
Seriousness	That crime occurs throughout the social structure and that the crimes of the powerful are more serious in their consequences than the crimes of the poor. That structural violence is more serious than criminal violence.
Selectivity	That criminal law, although phrased in a language of formal equality, is targeted in a way that is selective and substantially unequal.
Decentring	That the criminal justice system is not the front-line defence against crime but a minor part of the system of social control, itself crucially dependent on informal norms of civil society.
Counter-Productivity · and Self-Fulfilment	That the prison and the criminal justice system produce criminals rather than de-fusing criminality. That illusions and stereotypes of crime can be real in their consequences and self-fulfilling in reality.
Secondary Harm	That the primary harm of a social problem is frequently of a lesser order than the secondary harm accruing from the intervention to control it. The prime example of this being the regulation of drug use.

Critical Criminology in the Subsequent Years

Leaving aside the existence of . . . interesting disputes and divisions, it is clear that the new perspective overall has now become established and institutionalized. In the same way initially outrageous art movements (such as Dada and surrealism) eventually became respectable, so too has the new deviance and criminology become part of the accepted order of things. Its practitioners are ensconced in orthodox academic departments, journals, examining boards and publishing companies. No booklist would be complete without one. (Cohen, 1981, p. 241)

Thus Stan Cohen talks of the institutionalization of that which was once iconoclastic. Critical criminology has become a staple of textbooks, its concerns form the basis of secondary-school sociology exams, it runs conferences, journals and research programmes. Indeed, in Britain, outside of course Cambridge, which in origins and development has acted as an outpost of central government, the majority of centres which teach criminology are within the rubric of critical criminology.

Flourishing of Critical Criminology

My contention is that critical criminology in this age of the Gulag and the punitive turn is massively needed, it is the counter-voice to neo-liberalism and conservatism. And what is more critical criminology is flourishing. The most incisive recent textbooks are all in this genre, witness Piers Beirne and James Messerschmidt's *Criminology* (2010); Mark Lanier and Stuart Henry's *Essential Criminology* (2004); René van Swaaningen's *Critical Criminology: Visions from Europe* (1997); John Lea's *Crime and Modernity* (2002); Rob White and Fiona Haines' *Crime and Criminology* (2008); Gregg Barak's *Criminology: An Integrated Approach* (2009); John Tierney's *Criminology: Theory and Context* (2006); Wayne Morrison's *Theoretical Criminology: From Modernity to Post-Modernism* (1995); Roger Matthews' *Doing Time* (2010); Russell Hogg and Dave Brown's *Rethinking Law and Order* (1998); Jayne Mooney's *Gender, Violence and the Social Order* (2000); Ian Taylor's *Crime in Context* (1999); and Dario Melossi's *Controlling Crime: Controlling Society* (2008). It has produced the most exciting ethnography and critique of the last fifteen years. Read Philippe Bourgois' 'Just Another Night in a Shooting Gallery' (1998); Jeff Ferrell's 'Criminological Verstehen: Inside the Immediacy of Crime' (1997); Loic Wacquant's *Les Prisons de la Misère*; Nils Christie's *Crime Control as Industry* (2004), Vincenzo Ruggiero's *Crime and Markets* (2000), Damian Zaitch's (2001) wonderful study of Colombian cocaine dealing in Rotterdam; Pat Carlen's *Jigsaw* (1996); or look at Walter DeKeseredy and his associates' remarkable study of crime and poverty on a Canadian public housing estate with its acute awareness of gender and ethnicity (DeKeseredy et al., 2003). Critical criminology has been at the cutting edge of the discipline and is international in its scope; think of the burgeoning literature on governmentality (e.g. Stenson, 1998; Rose, 2000; O'Malley, 1999); on masculinity (Jefferson, 2002; Hall, 1997; Messerschmidt, 2000); Phil Scraton's intrepid investigative criminology in the harrowing *Hillsborough: The Truth* (2000); the opening up of the crime prevention discourses to critical analysis by Adam Crawford (1997) and Gordon Hughes (1998); the development of work on youth and justice by John Muncie (2009); Shahid Alvi (2000) and John Pitts (2001); Ruth Jamieson's pioneering work on the criminology of war (1998, 1999); or the extraordinary flourishing of cultural criminology (Ferrell et al., 2001; Ferrell and Saunders, 1995; Presdee, 2000, Ferrell et al., 2008; Hayward and Presdee, 2010).

What is of course true, is that the vast expansion of the criminal justice system has resulted in a plethora of evaluative studies, research programmes and vocational courses (see Robinson, 2001) which have generated a substantial institutional base for orthodox criminology. All of this further underscores the necessity of a critical voice to counter the minimalist, theoretical 'noise' constantly arising from out of the crime control complex.

Whatever Happened to Grand Theory: Mission Impossibilism and the Theorodactyl

If Abstracted Empiricism has become the orthodoxy of establishment criminology, what has happened to Mill's predictions with regard to Grand Theory? This – alas – has become a creature of the left and a constant flaw in the critical approach. It is characterized first of all by impossibilism (ten reasons why any extant policy will not work and no suggestions at all as to what might make things a even a little better and perhaps even offer transitional stepping stones to a genuine social trans-formation), secondly by a very high level of abstraction and the constant evocation of the latest, most fashionable theories. And whereas in the old days such a viewpoint was attached to a grand narrative of change – the view (however mistakenly) that nothing progressive could happen without first a total structural transformation with no steps in between, today the absence of narrative, of progress and the possible makes it even more detached from reality. Often this position is associated with a belief in the remorseless power of the system as if the 'masters of the universe' were indomitable and their techniques of control unassailable. It is as if neo-liberalism did not contain its own contradictions and instabilities (a view surely easily dispatched by recent events in the world of finance) and that such an ideology had invaded and demoralized the human spirit, leaving a barren world devoid of human creativity and resistance. (See, for instance, Steve Hall et al., 2007; Rose, 1999.)

Let us envisage this academic creature as another dinosaur like our old friend the datasaur, my metaphor for abstracted empiricism, that we met at the beginning of this book. It was you will recall a creature with a little brain wandering from dataset to dataset, grant to grant; it had a small head yet a huge gut for processing survey material; it was always on the move but it was strangely without direction or purpose. Grand Theory nowadays evokes another creature, a therodactyl, with a domed head and huge wings soaring high above reality in an endless quest for a fashionable perch, gliding from theory to theory, detected from below only by the trail of references it leaves behind, mouthing near incompre-hensible sentences with a hint of a French accent yet strangely like the datasaur, unsure of where it is going and what it is there for.

10
Rescuing the Imagination

Just now, among social scientists, there is a widespread uneasiness, both intellectual and moral, about the direction their chosen studies seem to be taking. This uneasiness, as well as the unfortunate tendencies that contribute to it are, I suppose, part of a general malaise of intellectual life. Yet perhaps the uneasiness is more acute among social scientists, if only because of the larger promise that has guided much earlier work in their fields, the nature of the subjects with which they deal and the urgent need for significant work today.

Not everyone shares this uneasiness, but the fact that many do not is itself a cause of further uneasiness among those who are alert to the promise and honest enough to admit the pretentious mediocrity of much current effort. It is quite frankly, my hope to increase this uneasiness, to define some of its sources, to help transform it into a specific urge to realize the promise of social science, to clear the ground for new beginnings: in short to indicate some of the tasks that must now be done.

(Wright Mills, 1959, pp. 26–7)

Criminology: The Lopsided Subject

Criminology is a strange subject, a cock-eyed, lopsided subject. It is unique, as the editors of *The Oxford Handbook of Criminology*, put it, in being 'the only highly developed social science which explicitly takes a social problem, and thus a political question ... as its defining subject matter' (Maguire et al., 1994, p. 5). As it is, from this perspective, the defining edge of the subject of criminology and, traditionally, the sociology of deviance is, as David Matza indicates in *Becoming Deviant* (1969), aimed at getting rid of what it is studying. Other sociologies study religion, youth, science, population; it is as if demography were re-titled the science of contraceptive studies. Would it not be better just to rid ourselves of this sad and crackpot affair? Many radicals have done exactly that from Carol Smart onwards, merging what criticism it has with critical sociology, incorporating the gender implications into mainstream feminism, its evidence of racism in post-colonialism, or constructing a more independent yardstick of infraction in human rights or perhaps, most ambitiously, to create a new 'ology', zemiology, the study of social harm (Hillyard et al., 2008). Indeed a somewhat revisionist account of the field would maintain that the very nature of criminology is suspect, that the history of the subject is one of constant domination by the criminal justice system for all but brief interludes, the critical debate in the late 1960s and early 1970s being perhaps the only exception. All other discourses are simply the manifestation of power, any changes in theory being merely a reflection of changes in the basis of such power in particular the shift from penal- welfarism to situational crime prevention (see Young, 2002b). Thus, in recent years a drastically different version of the subsequent history of critical criminology, and of criminology in general, has gained currency. This has involved perceiving the critical years of the 1960s and early 1970s as simply a brief interlude before orthodox criminology reasserted itself. The most elaborate presentation of such a revisionist history is that of David Garland in a series of pieces from *Punishment and Welfare* (1985) to *The Culture of Control* (2001; see also 1988, 1997, and with R. Sparks, 2000).

On the contrary, I think I have shown that the critical tradition in criminology has a long and continuing presence. But it also has a purchase on the world of great and increasing importance. It is not a discipline, of course, it is a field of study which focuses upon this process of power, inequality and stigmatization, this distillation of the excluded which gives rise to the sorry residents of the prison, which has become such a gargantuan apparatus and a major part of late modern society. It is this aspect of criminology which fascinates Zygmunt Bauman (2000a). He sees in the various forms of confinement: the concentration camps of totalitarianism, the Panopticons of early industrialization, the warehouse prisons of today as the 'laboratories' of their period, 'factories of exclusion' where the limitations of human routinization are experimented with. I am not sure about the concept of laboratories; it implies too much intent, but there can be little doubt that the social disposal systems of a society tell you much about their core nature. Thus it is difficult, particularly in the present period, to regard the criminal justice system as something external to the normal workings of the system and, hence, that criminology be consigned to the examination of the peripheral and the exceptional, an interesting but somewhat marginal discipline concerned with the study of the maladjusted individual set in some fringe annexes of social reality. Such a conception is palpably incorrect in the case of the liberal democracies of late modernity. Indeed in the United States, where the system of prison camps stretches from coast to coast, mass incarceration has taken on a signature quality. Instead it is preferable to view the process of criminalization as a critical and integral part of a core system of social inclusion and exclusion which reaches across the biographies of each citizen, selecting and rejecting and involving all the major institutions of society.

At heart the fundamental contradiction is that the system legitimates itself by proclaiming a meritocracy of effort and reward, an American Dream of distributive justice repeated in its counterparts across the Western World. Yet it endorses a class structure where wealth and reward are distributed with scant regard to such fairness and where social mobility is severely limited. It is a race track where some people start far from the finishing line with heavy burdens to carry and impediments to slow them down whereas others start one foot from the finish; indeed they very often own the track. And some, of course, are not allowed on the track at all and are only there as spectators to the distribution of prizes and the celebration of 'success'. It is a folly of a social structure where, as the comedian George Carlin put it, 'the only people who believe in the American Dream are asleep', where doubt and prejudice resound throughout a ramshackle polity and where society is held together by a tissue of dreams, of far-fetched hopes and a ragbag of cynical realism.

We live in a society which both includes and excludes, which attracts and repels, which evokes aspirations and generates disappointment. In such a socially bulimic society the criminal justice system is an institution which closely interlocks with all of the other institutions. Let us look a little at this process starting with the school, which in a liberal democracy is the supposed standard bearer of meritocratic values and the main avenue of opportunity. The schools of the poor in say New York and in London, with their wretched facilities and warehouse-like aspects, educate sufficiently to prepare the student for the lowest jobs in the social structure and enough for them to know that this is unfair. They are where for the poorest section of the population dreams are learnt and reality encountered. With their protective fences and their police guards they begin increasingly to look like a preparation for prison. Immigrants are attracted from across the world with hopes of a better life yet these great waves of immigration are quickly soured into a stoic realism in the process of assimilation, which is transformed by the second generation into dismay, disappointment and discontent. And for those without documentation they are subject to arrest and deportation when their cheap labour is no longer needed (Brotherton and Barrios,

2011). The disaffection that hangs over the poorest areas of our cities such as East New York in Brooklyn and the East End of London breeds among some macho-cultures and predatory behaviour: its roots in the contradictions of the system, its narratives based on the individualism and violence of the wider society. The mass media with their saccharine celebration of success, a celebratory meritocracy of sportsmen, rap artists and movie stars, provides for the poor a model of extreme reward and extremely unlikely chance of success, which has little to do with a genuine meritocracy. The narratives in videogame, movie and newscast constitute violence as one of the central tropes of our society. The media parades success stories of inclusion while, at the same time, they present us with a series of exclusions, folk devils who are presented as the prime causes of the manifest problems of society. Finally, the criminal justice system is seen as an essential part of this social order serving to protect us against crime, illegal immigration, drugs and terror but, in fact, creating a grotesque prison system, which criminalizes and hardens the offender, making sane people mad and mad people madder and then spilling them back into the most deprived areas of the city, further perpetuating the cycle of crime.

The criminal justice system is far from peripheral to the system, a backup when all else has failed, it has become encoiled in the day-to-day lives of so many, it is ubiquitous. The 4.2 million surveillance cameras in Britain where the average person is estimated to be caught on camera 300 times a day, it is the 2.3 million people in prison in the United States and 1 in 34 of the adult population under the supervision of the criminal justice system, it is a constant presence. Certainly if the Gulag told us important truths about Soviet society, the mass incarceration within liberal democracies in late modernity tells us much about the capitalist wing of modernity.

Critical Criminology as the Mainstream

There is a criminology which is informed by sociology, which concerns itself with meaning and power, and which understands that human beings create cultural solutions to their life problems in social structures which are largely not of their own making. This is a criminology which, as we have seen, traces its lineage through the Victorians, such as Mayhew, Booth and Engels, via the Chicago School of the 1930s to the revolutionary developments of the new deviancy theory in the US in the late 1950s and 1960s, and through to the new criminology and subcultural theory of Britain in the 1970s and early 1980s. It is this lineage which cultural criminology places itself in as a criminology of late modernity at the beginning of the twenty-first century. It is a criminology which is influenced by Marx, Weber and Durkheim, on one side, and the symbolic interactionism of George Herbert Mead and phenomenology of Alfred Schutz on the other. It is a criminology which exists *within* sociology; it is the application of sociological thought to the problem of crime and deviance. It denies criminology an independent existence: for crime and deviance is just the 'disorder' which mirrors order or, indeed, frequently very much part of that order itself. It is a subject which is not only central to the understanding of late modern society but is clearly in the mainstream of sociological thought.

There is a parallel criminology, minimalist in its theory, one-dimensional in its portrayal of human action. Its genealogy stretches from Lombroso in the late nineteenth century to the work of Travis Hirschi, James Q. Wilson and Marcus Felson today. It is the world of positivism and rational choice theory, a stance which denies meaning and minimalizes social structure; it is constructed around an analytical individualism which is contrary to the main thrust of sociological thinking. It is a subject which, as I have documented, is the very opposite of Mills' actor structure and history and the exact incarnation of abstracted empiricism. This criminology is, as David Garland (2001), so well articulated, a creation of the 'culture of control', indeed the movement from penal welfarism to situational crime prevention arises out of the changing 'surfaces' of control. It is a creature of the practicality of dominance and the conservatism of thought.

Such a criminology, as we have seen in its attempt at explanation, takes meaning away from human actors and distances crime from the wide social structure and values. It is the white noise generated by the criminal justice system, it is the criminology of denatured causes, of defective individuals and deficit cultures, it is the criminology of evaluation: of locks and bolts, of ten point drug treatment programmes and surveillance cameras. It is a criminology which has lost contact with reality, it is the most advanced stage of abstracted empiricism grown unwieldy yet self-confident in the massive shadow of an overbearing criminal justice system.

In substantial ways, then, Mills' predictions have been validated. There has been throughout the social sciences and particularly in criminology, a fetishization of method, the detachment of method from theory and a consequent aggrandisement of method and a shriveling of theory. Method has been bureaucratized, outsourced to independent, commercial research teams and administered by people who maintain great social distances from their subjects. Yet Mills himself, although scathing with regard to the direction that sociology was going, was, at the same time an optimist. He was so despite the incursions of abstracted empiricism and the political pressures upon him both from outside and within the academy. He warned about abstracted empiricism and the conformist tendencies of many of his colleagues, yet he was forthright about the rules of craftsmanship, inherited from the sociological tradition and eclectic and somewhat anarchic in his approach. Like the great philosopher of science Paul Feyerabend, Mills took what was useful from method, that which fitted a humanistic perspective while rejecting what was in the province of his 'cheerful robots'.

And there are grounds for optimism today, as we view the brittle foundations of positivism, unsteady in a world characterized by hyperpluralism and immense diversity and wonder at the banality of its world view and the inconsequential nature of its explanatory grasp and findings. For let us reiterate again that if a natural science of society were possible then, on this criterion alone, orthodox criminology would be inadequate. It confuses the ease of statistical manipulation with the rigours of science, it confuses scientific training with the rote learning from the recipe books of regression analysis. If a science of society were possible this is poor science; if a humanistic approach to society is correct this is tawdry scholarship.

None of this is to eschew the quantitative, a humanistic criminology needs numbers just as it is not restrained and defined by them. I have in this book attempted to utilize numbers effectively but, at the same time, indicated the limitations of what Sorokin called quantophilia. The criticism does not revolve round the imperfect and approximate nature of measurement, in the natural sciences the measurement of numerous things and events, outside of the laboratory, from climate change to the number of butterflies in the forest, is approximate and hesitant. Rather it is the false belief that, as Mills put it, truth is reflected in precision. Moreover, that very many measurements particularly of attitudes and reported behaviour far from revealing reality, obfuscate and conceal. Some of the data are inadequate, worse still some are toxic, corrupting argument and undermining sound judgement. Finally, 'hard' data change with culture and human interpretation and findings are historically situated and lack any nomothetic quality. They have a capriciousness which sits ill with pretensions of science.

I believe that recognition of the blurred, devious and ironic nature of social reality – although true of all time, presents itself all the more clearly in late modernity where the shift and pluralism of values encourage the double take, threatening daily what Alfred Schutz called the 'taken-for-granted world of everyday life'. Further, that it is such a questioning of the solidity of the social world and the stated purposes of its institutions which comes close to what we mean by the word 'critical'. Zygmunt Bauman in his interview with Keith Tester, ponders on the nature of critical theory: 'What I understand by that term is the kind of theorizing which accepts that, first, "things are not necessarily what they seem to be" and second that "the world may be different from what it is" ...' And Bauman is fiercely dismissive of those who would view human culture as a thing of inertia, the place of habit, routine, absence of reflection – a sort of stabilizing 'preservative' of humanity. For, as we have seen, as the taken-for-granted world begins to disintegrate in late modernity, reflex gives way to reflexivity. In contrast, he says: 'Once you accept culture with its endemic restlessness and its inborn inclination to transcendence as the fundamental characteristic of the human mode of being, the idea of "critical theory" appears pleonastic, like "buttery butter" or "metallic iron". Theory which wants to be faithful and adequate to its object cannot but be "critical" ' (Bauman and Tester, 2001, p. 33).

All good sociology is critical, as is all competent criminology. It is my belief that critical criminology is more relevant today than ever and that the critical attitude fits the experience of later modernity. If we return to the themes of the ten ironies it is striking how the problems faced in the 1970s are built larger today and how the concerns are more a harbinger of the present than a moment of the past. Every single one of the ironies, from the counterproductive nature of the prison to the role of stigmatization and othering in law-and-order politics, are of immense relevance. We are privileged to work in an area which has its focus on the fundamental dislocations of justice that occur throughout our social order, a place of irony and contest, of vituperation and transgression. Those who would seek to marginalize critical criminology fail to comprehend its purchase on the grain of social reality, those in our own camp who would narrow their definition of the 'critical' to the sectarian or the esoteric, fail to understand the central position of critique as a counterbalance to neoliberalism and its discourses of control. Let us set about our task, keeping in mind the urgency of opposition, yet with an eye for irony imbued, as always, with a sense of satire at the strange meanderings of the datasaur and the sad charade of science played out before us. Above all we must constantly be aware of the inherent creativity of human culture and of the rush of emotions and feelings which characterizes the human condition and the capacity for imagination which this demands and engenders.

References

ACSF Investigators, 1992, 'AIDS and Sexual Behaviour in France', *Nature* 360, 3 December: 407–9.

Adler, P. and Adler, P., 1998, 'Moving Backwards', in J. Ferrell and M. Hamm (eds), *Ethnography at the Edge*. Boston: Northeastern University Press.

Agee, J. and Evans, W., 1960/1941, *Let Us Now Praise Famous Men*. Cambridge, MA: The Riverside Press.

Agozino, B., 2003, *Counter-Colonial Criminology: A Critique of Imperialist Reason*. London: Pluto Press.

Alexander, J. and Smith. P. 2002 'The Strong Program in Cultural Theory', in J. Turner (ed.), *Handbook of Sociological Theory*. New York: Plenum.

Alvi, S., 2000, *Youth and the Canadian Criminal Justice System*. Cincinnati, OH: Anderson Publishing.

Anderson, E., 1999, *Code of the Street*. New York: W. W. Norton.

Arnott, J., 1999, *The Long Firm*. New York: Soho.

Baker, P., Harris, S., and Webbon, C., 2002a, 'Ecology: Effect of British Hunting Ban on Fox Numbers', *Nature* 419 (6902): 34.

Baker, P., Harris, S., and Webbon, C., 2002b, 'British Hunting Ban Had no Effect on Fox Numbers', from *Mammal Society Fact Sheet*: www.abdn. ac.uk/~nhi775/fox_hunting_reports.html.

Bakhtin, M., 1984, *Rabelais and this World*. Bloomington: Indiana University Press.

Bancroft, J., 1992, 'Sexual Behaviour in Britain and France', *British Journal of Medicine* 305: 447.12.

Barak, Gregg, 2009, *Criminology*. Lanham MD: Rowmam and Littlefield.

Barclay, G., Tavares, C. and Siddique, A., 2001, *International Comparisons of Criminal Justice Statistics 1999*. London: Home Office.

Bauman, Z., 1976, *Socialism: The Active Utopia*. New York: Holmes and Meier.

Bauman, Z., 1995, *Life in Fragments*. Oxford: Blackwell.

Bauman, Z., 1998a, *Globalization*. Cambridge: Polity.

Bauman, Z., 1998b, *Work, Consumerism and the New Poor*. Buckingham: Open University Press.

Bauman, Z. 1999, *Culture as Praxis*. London Sage.

Bauman, Z., 2000a, 'Social Uses of Law and Order', in D. Garland and R. Sparks (eds), *Criminology and Social Theory*. Oxford: Oxford University Press.

Bauman, Z., 2000b, *Liquid Modernity*. Cambridge: Polity.

Bauman, Z., 2004, *Wasted Lives*. Cambridge: Polity.

Bauman, Z. and Tester, K., 2001, *Conversations with Zygmunt Bauman*. Cambridge: Polity.

Baumer, E., 2007, 'Untangling Research Puzzles in Merton's Multilevel Anomie Theory', *Theoretical Criminology* 11(1): 63–93.

Beck, A. and Mumola, C., 1999, *Prisoners in 1998*. Washington DC: US Department of Justice.

Becker, H. S., 1963, *Outsiders*. New York: The Free Press.

Becker, H. S., 1965, 'Deviance and Deviates', in Boroff, D. (ed.), *The State of the Nation*. New Jersey: Prentice-Hall, reprinted in H. S. Becker, *Sociological Work*. London: Allen Lane.

Becker, H. S., 1967, 'Whose Side Are We On?', *Social Problems*, 14: 239–47.

Becker, H. S., 1999, 'The Chicago School So-Called', *Qualitative Sociology* 22(1): 3–12.

Becker, H. S., 2005, 'Introduction', in *Outsidere: Studier i Afvigelsessociologi*. Copenhagen: Hans Reitzel.

Beirne, Piers and Messerschmidt, James, 2010, *Criminology*. New York: Oxford University Press.

Benton-Short, L., Price, M. and Friedman, S., 2005, 'Globalization from Below: The Ranking of Global Immigrant Cities', *International Journal of Urban and Regional Research* 29(4): 945–59.

Berger, P. and Luckmann, T., 1966, *The Social Construction of Reality*. New York: Doubleday.

Berlanstein, L. (ed.), 1993, *Rethinking Labour History*. Urbana: University of Illinois Press.

Berman, M., 1983, *All That's Solid Melts Into Air*. London: Verso.

Bettelheim, B., 1943 'Individual and Mass Behavior in Extreme Situations', *Journal of Abnormal and Social Behavior* 38: 417–25.

Bhabha, H., 1993, *The Location of Culture*. London: Routledge.

Biderman, A., Johnson, L., McIntyre, J. and Weir, A., 1967, *Report on a Pilot Study in the District of Columbia on Victimization and Attitudes to Law Enforcement*. Washington DC: Government Printing Office.

Blok, Anton, 1998, 'The Narcissism of Minor Differences', *European Journal of Social Theory* 1: 33–56.

Blumer, H., 1956, 'Sociological Analysis and the "Variable"', *American Sociological Review* 21: 683–90.

Blumstein, A. and Wallman, J., (eds), 2000, *The Crime Drop in America*. Cambridge: Cambridge University Press.

Bottoms, A., 1995, 'The Philosophy and Politics of Punishment and Sentencing', in C. Clarkson and R. Morgan (eds), *The Politics of Sentencing Reform.* Oxford: Oxford University Press.

Bottoms, A. and Wiles, P., 1997, 'Environmental Criminology', in M. Maguire, R. Morgan and R. Reiner (eds), *The Oxford Handbook of Criminology* (2nd edn), pp. 305–60. Oxford: Clarendon Press.

Bourdieu, P. et al., 1999, *The Weight of the World.* Cambridge: Polity.

Bourgois, P., 1995, *In Search of Respect.* Cambridge: Cambridge University Press.

Bourgois, P., 1998, 'Just Another Night in a Shooting Gallery', *Theory, Culture and Society* 15(2): 37–66.

Bovenkerk, F. and Yesilgoz, Y., 2004, 'Crime, Justice and the Multicultural Administration of Justice' in J. Ferrell et al. (eds), *Cultural Criminology Unleashed.* London: Glasshouse.

Braine, R., Busway, S., and Paternoster, R., 2003, 'Examining the Prevalence of Criminal Desistance', *Criminology* 41(2): 423–48.

Braithwaite, J., 1981, 'The Myth of Social Class and Criminality Reconsidered', *American Sociological Review*, 46: 36–57.

Brake, M., 1980, *The Sociology of Youth Culture and Youth Subcultures: Sex and Drugs and Rock 'n' Roll.* London: Routledge.

Brake, M., 1985, *Comparative Youth Culture: The Sociology of Youth Cultures and Youth Subcultures in America, Britain, and Canada.* London: Routledge.

Brotherton, D., 2008, 'Beyond Social Reproduction: Bringing Resistance Back into Gang Theory', *Theoretical Criminology*: 12(1) pp 55–78.

Brotherton, D., 2010, 'Richard Coward' in K. Hayward, S. Maruna and J. Mooney (eds), *Fifty Key Thinkers in Criminology.* London: Routledge.

Brotherton, D. and Barrios, L., 2004, *The Almighty Latin King and Queen Nation.* New York: Columbia University Press.

Brotherton D. and Barrios L., 2011, *Banished to the Homeland.* New York: Columbia University Press.

Bureau of Justice Statistics, 1999, *Prison and Jail Inmates at Midyear 1998.* Washington DC: US Department of Justice.

Burney, Elizabeth, 2005, *Making People Behave.* Cullompton, Devon: Willan.

Bushway, S. and Weisburd, D., 2006, 'Acknowledging the Centrality of Quantitative Criminology in Criminology and Criminal Justice', *The Criminologist* 31(1): 3–4.

Campbell, C., 1987, *The Romantic Ethic and the Spirit of Modern Consumerism.* Oxford: Blackwell.

Carlen, P., 1996, *Jigsaw: A Political Criminology of Youth Homelessness.* Buckingham: Open University Press.

Carlen, P., 2010, 'Against Evangelism in Criminology: For Criminology as a Scientific Art'.

Cantor, D. and Lynch, J., 2000, 'Self-Report Surveys as Measures of Crime and Criminal Victimization' in National Institute of Justice (US). *Criminal Justice 2000*, Washington, DC: National Institute of Justice.

Christie, N., 2004, *Crime Control as Industry* (3rd edn). London: Routledge.

Clear T., 2007, *Imprisoning Communities*. Oxford: Oxford University Press.

Clemner, Donald, 1940, *The Prison Community*. Boston: The Christopher Publishing House.

Clinard, M. and Abbott, D., 1973, *Crime in Developing Countries*. New York: Wiley.

Cloward, R. and Ohlin, L., 1961, *Delinquency and Opportunity*. London: Routledge.

Cohen, A. K., 1955, *Delinquent Boys: The Culture of the Gang*. New York: The Free Press.

Cohen, A. K., 1965, 'The Sociology of the Deviant Act: Anomie Theory and Beyond', *American Sociological Review* 30: 5–14.

Cohen, A. K., 1978, 'The Study of Crime: Items for an Agenda' in *Major Social Issues* (eds.) J. Yinger and S. Cutler, New York: The Free Press.

Cohen, J., Gorr, W. and Singh, P., 2003, 'Estimating Intervention Effects in Varying Settings: Do Police Raids Reduce Illegal Drug Dealing at Nuisance Bars?' *Criminology*, 41(2): 257–92.

Cohen, P, 1972, 'Subcultural Conflict and Working-class Community', Centre for Contemporary Culture Studies, *Working Papers* 2: 5–53 (reprinted in Cohen, P., 1997).

Cohen, P., 1997, *Rethinking the Youth Question*. London: Macmillan.

Cohen, S., 1971, 'Introduction', in *Images of Deviance*, London: Penguin.

Cohen, S., 1972, *Folk Devils and Moral Panics*. London: McGibbon and Kee.

Cohen, S., 1981, 'Footprints in the Sand' in M. Fitzgerald, G. McLennan and J. Pawson, 1981, *Crime and Society*. London: Routledge.

Cohen S., 1985, *Visions of Social Control*. Cambridge: Polity.

Cohen S., 1988, *Against Criminology*. New Brunswick: Transaction.

Cohen, S., 1997, 'Intellectual Scepticism and Political Commitment', in P. Walton and J. Young (eds), *The New Criminology Revisited*. London: Macmillan.

Cohen, S. and Taylor, L., 1972, *Psychological Survival*. Harmondsworth: Penguin.

Cohn, E. and Farrington D., 1990, 'Differences between British and American Criminology: An Analysis of Citations', *British Journal of Criminology* 30(4): 467–80.

Cohn, E. and Farrington, D.,1994, 'Who are the Most Influential; Criminologists in the English-Speaking World?' *British Journal of Criminology* 34: 204–25.

Cohn, E. and Farrington, D., 1998, ' Changes in the Most Cited Scholars in Major International Journals Between 1991–1995', *British Journal of Criminology* 38(1): 156–67.

Coleman, C. and Moynihan, J., 1996, *Understanding Crime Data; Haunted by the Dark Figure*. Buckingham, UK: Open University Press.

Coleman, J., 1990, *The Foundations of Social Theory*. Cambridge, MA: Harvard University Press.

Conquergood, D., 1991, 'Rethinking Ethnography', *Communications Monographs* 58: 179–94.

Conquergood, D., 1992, 'On Reppin' and Rhetoric: Gang Representations',

Paper presented at the *Philosophy and Rhetoric of Inquiry Seminar*, University of Iowa, April.

Conquergood, D., 1993, 'Homeboys and Hoods: Gang Communication and Cultural Space, in L. Frey (ed), *Group Communication in Context: Studies of Natural Groups*. Hillsdale NJ: Laurence Erlbaum.

Cooper, C., 1967, *Psychiatry and Anti-Psychiatry*. London: Tavistock.

Correctional Association of New York, 2003, *Lockdown New York*. New York: Correctional Association of New York.

Corrigan, P., 1976, *Schooling the Smash Street Kids*. London: Macmillan.

Côté, J., 2000, 'The Mead–Freeman Controversy in Review', *Journal of Youth and Adolescence*, 29(5): 525–38.

Crawford, A., 1997, *The Local Governance of Crime*. Oxford: Oxford University Press.

Crawford, A., Jones, T., Woodhouse, T. and Young, J., 1990, *The Second Islington Crime Survey*. London: Middlesex University: Centre for Criminology.

Currie, E., 1985, *Confronting Crime: An American Challenge*. New York: Pantheon.

Currie, E., 1997, 'Market Society and Social Disorder', in B. Maclean and D. Milanovic (eds), *Thinking Critically About Crime*. Vancouver: Collective Press.

Currie, E., 1998, *Crime and Punishment in America*. New York: Metropolitan Books.

Curtis, R., 1998, 'The Improbable Transformation of Inner City Neighborhoods: Crime, Violence and Drugs in the 1990s', *Journal of Criminal Law and Criminology*, 88(4): 1233–76.

De Beauvoir, S., 1953, *The Second Sex*. London: Jonathan Cape.

De Certeau, M., 1984, *The Practice of Everyday Life*. Berkeley, CA: University of California Press.

Decker, S. and Curry, G., 1977, 'Gangs: What's in a Name?: A Gang by Any Other Name Isn't Quite the Same', *Valparaiso Law Review* 312: 501–14.

DeKeseredy, W., Alvi S., Schwartz M. and Tomaszewski A., 2003, *Under Siege: Poverty and Crime in a Public Housing Community*. Lanham, Md: Lexington Books.

Deutscher, I., 1973/1958, *What We Say/What We Do*. Glenview: Ill. Scott Foreman.

Dickson, D., 1968 'Bureaucracy and Morality', *Social Problems* 16: 143–56.

Ditton, J., 1981, *Contrology: Beyond the New Criminology*, London: Macmillan.

Dockery, T. and Bedeian, A., 1989, 'Attitude and Actions', *Social Behavior and Personality* 17: 9–16.

Douglas, J., 1967, *The Social Meanings of Suicide*, Princeton NJ: Princeton University Press.

Douglas, M., 1978, *Purity and Danger: An Analysis of the Concepts of Pollution and Taboo*. London: Routledge.

Downes, D., 1966, *The Delinquent Solution*. London: Routledge.

Downes, D., 1988, 'The Sociology of Crime and Social Control in Britain 1960–

1987', in P. Rock (ed), *The History of British Criminology*. Oxford: Oxford University Press.

Downes, D. and Rock, P., 1988, *Understanding Deviance*. Oxford: Clarendon Press.

Duneier, M., 2001, *Sidewalk*. New York: Farrar, Straus and Giroux.

Duneier, M., 2002, 'What Kind of Combat Sport is Sociology?', *American Journal of Sociology* 107(6): 151–76.

Durkheim, E., 1938 [1895], *The Rules of Sociological Method*. New York: The Free Press.

Durkheim, E., 1951 [1893], *The Division of Labour in Society*. New York: The Free Press.

Durkheim, E., 1952/1897, *Suicide*. London: RKP.

Edwards, A. and Hughes, G., 2005, 'Comparing Governance of Safety in Europe', *Theoretical Criminology* 3: 345–63.

Ehrenreich, B., 2001, *Nickel and Dimed*. New York: Henry Holt.

Ehrenreich, B. and Hochschild, A. (eds), 2002, *Global Woman: Nannies, Maids and Sex Workers in the New Economy*. New York: Metropolitan Books.

Elias, N., 1982, *State, Formation and Civilisation: The Civilising Process*. trans. E. Jephcott. Oxford: Blackwell.

Elias, N., 1994, *The Civilising Process*. New York: Blackwell.

Engels, F., 1969 [1844], *Conditions of the Working Class in England in 1844*. London: Panther.

Entwistle, C., 1987, 'Book Review', *New York Review of Books* 19, 31 December.

Erikson, K., 1966, *Wayward Puritans*. New York: John Wiley.

Eysenck, H. and Gudjonsson, G., 1989, *The Causes and Cures of Criminality*. New York: Plenum Press.

Fabianic, D., 1999, 'Educational Backgrounds of Most-Cited Scholars', *Journal of Criminal Justice* 27(6): 517–24.

Farrington, D., Joliffe, D., Hawkes, D., Catalano, R., Hull, R. and Kosterman, R., 2003, 'Comparing Delinquency Careers in Court Records and Self-Reports', *Criminology* 41(3): 933–58.

Featherstone, M.,1985, 'Lifestyle and Consumer Culture', *Theory, Culture and Society* 4: 57–70.

Felson, M. 2002, *Crime and Everyday Life*, 3rd edn. Thousand Oaks, CA: Sage.

Ferrell, J., 1997, 'Criminological Verstehen: Inside the Immediacy of Crime', *Justice Quarterly* 14: 3–23.

Ferrell, J., 1998, 'Criminological Verstehen', in J. Ferrell and M. Hamm (eds). *Ethnography at the Edge*. Boston: Northeastern University Press.

Ferrell, J., 1999, 'Cultural Criminology', *Annual Review of Sociology* 25: 395–418.

Ferrell, J., 2000, 'Making Sense of Crime: Review Essay on Jack Katz's Seductions of Crime' *Social Justice* 19(3):111–23.

Ferrell, J., 2004, 'Boredom, Crime and Criminology', *Theoretical Criminology* 8(3): 287–302.

Ferrell, J., 2005, 'Cultural Criminology', *Blackwell Encyclopaedia of Sociology*. Oxford: Blackwell

Ferrell, J., 2005, *Empire of Scrounge*. New York: New York University Press.

Ferrell, J. and Hamm, M., 1998, 'True Confessions: Crime, Deviance and Field Research', in J. Ferrell and M. Hamm (eds), *Ethnography at the Edge*. Boston: Northeastern University Press.

Ferrell, J. and Sanders, C., 1995, 'Culture, Crime and Criminology', in J. Ferrell and C. Sanders (eds), *Cultural Criminology*. Boston: Northeastern University Press.

Ferrell, J., Milovanovic, D. and Lyng, S., 2001, 'Edgework, Media Practices and the Elongation of Meaning', *Theoretical Criminology* 5(2):177–202.

Ferrell J., Hayward K. and Young J., 2008, *Cultural Criminology: An Invitation*. London: Sage.

Ferrell, J., Hayward, K., Morrison, W. and Presdee, M. (eds), 2004, *Cultural Criminology Unleashed*. London: Cavendish/Glasshouse.

Ferri E., 1895, *Criminal Sociology*, London: Unwin.

Feyerabend, P., 1978, *Science in a Free Society*. London: NLB

Field, S., 1990, *Trends in Crime and Their Interpretation*. London: HMSO.

Fitzgerald M. and Sim J., 1977, *Prisoners in Revolt*. London: Penguin.

Francome, C., 1993, 'Sexual Behaviour', *British Medical Journal* 306: 573.

Fraser, N., 1997, *Justice Interruptus: Critical Reflections on the Post-Socialist Condition*. New York: Routledge.

Freeman, M., 1983, *Margaret Mead and Samoa: The Making and Unmaking of an Anthropological Myth*. Cambridge, MA: Harvard University Press.

Freeman, M., 1999, *The Fateful Hoaxing of Margaret Mead*. Boulder, CO: Westview Press.

Freud, S., 1929, *Civilisation and its Discontents*. Harmondsworth: Penguin.

Friedan, B., 1960, *The Feminine Mystique*. Harmondsworth: Penguin.

Frith, S., 1983, *Sound Effects: Youth, Leisure and the Politics of Rock 'n' Roll*. London: Constable.

Gaines, D., 1998, *Teenage Wasteland: Suburbia's Dead End Kids*. Chicago: University of Chicago Press.

Gans, H., 1995, *The War Against the Poor*. New York: Basic Books.

Garland, D., 1985, *Punishment and Welfare*. Oxford: Oxford University Press.

Garland, D., 1988, 'British Criminology Before 1935', in P. Rock (ed.), *The History of British Criminology*. Oxford: Oxford University Press.

Garland, D., 1995, 'Penal Modernism and Postmodernism', in T. Bloomberg and S. Cohen (eds), *Punishment and Social Control*. New York: Aldine De Gruyer.

Garland, D., 1996, 'The Limits of the Sovereign State', *British Journal of Criminology* 36(4): 445–71.

Garland, D., 1997, 'The Development of British Criminology', in M. Maguire, R. Morgan and R. Reiner (eds.), *The Oxford Handbook of Criminology* (2nd edn). Oxford: Clarendon Press.

Garland, D., 2001, *The Culture of Control*. Oxford: Oxford University Press.

Garland D. and Sparks, R., 2000, 'Criminology, Social Theory and the Challenge of Our Times', in D. Garland and R. Sparks (eds), *Criminology and Social Theory*. Oxford: Oxford University Press.

Gartrell D. and Gartrell J., 2002 'Positivism in Sociological Research: USA and UK', *British Journal of Sociology* 53(4): 639–57.

Gayle, R., 1975, 'The Traffic in Women: Notes on the Political Economy of Sex', in R. Reiter (ed.), *Towards an Anthropology of Women*. New York: Monthly Review Press.

Geertz, C., 1973, *The Interpretation of Cultures*. New York: Basic Books.

Geis, G., 1991, 'The Case Study Method in Sociological Criminology', in J. Feagin, A. Orum, and G. Sjoberg (eds), *A Case for the Case Study*. Chapel Hill, NC: University of North Carolina Press.

Giallombardo, R., 1966, *Society of Women*. New York: Wiley.

Giddens, A., 1990, *The Consequences of Modernity*. Cambridge: Polity.

Giddens, A., 1991, *Modernity and Self-Identity*. Cambridge: Polity.

Giddens, A., 2001, *Sociology* (4th edn). Cambridge: Polity.

Giffen, P., 1965. 'Rates of Crime and Delinquency' in W. McGrath (ed.), *Crime and Treatment in Canada*. Toronto: Macmillan.

Gitlin, T., 1980, *The Whole World is Watching*. Berkeley: University of California.

Gitlin, T., 1995, *Twilight of Common Dreams*. New York: Henry Holt.

Goertzel, T., 2002, 'Econometric Modeling as Junk Science', *Skeptical Inquirer* 26(1): 19–23.

Goertzel, T., 2004, 'Myths of Murder and Multiple Regression', *Skeptical Inquirer* 28 (4): 23–7.

Goertzel, T. and Goertzel, B., 2008, 'Capital Punishment and Homicide', *Critical Sociology* 34(2): 239–54.

Goffman, E., 1968, *Asylums*. Harmondsworth: Penguin.

Goode, E., 1994, *Deviant Behaviour* (4th edn), Englewood Cliffs NJ: Prentice-Hall.

Goode, E., 2008, 'From the Western to the Murder Mystery: The Sociological Imagination of C. Wright Mills', *Sociological Spectrum* 28: 237–53.

Gordon, I., Travers, T. and Whitehead, C., 2007, *The Impact of Recent Immigration on the London Economy*. London: Corporation of London.

Gottfredson, M. and Hirschi, T., 1990, *A General Theory of Crime*. Stanford, CA: Stanford University Press.

Gouldner, A., 1968, 'The Sociologist as Partisan', *The American Sociologist*, May: 103–16.

Gouldner, A., 1973, 'Introduction', in I. Taylor et al., *The New Criminology*. London: RKP.

Grant, N., 1995, 'From Margaret Mead's Field Notes: What Counted as 'Sex' in Samoa?', *American Anthropologist* 97(4): 678–82.

Greenberg, D., 1985, 'Age, Crime and Social Explanation', *American Journal of Sociology* 91(1): 1–21.

Gupta, A. and Ferguson, J., 1997a, 'Culture, Power, Place: Ethnography at the End of an Era', in A. Gupta and J. Ferguson (eds), *Culture, Power, Place*. Durham NC: Duke University Press.

Gupta, A. and Ferguson, J., 1997b 'Beyond "Culture": Space, Identity and the Politics of Difference', in A. Gupta and J. Ferguson (eds), *Culture, Power, Place*. Durham NC: Duke University Press.

Hacking, I., 1981, 'How Should We Do a History of Statistics?', *Ideology and Consciousness* 8.

Hagedorn, J., 1991, 'Gangs, Neighborhoods and Public Policy', *Social Problems* 38(4): 429–42.

Hagedorn, J., 2001, 'Review of The Crime Drop in America', *Theoretical Criminology* 5(4): 492–7.

Hagedorn, J., 2006, *Gangs in the Global City*. Chicago: University of Illinois Press 2006.

Hall, S. (Steve), 1997, 'Visceral Culture and Criminal Practices', *Theoretical Criminology* 1(4): 453–78.

Hall, S., Chritcher C., Jefferson T., Clarke J. and Roberts B., 1978, *Policing the Crisis*. London: Macmillan.

Hall, S. and Jefferson, T. (eds), 1975, *Resistance Through Ritual*. London: Hutchinson.

Hall, S., Ancrum, C. and Winlow, S., 2007, *Criminal Identities and Consumer Culture*. Cullompton: Willan.

Hallsworth, S., 2000, 'Rethinking the Punitive Turn', *Punishment and Society* 2(2):145–60.

Hallsworth, S. and Young T., 'Gang Talk and Talkers', *Crime Media Culture* 4(2): 175–95.

Harcourt, B., 2001, *Illusion of Order*. Cambridge, MA: Harvard University Press.

Harrington, M., 1963, *The Other America*. New York: Macmillan.

Hayden, T., 2006, *Radical Nomad*. Boulder CO: Paradigm Publishers

Hayward, K., 2001 'Crime, Consumerism and the Urban Experience', PhD thesis, University of East London.

Hayward, K., 2004a, *City Limits: Crime, Consumerism and the Urban Experience*. London: Glasshouse Press.

Hayward, K., 2004b, 'Consumer Culture and Crime', in C. Sumner (ed.), *The Blackwell Companion to Criminology*. Oxford: Blackwell.

Hayward, K. and Presdee, M. (eds), 2010, *Framing Crime: Cultural Criminology and the Image*. London: Routledge.

Hayward, K. and Young, J., 2004, 'Cultural Criminology: Some Notes on the Script', *Theoretical Criminology* 8: 259–73.

Hayward, K. and Yar, M., 2006, 'The "Chav" Phenomenon: Consumption, Media and the Construction of a New Underclass', *Crime, Media, Culture* (2)1: 9–28.

Hebdige, D., 1979, *Subcultures: The Meaning of Style*. London: Methuen.

Hebdige, D., 1988, *Hiding in the Light*. London: Routledge.

Hebdige, D., 1990, 'Fax to the Future', *Marxism Today* (Jan.):18–23.

Hebdige, D., 1993, 'Redeeming Witness: In the Tracks of the Homeless Vehicle Project', *Cultural Studies* 7(3):173–223.

Hellman, H., 1998, *Great Feuds in Science: Ten of the Liveliest Disputes Ever*. New York: John Wiley.

Herlitz, C., 1990, 'Sexual Behaviour in the General Population of Sweden', *Social Science and Medicine* 36(12):1535–40.

Herrnstein, R. and Murray, C., 1994, *The Bell Curve*. New York: The Free Press.

Heydon, M. J. and Reynolds, J. C., 2000, 'Fox (Vulpes vulpes): Management in Three Contrasting Regions of Britain, in Relation to Agricultural and Sporting Interests', *Journal of Zoology* 251: 237–252.

Hillyard, P. et al., 2008, 'Social Harm and its Limits,' in D. Dorling, *Criminal Obsessions: Why Harm Matters More than Crime*. London: Centre for Crime and Justice Studies.

Hirschi, T. and Gottfredson, M., 2008, 'Critiquing the Critics', in E. Goode (ed.), *Out of Control*. Stanford: Stanford University Press.

Hobbs, D., 2006, 'East Ending: Dissociation, De-Industrialisation and David Downes', in T. Newburn and P. Rock (eds), *The Politics of Crime Control*. Oxford: Oxford University Press.

Hobsbawm, E., 1964, *Labouring Man: Studies in the History of Labour*. London: Weidenfeld and Nicolson.

Hobsbawm, E., 1994, *The Age of Extremes*. London: Michael Joseph.

Hobsbawm, E., 1996, 'The Cult of Identity Politics', *New Left Review* 217: 38–47.

Hofferth, S., Kahn, J. and Baldwin, W., 1987, 'Premarital Sexual Intercourse among US Teenage Women over the Past Three Decades', *Family Planning Perspectives* 19(2): 47.

Hogg, R. and Brown, D., 1998, *Rethinking Law and Order*. Annandale, NSW: Pluto.

Holmes, Malcolm and Taggart, William, 1990, 'A Comparative Analysis of Research Methods in Criminology and Criminological Journals', *Justice Quarterly* 7(2): 421–37.

Hough, M., 1986, 'Victims of Violent Crime, Findings from the British Crime Survey' in E. Fattah (ed.), *Crime Policy to Victim Policy*. London: St Martin's Press.

Hough, M. and Mayhew, P., 1983, *The British Crime Survey*. London: The Home Office.

Houghton, J. T., 2001, *Climate Change 2001: The Scientific Basis*. Cambridge, UK: Cambridge University Press.

Hughes, E., 1958, *Men and Their Work*. Glencoe: The Free Press.

Hughes, G., 1998, *Understanding Crime Prevention: Social Control, Risk, and Late Modernity*. Buckingham: Open University Press.

Ignatieff, Michael, 1999, *The Warrior's Honor*. London: Vintage.

Jackson, M., 1989, *Paths Towards a Clearing*. Bloomington: Indiana University Press.

Jamieson, R., 1998, 'Towards a Criminology of War in Europe', in V. Ruggiero, N. South and I. Taylor (eds), *The New European Criminology*. London: Routledge.

Jamieson, R., 1999, 'Genocide and the Social Production of Immorality', *Theoretical Criminology* 3(2): 131–46.

Jefferson, T., 2002, 'Subordinating Hegemonic Masculinity', *Theoretical Criminology* 6(1): 63–88.

Jeffrey, Clarence, 1980, 'Sociobiology and Crime', in E. Sagarin (ed.), *Taboos of Criminology*. Beverley Hills: Sage.

Johnson, David, 2008, 'The Homicide Drop in Post War Japan', *Homicide Studies* 12: 146–60.

Jones, T., MacLean, B. and Young, J., 1986, *The Islington Crime Survey*. Aldershot: Gower.

Jones, T. and Newburn, T., 2002, 'The Convergence of US and UK Crime Control Policy', *Criminal Justice* 2(2): 173–203.

Kanin, J., 1957, 'Male Aggression in Dating Courtship Relationships,' *American Journal of Sociology* 62(2): 197–204.

Kara, M. and Upson, A., 2006, *Crime in England and Wales: Quarterly Update to 2005*. London: Home Office.

Karmen, A., 2000, *New York Murder Mystery*. New York; New York University Press.

Katz, I., 1994, 'Rights Groups Scorn "1 in 90 gay" Survey', *Guardian*, 22 January, p. 5.

Katz, J., 1988, *Seductions of Crime: The Moral and Sensual Attractions of Doing Evil*. New York: Basic Books.

Katz J., 2001, *How Emotions Work*. Chicago: Chicago University Press.

Katz, J., 2002, 'Start Here: Social Ontology and Research Strategy', *Theoretical Criminology*, 6(3), pp. 255–78.

Katz, J. and Jackson-Jacobs, C., 2004, 'The Criminologist's Gang', in P. Beirne and C. Sumner (eds). *Blackwell Companion to Criminology*. Oxford: Blackwell, pp. 106–7.

Keen, M., 2004, *Stalking Sociologists*. New Brunswick: Transaction.

Kershaw, C., Nicholas S. and Walker A. (eds), 2008, *Crime in England and Wales, 2007–8*. London:Home Office.

Klein, M. W., 1971, *Street Gangs and Street Workers*. Englewood Cliffs, NJ: Prentice-Hall.

Klockars, C., 1980, 'The Contemporary Crisis of Marxist Criminology', in *Radical Criminology: The Coming Crisis*. Beverly Hills, CA: Sage.

Kontos, L., Brotherton, D. and Barrios, L. (eds), 2003, *Gangs and Society*. New York: Columbia University Press.

Kuhn, T., 1970, *The Structure of Scientific Revolutions*. London: University of Chicago Press.

Laing, R., 1965, *The Divided Self*. Harmondsworth; Penguin.

Lanier, M. and Stuart, H., 2004, *Essential Criminology*. Boulder, Colorado: Westview Press.

La Piere, R., 1934, 'Attitudes and Actions', *Social Forces* 13: 230–7.

Lasalle, Y. and O'Dougherty, M., 1997, 'The Search of Weeping Worlds', *Radical History Review* 69: 243–60.

Latzer, B., 2008, 'The Great Black Hope', *Claremont Review of Books* (Winter).

Laub, J., 2004, 'The Life Course of Criminology in the United States: The

American Society of Criminology 2003 Presidential Address', *Criminology* 42(1): 1–26.

Laumann, E., Gagnon, J., Michael, R. and Michaels, S., 1995a, *The Social Organisation of Sexuality: Sexual Practices in the United States*. Chicago: University of Chicago Press.

Laumann, E., Gagnon, J., Michael, R. and Michaels, S., 1995b, 'Letter to Editor', *New York Review of Books* 42(9) (May): 43.

Lazarsfeld, P. and Thielens W., 1955/1958, *The Academic Mind*. New York: The Free Press.

Lea, J., 2002, *Crime and Modernity*. London: Sage.

Lea, J. and Young, J., 1984, *What is to be Done about Law and Order?* Harmondsworth: Penguin.

Lemert, C., 2003, 'Forward to the 2003 Edition', in E. Liebow, *Tally's Corner*. Lanham, MA: Rowman and Littlefield.

Lemert, E., 1967, *Human Deviance, Social Problems and Social Control*. New Jersey: Prentice-Hall.

Lévi-Strauss, C., 1966, 'Anthropology: Its Achievement and Future', *Current Anthropology* 7: 124–7.

Lewontin, R., 1995a, 'Sex in America', *The New York Review of Books* 42(7) (21 April): 24–9.

Lewontin, R., 1995b, 'Letter to Editor', *The New York Review of Books* 42(9) (May): 43–4.

Lewontin, R., Rose, S. and Kamin, L, 1984, *Not in Our Genes*. New York: Random House.

Liberty, 2006, 'New Respect Action Plan. Measures Off Target', Press Release 10 January.

Librett, M., 2005, 'The Spoils of War: Divergent Lifestyles and Identity Formation Among Undercover Vice Cops in the Burbs', CUNY, PhD.

Liebow, E., 2003/1968, *Tally's Corner* (new edn). Lanham, MA: Rowman and Littlefield.

Lilly, J. R., Cullen, F. T. and Ball, R. A., 2009, *Criminological Theory: Context and Consequences*. Newbury Park, CA: Sage Publications.

Lindesmith, A., 1968, *Addiction and Opiates*. Chicago: Aldine.

Livingstone, S., 1996, 'On the Continuing Problem of Media Effects' in J. Curran and M. Gurevitch (eds). *Mass Media and Society*. London: Arnold.

Lombroso, C., 1896, *L'Uomo Delinquente*. Milan: Hoepli.

Luttwak, E., 1995, 'Turbo-Charged Capitalism and Its Consequences', *London Review of Books* 17(21), 2 November: 6–7.

Lyng, S., 1990, 'Edgework: A Social Psychological Analysis of Voluntary Risk-Taking', *American Journal of Sociology* 95(4): 876–921.

Lyng, S., 1998, 'Dangerous Methods: Risk Taking and the Research Process', in J. Ferrell and M. Hamm (eds), *Ethnography at the Edge*. Boston: Northeastern University Press.

Lynch, J., 2006, 'Cross-National Victimization Research', in M. Tonry (ed.), *Crime and Justice*, Vol. 34. Chicago: Chicago University Press.

MacLeod, J., 1995, *Ain't No Makin' It*. Boulder, CO: Westview.

Macpherson, C. B., 1977. *The Life and Times of Liberal Democracy*. Oxford: Oxford University Press.

McRobbie, A., 1994, *Postmodernism and Popular Culture*. London: Routledge.

McRobbie, A. and Thornton, S., 1995, 'Rethinking Moral Panic for Multi-Mediated Social Worlds', *British Journal of Sociology* 46(4): 559–74.

McVicar, J., 1979, *McVicar*. London: Arrow.

Maffesoli, M., 1996, *The Time of the Tribes*. London: Sage.

Maffesoli, M., 2004, 'Everyday Tragedy and Creation', *Cultural Studies* 18(2/3): 201–10.

Maguire, M., Morgan R. and Reiner, R. (eds), 1994, *The Oxford Handbook of Criminology*. Oxford: Oxford University Press.

Maguire, K. and Pastore, A., 2001, *Sourcebook of Criminal Justice Statistics 2000*. Washington: Bureau of Justice Statistics.

Mannheim, H., 1948, *Juvenile Delinquency in an English Middletown*. London: Routledge.

Marcus, G. and Fischer, M., 1999, *Anthropology as Cultural Critique* (2nd edn). Chicago: University of Chicago Press.

Marshall, I. H., 2001, 'The Criminological Enterprise in Europe and the United States', *European Journal of Criminal Policy and Research* (3): 235–57.

Martin, P., 2004, 'Culture, Subculture and Social Organisation', in A. Bennett and K. Kahn-Harris (eds), *After Subculture*. Basingstoke: Palgrave.

Maruna, S., 2001, *Making Good: How Ex-Convicts Reform and Rebuild their Lives*. Washington, DC: American Psychological Association.

Marx, K., 1844 [1967], *Economic and Philosophic Manuscripts* in L. Easton and K. Guddat (eds), *Writings of the Young Marx on Philosophy and Society*. New York: Anchor Books.

Massing, M., 1995, 'Hanging Out', *New York Review of Books* 42(9): 34–6.

Matthews, R., 2010, *Doing Time*. London: Macmillan.

Matthews, R. and Pitts, J., 2001, 'Beyond Criminology?', in R. Matthews and J. Pitts (eds), *Crime, Disorder and Community Safety*. London: Routledge.

Matza, D., 1964, *Delinquency and Drift*. New York: John Wiley.

Matza, D., 1969, *Becoming Deviant*. Englewood Cliffs, NJ: Prentice-Hall.

Matza, D. and Sykes, G., 1961, 'Juvenile Delinquency and Subterranean Values', *American Sociological Review* 26: 712–19.

Mead, M., 1949/1928, *Coming of Age in Samoa: A Psychological Study of Primitive Youth for Western Civilization*. New York: Mentor Books.

Melossi, D., 2001, 'The Cultural Embededness of Social Control', *Theoretical Criminology* 5(4): 403–24.

Melossi, D., 2008, *Controlling Crime, Controlling Society*. Cambridge: Polity.

Merton, R. K., 1938, 'Social Structure and Anomie', *American Sociological Review* 3: 672–82.

Merton, R. K., 1940, 'Fact and Factitiousness in Ethnic Opinionnaires', *American Sociological Review* 5(1): 13–28.

Merton, R. K.,1957, *Social Theory and Social Structure*, rev. edn. Glencoe: The Free Press.

Messerschmidt, James W., 2000, *Nine Lives: Adolescent Masculinities, The Body, and Violence*. Boulder, CO: Westview Press.

Michael, R., Gagnon, J., Laumann, E. and Kolata, G., 1995, *Sex in America: A Definitive Survey*. Boston: Little Brown.

Miller, W., 1958, 'Lower Class Culture as a Generating Milieu of Gang Delinquency', *Journal of Social Issues* 14(3): 17–23.

Miller, W., 1964, Foreword to Sydney E. Bernard, *Fatherless Families: Their Economic and Social Adjustment*. Waltham, MA: Brandeis University Research Center, Papers in Social Welfare No. 7.

Mills, C. W., 1940, 'Situated Actions and Vocabularies of Motive', *American Sociological Review* 5(6), December.

Mills C. W., 1943, 'The Professional Ideology of Social Pathologists', *American Journal of Sociology* 49: 65–80.

Mills, C. W., 1959, *The Sociological Imagination*. New York: Oxford University Press.

Mills, C. W., 1963/1954, 'IBM Plus Reality Plus Humanism = Sociology', in I. L. Horowitz (ed.), *Power, Politics and People: The Collected Essays of C. Wright Mills*. New York: Ballantine Books.

Mirlees-Black, C., Mayhew, P. and Percy, A., 1996, *The 1996 British Crime Survey*. London: The Stationery Office.

Monkkonen, E. H., 1978, *The Dangerous Class: Crime and Poverty in Columbus Ohio*. Cambridge: Harvard University Press.

Mooney, J., 1997, 'Single Mothers and Feckless Fathers', in P. Walton and J. Young (eds), *The New Criminology Revisited*. London: Macmillan.

Mooney, J., 2000, *Gender, Violence and the Social Order*. London: Macmillan.

Mooney, J., 2003, 'It's the Family, Stupid: New Labour and Crime', in R. Matthews (ed.), *The New Politics of Crime and Punishment*. Cullompton, Devon: Willan.

Mooney J., and Young, J., 2000, 'Policing Ethnic Minorities', in B. Loveday and A. Marlow (eds), *Policing After the Stephen Lawrence Inquiry*. Lyme Regis: Russell House.

Mooney, J. and Young, J., 2002, 'Video Games: Overview Research', *Video Games and Aggression*. Middlesex University: Centre for Criminology.

Morley, D., 2000, *Home Territories: Media, Mobility and Identity*. London: Routledge.

Morley, D. and Robins, K., 1995, *Spaces of Identity*. London: Routledge.

Morris, T., 1957, *The Criminal Area*. London: Routledge.

Morris, T. and Morris, P., 1963, *Pentonville*. London: Routledge.

Morrison, W., 1995, *Theoretical Criminology: From Modernity to Post-Modernism*. London: Cavendish.

Morrison, W., 2004, 'Criminology, Genocide and Modernity: Remarks on the Companion that Criminology Ignored', in P. Beirne and C. Sumner (eds), *Blackwell Companion to Criminology*. Oxford: Blackwell.

Morrison, W., 2006, *Criminology, Civilisation and the New World Order*. Abingdon: Routledge/Cavendish.

Mouzelis, N., 1995, *Sociological Theory: What Went Wrong?* London: Routledge.

Moynihan, D., 1993, 'Defining Deviancy Down', *American Scholar* 62, Winter: 17–30.

Muncie, J., 1999, 'Institutionalised Intolerance: Youth Justice and the 1998 Crime and Disorder Act', *Critical Social Policy* 19(2): 147–75.

Muncie, J., 2009, *Youth and Crime*. London: Sage.

Murray, C., 1984, *Losing Ground*. New York: Basic Books.

Myhill, A. and Allen, J., 2002, *Rape and Sexual Assault of Women: The Extent and Nature of the Problem*. London: Home Office.

Nagin, D. and Tremblay, R., 2005, 'From Seduction to Passion: A response to Sampson and Laub', *Criminology* 43(3): 915–18.

NASA, 2004, *Near Earth Objects Program*. Retrieved 5/26/09. from nasa.gov/vision/universe/watchtheskies/near-earth052104.html.

Newburn, T., 2002, 'Atlantic Crossings: Policy Transfer and Crime Control in England and Wales', *Punishment and Society* 4(2):165–94.

Newman, K., 1999, *Falling from Grace*. Berkeley, CA: University of California Press.

Nicolaus, M., 1968, 'Fat Cat Sociology: Remarks at the American Sociological Association Convention', Boston, August.

Nicolaus, M., 1969, 'The Professional Organization of Sociology: A View from Below', *Antioch Review* (Fall): 375–87.

Nietzsche, F., 2005, *The Genealogy of Morals* (trans. Richard Hooker), www.wsu.edu:8080/~dee/MODERN/GENEAL.HTM.

Nightingale, C., 1993, *On the Edge*. New York: Basic Books.

O'Malley, P., 1999, 'Volatile Punishments: Contemporary Penality and Neo-Liberal Government', *Theoretical Criminology* 3(2): 175–96.

O'Malley, P. and Mugford, S., 1994, 'Crime, Excitement and Modernity', in G. Barak (ed.), *Varieties of Criminology*. Westport, CT: Praegar.

Oosthoek, A., 1978, *The Utilization of Official Crime Data*. Ottawa: Supply and Services.

Ouimet, M., 2002, 'Explaining the American and Canadian Crime "Drop" in the 1990s', *Canadian Journal of Criminology* 44(1): 33–50.

Painter, K., 1991, *Wife Rape, Marriage and the Law*. Manchester: Faculty of Economic and Social Studies, University of Manchester.

Parenti, C., 2000, *Lockdown America*. London: Verso.

Park, R., 1927 'Cultural Conflict and the Marginal Man', in E. Stonequist, *The Marginal Man*. New York: Charles Scribner.

Parsons, T., 1951, *The Social System*. Glencoe, Ill: The Free Press.

Pavarini, M., 1994, 'Is Criminology Worth Saving?' in *Future of Criminology* (ed.) D. Nelken, London: Sage.

Pavlich, P., 1999, 'Criticism and Criminology,' *Theoretical Criminology* 3(1): 29–51.

Pearson G., 1978, 'Goths and Vandals: Crime in History', *Contemporary Crises* 2(2), 119–40.

Peterson, A., 1997, Review: [untitled]. *Acta Sociologica* 40 (3): 323–7.

Pitts, J., 2001, *The New Politics of Youth Crime*. London: Palgrave.

Plummer, K., 1995, *Telling Sexual Stories*. London: Routledge.

Plummer, K., 2003, *Intimate Citizenship: Private Decisions and Public Dialogues*. Seattle: University of Washington Press.

Polsky, N., 1967, *Hustlers, Beats, and Others*. Observations. Chicago: Aldine.

Pountain, D. and Robins, D., 2000, *Cool Rules: Anatomy of an Attitude*. London: Reaktion.

Presdee, M., 2000, *Cultural Criminology and the Carnival of Crime*. London: Routledge.

Presdee, M., 2004a, 'The Story of Crime: Biography and The Excavation of Transgression', in J. Ferrell et al. (eds), *Cultural Criminology Unleashed*. London: Glasshouse.

Presdee, M., 2004b, 'Cultural Criminology the Long and Winding Road', *Theoretical Criminology* 8(3): 275–85.

Presdee, M., 2006, 'Working It Out', in S. Muzzatti and C. Samarco (eds), *Reflections from the Wrong Side of the Tracks: Class, Identity and Working Class Experience in Academe*. New York: Roman and Littlefield.

Provine, D., 2008, 'Review of The Great American Crime Decline', *Law and Society Review* 42(3): 692–4.

Pryce, K., 1979, *Endless Pressure*. Harmondsworth: Penguin.

Quetelet, A., 1842, *Treatise on Man*. Paris: Bachelier (first published in 1835 as *Sur l'homme et le dévelopment de ses facultés ou Essai de physique sociale*, 2 volumes).

Raban, J., 1974, *Soft City*. London: Hamilton.

Radzinowicz, L., 1999, *Adventures in Criminology*. London: Routledge.

Ranulf, S., 1964/1938, *Moral Indignation and Middle Class Psychology*. New York: Schocken.

Rieff, D., 1993, *Los Angeles: Capital of the Third World*. London: Phoenix/Orion.

Robinson, M., 2001, 'Whither Criminal Justice: An Argument for a Reform of Discipline', *Critical Criminology* 10(2): 97–106.

Rock, P., 1973, *Deviant Behaviour*. London: Hutchinson.

Rosaldo, R., 1993, *Culture and Truth*. Boston: Beacon Press.

Rose, N., 1999, *Powers of Freedom: Reframing Political Thought*. Cambridge: Cambridge University Press.

Rose, N., 2000 'Government and Control', in D. Garland and R. Sparks (eds), *Criminology and Social Theory*. Oxford: Oxford University Press.

Rosenfeld, R., 2000, 'Patterns in Adult Homicide: 1980–1995', in A. Blumstein and J. Wallman (eds), *The Crime Drop in America*. Cambridge: Cambridge University Press.

Rowbotham, S., 1973, *Hidden from History*. London: Pluto.

Rubin, G., 1975, 'From Mead's Field Notes: What Counted as "Sex" in Samoa?' *American Anthropologist* 97(4): 678–82.

Ruggiero, V., 2000, *Crime and Markets*. Oxford: Oxford University Press.

Russell Sage Foundation, 1914, *West Side Studies*. New York: Russell Sage Foundation.

Sahlin, M., 1976, *Culture and Practical Reason*. Chicago: University of Chicago Press.

Said, E., 1993 (1979), *Orientalism.* New York: Vintage.

Sampson, R., 2008, 'Rethinking Crime and Immigration', in *Contexts,* Winter 2008, American Sociological Association.

Santelli, J., Lindberg, L. and associates, 2000, 'Adolescent Sexual Behavior: Estimates and Trends from Four Nationally Representative Surveys', *Family Planning Perspectives* 32(4): 156–65.

Sassen, S., 2002, 'Global Cities and Survival Circuits', in B. Ehrenreich and A. Hochschild (eds), *Global Woman: Nannies, Maids and Sex Workers in the New Economy.* New York: Metropolitan.

Sayer, A., 1992, *Method in Social Science,* 2nd edn. London: Routledge.

Scheff, T., 1968, 'Negotiating Reality', *Social Problems* 16: 3–17.

Scheff, T., 2006, *Goffman Unbound,* Boulder, CO: Paradigm Books.

Scheler, M., 1923, 'Das Ressentiment im Aufbau der Moralem', in *Van Umsturz der Werte* I, Leipzig

Schelsky, H., 1957, 'Ise die Dauerreflektion Institutionalisierbar?' *Zeitschrift für Evangelische Ethik* 1: 153–74.

Scheper-Hughes, N., 1984, 'The Margaret Mead Controversy: Biological and Anthropological Inquiry', *Human Organization* 43(1): 85–93.

Shrecker, E., 1986, *No Ivory Tower.* New York: Oxford University Press.

Schwendinger, H. and Schwendinger, J., 1985, *Adolescent Subcultures and Delinquency.* New York: Praeger.

Schutz, A., 1962, *Collected Papers. Vol.1, The Problem of Social Reality.* The Hague: Nijhoff.

Scraton, P., 2000, *Hillsborough: The Truth.* Edinburgh: Mainstream.

Scull, A., 1977, *Decarceration.* New Jersey: Prentice Hall.

Sellin, T., 1938, *Culture, Conflict and Crime.* New Jersey: Social Science Research Council.

Sennett, R., 1995, 'Letter to Editor', *New York Review of Books* 42(9) (May): 43.

Sennett, R. and Cobb, J., 1993, *The Hidden Injuries of Class.* London: Faber and Faber.

Shankman, P., 1996, 'The History of Samoan Sexual Conduct and the Mead–Freeman Controversy', *American Anthropologist* 98(3): 555–67.

Shelden, R., 1999, 'The Prison Industrial Complex and the New American Apartheid', *The Critical Criminologist* 10(1) Fall: 1–9.

Sherwood, S., Smith, P. and Alexander, J., 1993, 'The British are Coming . . . Again! The Hidden Agenda of Cultural Studies', *Contemporary Sociology* 22(3): 370–5.

Shore, B., 1982, *Sala'ilua: A Samoan Mystery.* New York: Columbia University Press.

Shorter, E., 1977, *The Making of the Modern Family.* London: Fontana.

Sibley, D., 1995, *The Geographies of Exclusion.* London: Routledge.

Siegel, F., 2005, *The Prince and the City: Giuliani, New York and the Genius of American Life.* New York: Encounter Books.

Simmel, G., 1903/1950 'The Metropolis and Mental Life in *The Sociology of George Simmel,* trans. K. H. Wolff. New York: The Free Press.

Simmons, J. and Dodd, T. (eds), 2002/3, *Crime in England and Wales*. Home Office Statistical Bulletin 07/03.

Simon, J., 2007, *Governing Through Crime: How the War on Crime Transformed American Democracy and Created a Culture of Fear*. Oxford: Oxford University Press.

Skogan, W., 1986, 'Methodological Issues in the Study of Victimization', in E. Fattah (ed.), *Crime Policy to Victim Policy*. London: St Martin's Press.

Smelser, N. 1997, 'Sociology as Science, Humanism and Art' in *Sociological Visions* (ed). K. Erikson, Oxford: Rowman and Little.

Smith, N., 1996, *The New Urban Frontier: Gentrification and the Revanchist City*. London: Routledge.

Smith, P., 1998, *The New American Cultural Sociology*. Cambridge: Cambridge University Press.

Sparks, R. F., 1981, 'Surveys of Victimization – An Optimistic Assessment' in M. Tonry and N. Morris (eds), *Criminal Justice* Vol. 3. Chicago: University of Chicago Press.

Sparks, R. F., Genn, H., and Dodd, D., 1977, *Surveying Victims*. London: Wiley.

Squires, P. and Stephen, D. E., 2005, *Rougher Justice: Anti-Social Behaviour and Young People*. Devon: Collompton.

Stenson, K, 1998, 'Beyond Histories of the Present', *Economy and Society* 27 (4): 333.

Stevens, P. and Willis, C., 1979, *Race, Crime and Arrests*. London: Home Office Research Study No. 58.

Sumner, C., 1982, *Crime, Justice and Underdevelopment*. London: Heineman.

Sykes, G., 1958, *The Society of Captives*. Princeton NJ: Princeton University Press.

Sykes, G. and Matza, D., 1957, 'Techniques of Neutralization', *American Sociological Review* 22: 664–70.

Sztompka, P., 1990, 'Conceptual Frameworks in Comparative Research: Divergent and Convergent', *Justice Quarterly* 7: 421–39.

Taylor, I., 1999, *Crime in Context*. Oxford: Polity.

Taylor, I., Walton, P. and Young, J., 1973, *The New Criminology*. London: Routledge.

Taylor, L., 1971, *Deviance and Society*. London: Michael Joseph.

Thompson, E. P., 1968, *The Making of the English Working Class*. Harmondsworth: Penguin.

Thornton, S., 1995, *Club Cultures: Music, Media, and Subcultural Capital*. Cambridge: Polity.

Thrasher, F., 1963/1927, *The Gang*. Chicago: University of Chicago Press.

Tierney, J., 2006, *Criminology: Theory and Context*. London: Pearson Education.

Tittle, C., Villemez, W., and Smith, D., 1978, 'The Myth of Social Class and Criminality', *American Sociological Review* 43: 643–56.

Trumka, R., 2009, 'Where Things are Made', Speech on Building the New Economy, Washington DC, 29 October.

Turner, V., 1982, 'Dramatic Ritual/Ritual Drama: Performative and Reflexive

Anthropology', in *From Ritual to Theater: The Human Seriousness of Play*. New York: Performing Arts Journal Publications.

Turner, V., 1986, *The Anthropology of Performance*. Baltimore: PAJ Publications.

Turner, V., 1982, *From Ritual to Theatre*. Baltimore: PAJ Publications.

Weisburd, D. and Piquero A., 2008, 'Taking Stock of How Well Criminologists Explain Crime: Statistical Modeling in Published Studies', *Crime and Justice* 17: 453–502.

Van Dijk, J., 2008, *The World of Crime: Breaking the Silence on Problems of Security, Justice, and Development across the World*. Los Angeles: Sage Publications.

Van Kesteren, J., Mayhew, P. and Nieuwbeerta, P., 2000, *Criminal Victimization in 17 Industrialized Countries: Key Findings from the 2000 International Crime Survey*. The Hague, Ministry of Justice, WODC.

Van Maanen, J., 1995, 'An End to Innocence: The Ethnography of Ethnography', in J. Van Maanen (ed.), *Representations in Ethnography*. Thousand Oaks, CA: Sage.

Van Swaaningen, R., 1997, *Critical Criminology: Visions from Europe*. London: Sage.

Velez, M., Krivo, L. and Peterson, K., 2003, 'Structural Inequality and Homicide: An Assessment of the Black–White Gap', *Criminology* 41(3): 645–72.

Vidal, J., 2005, 'The End of Oil is Closer than You Think', *Guardian*, 21 April.

Vold, G. B., Bernard, T. J. and Snipes, J. B., 1998, *Theoretical Criminology*. New York: Oxford University Press.

Wacquant, L., 1997, 'Three Pernicious Premises on the Study of the American Ghetto', *International Journal of Urban and Regional Research* 20(2): 34–53.

Wacquant, L., 1998, 'Inside the Zone: The Social Art of the Hustler', *Theory, Culture and Society* 15(2):1–36.

Wacquant, L., 1999, *Les Prisons de la Misère*. Paris: Éditions Rasions d'agir.

Wacquant, L., 2000, 'The New "Peculiar Institution": On the Prisoners Surrogate Ghetto', *Theoretical Criminology* 4(3): 377–89.

Wacquant, L., 2001, 'Deadly Symbiosis: When Ghetto and Prison Meet and Merge', *Punishment and Society* 3(1): 95–134.

Wacquant, L., 2002a, 'From Slavery to Mass Incarceration', *New Left Review* 13 (Jan/Feb).

Wacquant, L., 2002b, 'Scrutinizing the Street: Poverty, Morality, and the Pitfalls of Urban Ethnography', *American Journal of Sociology* 107(6):1468–1532.

Wacquant, L., 2004, *Body and Soul: Notebooks of an Apprentice Boxer*. Oxford: Oxford University Press.

Ward, D. and Kassebaum, G., 1966, *Women's*. London: Weidenfeld and Nicolson.

Warriner, C., 1958, 'The Nature and Functions of Official Morality', *American Journal of Sociology* 64(2):165–8.

Weiss, J., 1971, 'Dialogue with David Matza', *Issues in Criminology* 6(1): 33–53.

West, D.,1968, *Homosexuality*. London: Penguin.

Wheen, F., 1999, *Karl Marx*. London: Fourth Estate.

White, R. and Haines, F., 2008, *Crime and Criminology*. Melbourne: Oxford University Press.

Whiteman, G., Muller, T., Johnson, J., 2009, 'Strong Emotions at Work', *Qualitative Research in Organizations and Management* 4(1): 46–61.

Whyte, W. F., 1955, *Street Corner Society*. Chicago: University of Chicago Press.

Wicker, A., 1969, 'Attitudes versus Actions', *Journal of Social Issues* 25: 41–78.

Williams, T. R., 1958, *Culture and Society*. London: Chatto and Windus.

Williams T. R., 1959, 'A Critique of Some Assumptions of Social Survey Research', *Public Opinion Quarterly* 23: 55–62.

Willis, C., Evans, T. and LaGrange, R., 1999, '"Down Home" Criminology: The Place of Indigenous Theories of Crime', *Journal of Criminal Justice* 27(3): 227–38.

Willis, P., 1977, *Learning to Labour*. Aldershot: Gower.

Willis, P., 1978, *Profane Culture*. London: Routledge.

Willis, P., 1990, *Common Culture*. Milton Keynes: Open University Press.

Willis, P., 2000, *The Ethnographic Imagination*. Cambridge: Polity.

Wilson, J. Q., 1975, *Thinking About Crime*. New York: Basic Books.

Wilson, W. J., 1996, *When Work Disappears: The World of the New Urban Poor*. New York: Knopf.

Wirth, L., 1938, 'Urbanism as a Way of Life', *American Journal of Sociology* 44(1): 1–24.

Wolfe, T., 1988, *The Bonfire of the Vanities*. New York: Bantam Books.

Wooton, B., 1959, *Social Science and Pathology*. London: Allen and Unwin.

Wright, R. and Cohn, E., 1996, 'The Most-Cited Scholars in Criminal Justice Textbooks', *Journal of Criminal Justice* 24: 459–67.

Yablonsky, L., 1962, *The Violent Gang*. New York: Macmillan.

Young, I. M., 1990, *Justice and the Politics of Difference*. Princeton, NJ: Princeton University Press.

Young, J., 1971a, 'The Role of Police as Amplifiers of Deviancy, Negotiators of Reality and Translators of Fantasy', in S. Cohen (ed.), *Images of Deviance*. Harmondsworth: Penguin.

Young, J., 1971b, *The Drugtakers*. London: Paladin.

Young, J., 1973, 'The Hippie Solution: An Essay in the Politics of Leisure', in I. Taylor and L. Taylor (eds), *The Politics of Deviancy*. London: Penguin.

Young, J., 1981, 'Beyond the Consensual Paradigm', in S. Cohen and J. Young (eds), *The Manufacture of News* (rev. edn). London: Constable.

Young, J., 1988, 'Risk of Crime and Fear of Crime: A Realist Critique of Survey-Based Assumptions', in M. Maguire and J. Pointing (eds), *Victims of Crime: A New Deal*. Milton Keynes; Open University Press.

Young, J., 1992, 'Ten Points of Realism', in J. Young and R. Matthews (eds), *Rethinking Criminology*. London: Sage.

Young, J., 1994, 'Incessant Chatter', in M. Maguire, R. Morgan and R. Reiner (eds), *The Oxford Handbook of Criminology* (1st edn). Oxford: Oxford University Press.

Young, J., 1998, 'Breaking Windows: Situating the New Criminology', in P. Walton and J. Young (eds), *The New Criminology Revisited*. London: MacMillan.

Young, J., 1999, *The Exclusive Society*. London: Macmillan.

Young, J., 2000, 'Globalization, Chaos and the Narcissism of Minor Differences'. Middlesex University: Centre for Criminology. Paper first given at The American Society of Criminology, Toronto, 1999.

Young, J., 2001, 'Identity, Community and Social Exclusion', in R. Matthews and J. Pitts (eds), *Crime, Disorder and Community Safety*. London: Routledge.

Young, J., 2002a, 'Crime and Social Exclusion', in M. Maguire, R. Morgan and R. Reiner (eds), *The Oxford Handbook of Criminology*, 3rd edn. Oxford: Oxford University Press.

Young, J., 2002b, 'Critical Criminology in the Twenty First Century: Critique, Irony and the Always Unfinished', in K. Carrington and R. Hogg (eds), *Critical Criminology: Issues, Debates, Challenges*. Cullompton, Devon: Willan.

Young, J., 2002c, 'Searching for a New Criminology of Everyday Life, review of D. Garland, *The Culture of Control*', *British Journal of Criminology* 42; 445–61.

Young, J., 2003a, 'Winning the Fight Against Crime', in R. Matthews and J. Young (eds), *The New Politics of Crime and Punishment*. Cullompton, Devon: Willan.

Young, J., 2003b, 'Merton with Energy, Katz with Structure', *Theoretical Criminology* 7(3); 389–414.

Young, J., 2004, 'Voodoo Criminology and the Art of Skating on Thin Ice', in J. Ferrell et al. (eds), *Cultural Criminology Unleashed*. London: Glasshouse.

Young, J., 2007, *The Vertigo of Late Modernity*. London: Sage.

Young, J., 2009, 'Moral Panic: Its Origins in Resistance, *Ressentiment* and the Translation of Fantasy into Reality', *British Journal of Criminology* 49(1): 4–16.

Young, J., 2010, 'Robert Merton', in K. Hayward, S. Maruna and J. Mooney (eds), *Fifty Key Thinkers in Criminology*. London: Routledge.

Young, J. and Matthews, R., 2003, 'New Labour, Crime Control and Social Exclusion', in R. Matthews and J. Young (eds), *The New Politics of Crime and Punishment*. Cullompton, Devon: Willan.

Young, R., 1990, *White Mythologies: Writing History and the West*. London: Taylor and Francis.

Zaitch, D., 2001, *Traquetos*. Amsterdam School for Social Science Research.

Zimring, F., 2007, *The Great American Crime Decline*. New York: Oxford University Press.

Zimring, F. and Hawkins, G., 1997, *Crime is Not the Problem*. New York: Oxford University Press.

Index

Lightning Source UK Ltd.
Milton Keynes UK
UKHW022041050121
376478UK00005B/341